Africa's Greatest
Entrepreneurs

AFRICA'S GREATEST ENTREPRENEURS

Moky Makura

PENGUIN BOOKS

Published by Penguin Books
an imprint of Penguin Random House South Africa (Pty) Ltd
Reg. No. 1953/000441/07
The Estuaries No. 4, Oxbow Crescent, Century Avenue, Century City, 7441
PO Box 1144, Cape Town, 8000, South Africa
www.penguinrandomhouse.co.za

Penguin
Random House
South Africa

First published 2008
Reprinted 2009 (twice), 2011, 2012, 2013, 2015 , 2017 and 2019

10 9

Publication © Penguin Random House 2008
Text © Moky Makura 2008

All photographs © the respective entrepreneurs

Cover designer: Flame Design

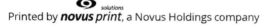
Printed by **novus print**, a Novus Holdings company

This book is printed on FSC® certified and controlled sources. FSC (Forest Stewardship Council®) is
an independent, international, non-governmental organization. Its aim is to support environmentally
sustainable, socially and economically responsible global forest management.

ISBN 978 0 1430 2430 9 (print)
ISBN 978 0 1430 2736 2 (ePub)

Contents

For Kunle, Peju, Nakai and Tawana

Acknowledgements

I could never have written this book without the help of my network of friends across the continent. There were many, many people who assisted me with invaluable research, contacts and information. In particular, I'd like to thank Adega Ouma, Philippe Armeding, Isabelle Bra and Martyn Mensah, all of whom went above and beyond the call of duty.

I would also like to thank every single one of the 15 entrepreneurs in this book and Albert Gatare, Miko Rwayitare's brother, who gave me their time and trusted me to tell their stories. Thank you for this opportunity.

My biggest thank you goes to my husband, Stewart Makura, for giving me the space to dream.

Moky Makura (neé Akinsemoyin)
www.africaourafrica.com
September 2008

Foreword by Sir Richard Branson

Entrepreneurs have been the driving force for growth in countries around the world. Their ability to see opportunities, where others only see issues, has helped transform communities and economies. One of the most exciting places where this entrepreneurial spirit is very alive is across Africa. I've had the great privilege to be involved in several new businesses in Africa and I'm constantly amazed by the incredible energy, determination and innovation coming from entrepreneurs across the continent. They give me great hope in a bright future for one of the most incredible regions of the world.

Each of the stories in this book about what these 16 entrepreneurs have achieved not only highlights the work of some wonderful individuals, but also highlights the impact of some great leaders. Their businesses have all reached beyond the individual and uplifted communities and countries across Africa. For example, the millions of phones that Mo Ibrahim has put into people's hands have created thousands more entrepreneurial opportunities and helped give people the economic freedom they need to lift their communities out of poverty.

A massive opportunity lies ahead on the continent for these entrepreneurs and those who will follow in their footsteps. The opportunity is not just about making money and acquiring wealth; it's a unique window to provide communities and nations access to new products and services that can transform lives and uplift economies nationally and on grassroots levels. It is a chance to embrace the spirit of *ubuntu* – we exist only because of others – that defines communities in South Africa and across the continent.

While the remarkable business leaders in the following chapters have broken unimaginable ground, I encourage all of us to come together to protect and grow this entrepreneurial spirit in communities across Africa. On my visits to Africa, it is devastating to see downward transition in some communities, marked by funeral signs overtaking adverts for local businesses that once signified a bubbling spirit of entrepreneurship right at the grassroots. Are we going to continue to let preventable diseases ravage communities? We must all look at how we can prevent these diseases and each play a role in helping thousands of others to follow in the footsteps of the great entrepreneurs whose stories are told so beautifully in this book.

I recently spent my birthday with some young people from the Branson School of Entrepreneurship in South Africa. Nowhere in the world have I ever experienced such a wonderful concentration of hope and pure determination for the future. Within all of these students is also an amazing sense of being in business, not only to better themselves and their families, but just as importantly to better their communities and countries. These students will be the next Ndaba Ntsele and Strive Masiyiwa. We must look at the ways that we can spread the wonderful entrepreneurial revolution happening across the continent to build an empowered next generation that will truly help to harness Africa's powerful entrepreneurial spirit.

As readers will discover from the stories of these incredible individuals, entrepreneurs are doers rather than preachers. They have a renegade, sky's-the-limit approach and lead by example. Frontline leaders fighting poverty, disease and environmental degradation can all benefit by taking an entrepreneurial approach and learning how to drive sustainable solutions that can be scaled and freed from donor dependency.

Congratulations to Moky Makura for having the vision to capture and spread the stories of the 16 entrepreneurs in this book. I truly hope that this book inspires many more people to use their entrepreneurial energy to change the world through creating opportunities for others.

Richard Branson
September 2008

Introduction

As Africans we often hesitate to tell our own positive stories, yet if we don't remember and record our past, if we don't highlight our achievements, showcase our heroes and take responsibility for the future image of Africa, nobody else will. I believe it is our responsibility.

Africa's Greatest Entrepreneurs is my attempt at showcasing some of our heroes in the business world. In it, you will meet 16 of the continent's most inspiring entrepreneurs – self-starters and patriotic Africans who share the distinction of having made it in Africa. These are people who have created not just personal wealth for themselves, but sustainable businesses that can be benchmarked alongside the best in the world.

What makes their stories more remarkable is seeing how they all worked ingeniously within the context of the historical, economic and political climates of their respective countries. How they manoeuvred their way through what many would describe as hostile business environments. A number of the entrepreneurs battled with antagonistic governments; on the other hand, a few built their businesses on the back of government contracts. Some found ways of operating under repressive systems or frequent governments changes. Others battled against personal poverty and lack of a good education. A small number had it all. Some of them risked nothing; some risked everything – including their lives. But they all made it, spectacularly. And these are their stories.

The characters you will meet in this book are by no means a comprehensive list of successful entrepreneurs in Africa – one book could not possibly do justice to that title. What *Africa's Greatest Entrepreneurs* sets out to do is to make a start at creating and profiling new heroes not only for Africans, but for the rest of the world to respect and admire.

In compiling this book I looked for entrepreneurs who had single-handedly started a multimillion-dollar business in Africa, individuals who were well known for their business successes in their countries, and in some cases, beyond. I considered key drivers like employment and turnover, or profit, where it was available. But most importantly, I looked for mavericks – pure capitalists who, like the visionary Martin Luther King, had a dream, a dream they had the drive to realise.

Africa's Greatest Entrepreneurs is a work in progress. It highlights sub-Saharan African entrepreneurs and even within that, there are obvious countries and entrepreneurs not represented. For example, some entrepreneurs I would have liked in the book, including women and francophone Africans, were not always available to participate. Secondly, there are more South Africans represented in these pages than other nationalities. Rather than any statement on my part, this is because the book is being published and marketed predominantly in South Africa. But my intention is not to end this book with just one volume. Like the entrepreneurs profiled here, I too have a dream, and this is just the beginning.

A wise man once said to me: 'when you publish, people will criticise but they can only do that because there is something tangible to criticise'. At best, I hope *Africa's Greatest Entrepreneurs* will act as a catalyst to stimulate debate about who the greatest entrepreneurs are on this continent. At the very least, I hope this book will be an enjoyable read.

'Until lions learn to write, hunters will tell their
history for them'

Wale Tinubu – The Upstart Entrepreneur

VITAL STATISTICS

Name: Wale Tinubu
Country: Nigeria
Born: 26 June 1967
Position/Title: CEO Oando
Nationality: Nigerian
Industry: Oil and gas
**Highest education qualification: LLM (Masters in Law),
London School of Economics**

I remember we would pay for our cargo in Lagos and get on the plane carrying 3 million naira cash (US$7000) in 50-naira bills to pay port charges at the other end. We would land at the airport with a duffel bag full of cash, pay the port charges, go straight to the refinery, and sit there and wait for the ship to load. We would sail with the ship and deliver to some of the customers offshore. Then we would immediately invoice the client, get the money wired to France, get on the next Air France flight to Paris and get the invoice discounted and collect the cash.

The same night we'd go out to a night club in Paris and then get on a flight the next day back to Nigeria. We'd change the cash, pay again for another load of cargo and then off we'd go again. That's what I did non-stop for two years as we built capital in the business.

That was the oil trading business in Nigeria 14 years ago but today you can still sense the energy and the passion in everything Wale Tinubu does. As he puts it: 'work is play' and he is having as much fun building what he describes as a 'world class Nigerian company' as he did trawling the clubs in Paris. Tinubu is well on his way to achieving his vision of making his company Oando a leader in the African energy sector. From his first office, which doubled as the family's garage, and his first business loan, which came from his mother, Tinubu has come a long way. Today he is CEO of a company with a market capitalisation of US$2 billion and a presence across most of West Africa.

Under Tinubu's leadership, Oando has grown from a downstream petroleum product marketing company to a diversified oil and gas company with interests in oil exploration, refining, gas distribution and power plant development. Since 1994 when he started the company along with his two best friends, Tinubu has steered it towards massive growth. Oando is now the largest publicly quoted oil company in Nigeria and one of the top-10 Nigerian-controlled companies quoted on the Nigerian Stock Exchange (NSE). Oando consistently achieves returns that would get even the most jaded of analysts excited.

According to their financial results for the year ending December 2007 Oando delivered pre-tax profits of seven billion naira (about US$60 million) and have delivered consistent shareholder value year on year. It is the second-largest petroleum marketer in Nigeria based on turnover and became the only Nigerian company to have decided he was tired and was no longer doing any more work and promptly left the building. A deeply insulted Tinubu decided that being a lawyer left him with very little control.

> I imagined the difference with business was that if you were waiting for three hours you were waiting for something positive to happen. You could choose which appointments you were going for and you wouldn't go to an appointment unless you knew it was going to add value.

So he resigned from the law firm. His intention was to work for himself as a corporate lawyer and, far more importantly, to do 'deals' on the side. So, just like Bill Hewlett and David Packard of Hewlett Packard, and Bill Gates of Microsoft, Tinubu set up shop in his garage. Well, if the truth be told, it was his father's garage.

> I asked my dad if I could use the garage, so we moved the cars out and I moved in. My mum gave me a little bit of money; I bought a second-hand carpet, painted the walls and took the phone from the house and connected the wires, and the home phone became my office phone. Then I took the desk from inside the house and on the first day I wore a jacket and tie, sat on the chair and said, 'I am open for business.' I didn't know what I was going to do.

On the street across from his office was a company called the Pipe-line and Products Marketing Company – a subsidiary of the now-defunct Nigerian National Petroleum Corporation (NNPC) which managed all government interests in the Nigerian oil industry. Tinubu said to himself: 'One day we are going to do business.' In the meantime he was undaunted by the fact that he was the butt of his family's jokes about his 'office-cum-garage', he duly turned up for 'work' every day and thought about ways to 'do deals' in between hiring himself out as a legal consultant.

It didn't take him long to leave the ignominious beginnings of his father's garage; he had his eyes set on something a little more in keeping with his vision. His mind was set on a new building that was still under construction. It was the most expensive building in the street, and as is the usual practice in Nigeria, the landlord wanted the entire three-year lease's rent in advance. Of course, Tinubu didn't have enough money to pay for the total rent upfront, but he wasn't going to let that stand in the way of something he wanted. Although he was earning money from small corporate legal assignments, regular cash flow continued to elude him due to customers not paying on time. But he had made a bet with himself that he would somehow pay it off before the building was completed. Through a combination of luck and sheer willpower, Tinubu managed to collect the money he was owed and win the bet with himself.

> I got the first year's rent and paid it, struggled to get the second year, but finally I got all the cash I could muster, and when it was time to move in I had the balance. I realised then that if you set yourself a target even if it is above what you can achieve today, nine times out of 10, because of your desire for something bigger, you will achieve it. Your reality is only as good as your dreams.

Although he paid the rent, Tinubu didn't have money for much else, including office equipment. He was also about to get married to his girlfriend at the time, Bola. Rather romantically, he told his wife-to-be that they had a choice of where to go on honeymoon with the £1 000 budget he had set aside. The choice was to blow the full amount on the honeymoon away, or spend half of it on a cheaper honeymoon and the rest on two much-needed computers for his ill-equipped offices. Tinubu's powerful persuasive skills aside (they do say that behind every fledgling entrepreneur is an understanding wife, and in this case, it was very true), the happy couple returned from a cut-price honeymoon with two computers in their suitcases. With two computers and a very expensive office to service, Tinubu continued his legal practice until the opportunity arose to start formally trading oil.

A potential deal presented itself when a friend, Jite Okoloko, who later became his partner, had an opportunity to transport diesel from the government-owned Port Harcourt refinery in the oil-producing Niger Delta, to Lagos to fill up fishing trawlers. The contract was for Unipetrol, a government-owned petroleum marketing company that Tinubu would soon take over. At the same time, one of Tinubu's best friends, Mofe Boyo, also a lawyer, represented a US oil services company which had supply boats and an oil tanker which fuelled them while they were working offshore. The company, which was in financial difficulty, had an old 1945 World War II tanker called

The Carolina which Tinubu and Boyo thought they could charter in order to fulfil the Unipetrol contract. The two friends went out to Bonny Island, which is situated at the southern edge of Rivers State in the Niger Delta, to look at the ship which was anchored off shore.

> We were on this out-board engine speed boat, I had no life jacket, it was raining heavily, the boat was going at 60 km per hour and all we had was a rain sheet over our heads. I kept asking myself: 'What am I doing here?' But as soon as I saw the ship – it was an old ship bobbing in the water – I just knew it was my destiny.

Love at first sight or not, Tinubu just didn't have the cash to buy *The Carolina*. Nevertheless, he and Boyo got on board to find that the crew were upset because they hadn't been paid for months by the ship's owners; and there and then, Tinubu made an offer to charter the boat. His next challenge was to find the money for the deal, but this time he didn't need to look too far. His mother and father financed his deal to the tune of US$10 000, which in 1994 was, to Tinubu, 'a huge amount of money … It was everything.'

With his financial backers on board, Tinubu chartered the tanker. His next stop was to tell his friend Okoloko that he had a ship that could move the fuel. Tinubu was in business. After two months of *The Carolina* being in service, Tinubu learnt his first business lesson: the importance of working capital. Payments for the services that they were rendering were just too slow. They were transporting the equivalent of 1 000 tons of diesel every 15 days from the refinery to Lagos for the fishing trawlers. Theoretically they were making money, but they had no cash. They fell behind with their payments to the ship owners who then threatened to pull the vessel. Tinubu came up with an unexpected solution to the problem. After giving the ship owners the runaround for three months, he approached them and pointed out that since he owed them money anyway, they should consider extending his debt further and selling him the ship.

> They thought this was rich coming from someone who could not pay their bills. So I said: 'Look, I owe you the money anyway so I might as well buy it from you and that way you know that my debt is going to lead to a complete transfer of ownership and you no longer have the

liability of chasing after me.'

It was difficult to fault his logic. 'They thought this was an interesting concept. So they said yes.' Tinubu went on to finance the
US$100 000 the ship owners wanted through a finance house, a
small-scale licensed industry lender, which agreed to give him the
full amount and charged him a whopping 10% interest per month.
Naïve and eager to close the contract he signed. 'I thought it was
a good deal that somebody loaned me money in the first place, so
I was happy. I didn't realise that it was practically usury,' he says
wryly. Gradually Tinubu paid off the debt and eventually owned
the ship. '*The Carolina* used to make her value every month', he
remembers fondly. 'She was very profitable.'

Tinubu soon discovered there was a bigger market selling to
oil companies than solely fishing trawlers. He ended up making
more profit selling 10% of his fuel to an oil company than he made
from selling the remaining 90% to fishing trawlers. What he hadn't
realised at the time was that the oil service companies were willing
to pay a premium for a reliable service and that there was only one
other competitor in the market.

> Every time we had one satisfied customer they would say: 'You mean a
> Nigerian company can say they will deliver at 3pm and mean it? Here
> are two business cards, go talk to my buddy at this place.'

Tinubu's company, then called Ocean and Oil, moved from one ship
to two, to three and then eventually boasted a fleet of seven ships
ranging from 1 000 to 30 000 tons. *The Carolina* was the smallest
of them. Ocean and Oil was one of the very few local companies
operating in the oil and gas sector because most of the business
usually went to foreign companies. The modus operandi was for
Nigerian companies to secure the contracts, take a commission and
pass the work on to foreign companies. This was mainly because
the infrastructure to allow international trade from Nigeria simply
didn't exist – including a payment transfer system. But Tinubu,
once again, wasn't going to let that stand in his way.

This was the period in his life when he worked hard and partied
hard in clubs in Paris and London. He was working hard and playing
even harder to build up capital in the business, which he then
invested into big financially risky projects, like the importing of

Bitumen into Nigeria to improve the country's dire road network. There is no doubt that Tinubu and his partners took what could be described as bold – but were much closer to high-risk – career steps, and they clearly had fun doing it. But their maverick style of doing business was about to pay off and jettison them into the big league.

The birth of Oando

Initially called Ocean and Oil, Oando's entrance into the corporate world is evidence of one of Tinubu's fundamental beliefs: 'Set a goal bigger than you are.' In fact the story of how three young upstarts; Tinubu and his two best friends, Mofe Boyo (now Oando's deputy chief executive) and Jite Okoloko (who served as Oando's group executive director for a while), took over a well-established government parastatal which was listed on the NSE in the highly regulated oil and gas sector, is not only legendary but reads like a David and Goliath tale. Unipetrol, a petroleum marketing company, was established in 1976 when the Nigerian government bought out all of Exxon's interests. In 1992, the company was floated on the NSE and 60% went into the hands of the Nigerian public. Eight years later, in 2000, during the second phase of the government's privatisation programme, 10% of the shares were to be offered to the public and the balance of 30% was to be put up for sale to the private sector. It was this 30% that Tinubu, Boyo and Okoloko were after.

> We put in our bid and everybody thought it was a joke. It was valued at US$16 million and of course we didn't have the money. At best maybe we had US$3 million. We went to all the banks. I remember my meeting with the First Bank manager. I told him we wanted to buy Unipetrol. He burst out laughing.

But Tinubu and his team knew an opportunity when they saw it. Unipetrol was small enough for them to believe they could actually acquire it – it had a solid base and what Tinubu believed was a good balance sheet. The Nigerian government, in turn, were looking for core shareholders who would not only buy the business, but would also take on the responsibility for its strategic direction. And Tinubu badly wanted to win.

We presented with such passion to the panel that they thought, 'Let's give these young guys a chance.' I had never met anyone on the panel before – I didn't know anyone big or impressive.

Tinubu believes that what made the three young men stand out from the other bidders, apart from their age and the lack of a necktie in his case, was the combination of a first-class business plan, aggressive pricing and their absolute drive to succeed. One of the board members of Unipetrol who was part of the panel on that day remembers how impressive the three were: 'They were very direct. They were clear risk-takers and consummate entrepreneurs – I liked their style. Tinubu was very eloquent, he presents exceptionally well and like the trained lawyer he is, he knows how to argue a case well.'

They were the underdogs but Tinubu and his team, much to everyone's surprise, pulled it off. However, the decision to award them the bid was a controversial one. Many people simply could not believe that these young boys – Tinubu was 30 at the time – who appeared to come from nowhere, could have blindsided everyone and bought the Nigerian government's share of Unipetrol. It caused outrage in some quarters because no one believed it was possible for three young men in their early thirties to have the money and the business experience to buy and effectively manage what was then a top-10 publicly quoted company on the Nigerian Stock Exchange. 'Government was under pressure to cancel, because we had no pedigree, no balance sheet and no money,' says Tinubu, who clearly relished the challenge ahead.

To address the lack of public confidence in the award of the bid, the Nigerian government moved the goalposts and reduced the amount of time Tinubu and his team had to raise the money. Suddenly they had 15 days instead of 20 to find US$15 million and the clock was ticking – fast. Much was at stake. Apart from their personal reputations, the loss of face to the government if Tinubu and his team did not deliver was not worth thinking about. It was not the first time that Tinubu had found himself in the position of having to raise money, but this time the stakes were much, much higher.

He eventually raised the funds by selling a 25% stake to a Venture Capital affiliate of a local bank for US$5 million and raising a US$10 million loan, payable over four years at 30% per annum from Oceanic Bank. The thrill of the chase and catching the prey was only the beginning, because, as they soon found out, the real challenge lay ahead.

Tinubu and his team had to move into the Unipetrol building and take over the management of the company they had just bought and promised to turn around. In recognition of the new management's win, the unions promptly went on strike. Each day the new team arrived at their office building to welcoming placards carried by their new staff branding them 'eaglet managers'. It was a reference to their ages, which were not far off from those of the Nigerian junior football team, the Eaglets. Some placards plainly stated that Tinubu and this team knew nothing, were undoubtedly coming to loot the company and would ultimately run it into the ground.

> It was a long drawn-out process and we tried to go the legal route, but we realised that without the cooperation of the work force we would never succeed. So we went on a series of consultations with the union leaders inside and outside the company in the middle of the night, because we realised we could never address them as a whole. The only way to get anything done was to identify and isolate the leaders and influencers and convince them. We gradually broke the ice and reached a settlement.

The team showed immense maturity and understanding beyond their years in turning a potentially catastrophic situation around. Employees who had suffered for years under government mis-management now enjoyed better working conditions, better salaries and a much better management team, that introduced the concept of meritocracy.

> We started off by demonstrating that every promise we made we would deliver on. We promised we were going to review all the employees and make some appropriate promotions. We had people who had not had a promotion for 17 years for no reason apart from the fact that the HR system was archaic.

Like any new management team brought on to make changes and deliver profit, they opened up the rule book and started with rule number one. First to feel the impact were the staff. Out went all the ineffective, non-delivering, government-style workers and in came fresh, new, young, dynamic blood, just like Tinubu and his team.

Today Oando is 20 times bigger than it was on the day the 'young upstarts' took over, despite shedding nearly 50% of its staff. Tinubu and his team successfully turned a 31-year-old government institution into a modern corporation and created real growth from which employees, shareholders and other stakeholders have benefited.

Tinubu believes that Oando is a 'magical' place to work. That's because: 'People get the opportunity of discovering things about themselves they never knew existed and that comes from being challenged and being given opportunities.' 'The differentiator for working here', he explains passionately, 'is that you will work very hard. You will be given responsibility, be allowed to lead and realise your own potential. You will know you are part of something different, something magical.'

Tinubu's success in the context of Nigeria

Looking up at the multi-storey building at 2 Ajose Adeogun Street, which houses Oando's 400-strong headquarters staff in Lagos's upmarket commercial centre, Victoria Island, it is easy to imagine a magical place, where young leaders are groomed and rewarded. However, Tinubu's success in building Oando has been achieved against the backdrop of a country where the terrain is not always that easy to navigate.

> You have to learn to be politically savvy, you don't have a choice. It's not something you can run away from, because the government in Nigeria truly dominates the economy and the private sector is only just beginning to get a voice of its own.

Despite this fact, Tinubu says he tries hard to be 'less a friend of government' and more 'the best at what he does' – which is to be politically savvy and the best commercially. But he recognises the need to do both. 'You have to win politically to get included on the bidding list and then you have to win convincingly on the bid to get the business.' Tinubu is outspoken about what he believes is the government's interference in business:

> Government can't create jobs, that is the private sector's role. I am a firm believer that they should just collect taxes and regulate. If they

want to be capitalists they can be stimulants for growth, but they should never attempt to run businesses – they are hopeless at it.

If you own a car, you keep it fixed. If the government owns it, and a screw has to be tightened, it remains loose, whilst numerous layers of bureaucracy must be scaled to get simple approval to spend.

Tinubu is equally dismissive about the perception that doing business in Nigeria must necessarily be fraught with issues around corruption. He believes there are ways and means of stepping away from corruption, by simply running a business based on merit.

Those who rely on corruption to survive don't want to compete. We *want* to compete; we *love* tenders, that's where we showcase our talent – openly and transparently. At the end of the day, to deal with corruption means managing from both sides. It exists but it doesn't stop businesses that truly want to distinguish themselves.

He does, however, point out that like a good tango, it takes two to make corruption work: 'Nine times out of 10, this so-called corruption is a foreigner paying money into an African's bank account.' But one of the biggest challenges he has faced building his business in Nigeria has been convincing regulators, bureaucrats even shareholders and staff that an indigenous company can deliver the goods. He cites several examples where he believes his company would offer a better quality product or service to a Nigerian government buyer and because they were a Nigerian company, they would lose the bid.

There is a scepticism that borders on paranoia that you can't actually have an African success story in business. So I have to go out of my way to prove that we are an indigenous company – we don't employ foreigners – we employ the best Africans we can find worldwide from Canada, Asia and the US. It is not a case of being discriminatory; it's more a case of saying 'we can do it'.

The personality behind the success

That 'can-do' attitude stems from a confidence Tinubu says was instilled in him by his parents when he was growing up in Nigeria with what he describes as a 'true middle-class upbringing'.

Accountancy

> The training was tough, the feeding erratic because we were given five
> minutes to finish our food and then it was out! It was physically hectic.
> I quickly realised that if you did your work promptly and well, you
> were left alone. So instead of idling and drawing attention to myself I
> did everything quickly. I learned quickly. I was a good soldier.

But Prince Kofi Amoabeng was destined for a life in the army, not
in business. He loved the order, the drills, the turning and the
'sharp commands', but most of all, he loved the lifestyle and the
discipline that the army imposed. The army taught him that he
could do without material things:

> Most people wonder why I am not a typical African in that I have made
> some money and I haven't moved into a big house with lots of servants
> and wives. Once you have lived in a trench for a week in the middle
> of nowhere you realise that you don't need material things, what is
> important is the will to live and living with people.

Today, Amoabeng is the CEO of a financial services company that
was rated as the best financial institution in Ghana and ranked as
the second-best company on the prestigious Ghana Club 100 (GC
100) in 2005, which recognises the best-performing companies
in Ghana. From an informal 'free service' in which Amoabeng
dabbled – where he introduced friends who had money to invest to
friends who needed money quickly for business – grew a company
that boasted a 28.7 million Ghanaian cedi (about US$24 million)
turnover in 2007 and a staff count of 300. Unique Trust now
operates from eight offices in Ghana and is looking to spread its
wings further into Africa and Europe. Earlier in his life, the army
was possibly the most unexpected place for Amoabeng to end up in
yet it turned out to be his salvation. It was exactly what he needed
– a place where 'you didn't have options, where it was quite clear
what you were supposed to do'.

In his youth, he had been a troublemaker who, because he was
smart, managed to coast through school and university without
being kicked out. He described himself back then as 'quite brilliant
but notorious'. He was that rare thing – a very smart student who
was also a borderline delinquent.

The army changed my whole perspective on life. It changed me from a player to a highly disciplined person. Even though it didn't change the core me, it changed my outlook on life and my attitude towards people.

To this day, Amoabeng admits he was – and some would argue, still is – an army man through and through. An unconventional character who thrives on routine, Amoabeng could possibly be one of the most organised and eccentric business people you will ever meet. He has even been known to start meetings with no one present!

People think I am crazy because I turn up at all my appointments on time even though I know the people I am meeting won't be there. I hate things being moved around; if things need to be changed, they need to be changed permanently. Right now I can walk in to my house and find the aftershave I want in the dark.

And if you walk in to the offices of Unique Trust, the company which Amoabeng started in 1997, you'll find him sitting in his office, the door open. He is almost a permanent fixture – he rarely goes out to meetings, preferring to be available to his clients as and when they need him, and he rarely travels out of the country, because, quite simply, he hates travelling.

About Unique Trust

In spite of, or because of, his idiosyncrasies, Amoabeng has managed to create a unique business whose success awes him.

It's beyond my wildest dreams. When I started I thought I was going to build a small financial outfit, but the opportunity came so we took advantage of it, to the point where today we are ranked as the best indigenous company in Ghana and we have become a household name.

Unique Trust's business model is not just simple, fast and very efficient – it also works brilliantly. Its official description is that of a non-bank financial institution and its licence doesn't allow it to take deposits like a conventional bank. However, it specialises in lending money to businessmen in need of short-term finance, businesses with no safety net. 'When I have to walk out, I don't need a plan B, I have so much faith in myself. I don't need much to live.' Although he didn't have a plan B after the saw mill episode, he continued to keep himself busy with a hobby that earned him no money whatsoever. Amoabeng was a self-styled investment consultant in his spare time – a service he offered, like his time, for free. It was quite simple, really. Friends would come to him with a proposal looking for help to raise money. Amoabeng would never approach banks as they always refused such loans. Instead, he would approach other friends and acquaintances who had some money to invest and pair the two up for no commission. This free matchmaking service eventually grew to be the basis of Unique Trust but Amoabeng did not see it as a source of income at the time. He continued to look for opportunities while the perfect business venture was staring him right in the face.

Between 1992 and 1996 his 'easy come easy go attitude' to business partnerships led him to a point where he admits: 'I was down'. But before he hit rock-bottom he was to take a few more blows. He fell out with an old German man with whom he had partnered to import and sell air-conditioning units in Ghana. It all started well; he put in the local money and his German partner sent in the air conditioners from Germany. He employed two directors to run the business while he spent time working on another business that imported various consumer goods into Ghana. His two directors proved to be his downfall. They stabbed him in the back by 'reporting' him to his German partner saying that he was not really doing much for the business. His partner came down to Ghana and demanded a meeting. Amoabeng's answer was that if his German partner believed that the two disloyal directors could really run the business, he should go ahead and work with them. Then he walked away.

He walked away again a month later in different circumstances. During his partnership with the German businessman, Amoabeng had also been acting as the local representative for a French-based oil company, Elf, which later became Total. When Elf acquired the business interests of BP in Ghana, they no longer needed his services. In order to pay him off, they offered him the opportunity to run some petrol stations without paying the usual franchise fee upfront. And so he became a reluctant petrol station proprietor. Shortly after, the new country manager for Elf arrived in Ghana and took an instant disliking to Amoabeng on the basis that Amoabeng drove a nice car – a BMW – and played a lot of golf. The new country manager could not understand how he managed to do this on the salary he earned as a dealer. When he was called to explain his lifestyle choices, Amoabeng, typically unrepentant, responded as expected: 'I gave him a piece of my mind and then I left.'

He rationalises what some would argue were rather rash decisions. 'I know in this world that nothing is permanent. That is a fact, so I don't fear walking away from something.' At this point though, Amoabeng had hit rock-bottom. And it took a little while to piece together a plan B. It turned out to be one that had actually always been staring him in the face. His work as a no-fee investment consultant was about to start yielding a return.

> After I lost Elf, I still had to wake up in the morning and go and chase friends to pay other friends. I was working for nothing. Somewhere along the line it hit me that why didn't I just formalise this. People need money, people have money to invest. The banks are not serving the majority of people in Ghana, so let me start something that answers the needs that the banks cannot service. Why not get a licence and do it properly?

The path to Unique Trust

Over the years, Amoabeng had done his research on the business:

> I had been to the market myself, I had talked to the traders and I knew they were borrowing money at anything from 30 to 50 to even 100% interest rates per month. In one incident which I found very exciting, the traders were lending amongst themselves at a rate of 10% per day! The moneylenders who were charging these interest rates and getting away with it were fellow market traders and informal moneylenders.

So Amoabeng put in his application for a banking licence and waited and waited. Like many entrepreneurs before him, he started the business from home so when the Bank of Ghana came knocking on the door to inspect his premises as part of the licence application process, Amoabeng had to think quickly. He eventually ended up borrowing and later officially moving into an office which housed a small business owned by a US-based friend of his. The friend, in return for the office space, became a silent partner and investor with a 50% shareholding in the business. This was the value Amoabeng put on the physical space and the office equipment he took over. The only tangible thing that Amoabeng brought to the deal was the banking licence and he figured that was worth at least 50% of the equity of the business. He easily justifies what many have said is an overly generous shareholding offer to a silent partner who also became the chairman of his company's board. Amoabeng is very clear:

> If I didn't have him at the time, I wouldn't have been where I am today. It's not a matter of how much one has put in, it's a matter of when it was critical, who was there?

He recalls the euphoria of the day the licence was granted, a day marked with much quaffing of champagne and smoking of expensive cigars with some of his wealthy friends who had promised to invest in his business. Amoabeng now had an office, three members of staff and something that was worth its weight in gold: a banking licence. Now all he needed was the money. So he called up the wealthy friends with whom he had shared champagne and cigars, who had promised to put in money once he got the licence. 'I went round to every one of those friends I celebrated with and not a single one of them put in any money. They all felt it was too risky.' This was despite a detailed feasibility study and a five-year projection plan he had presented to them. Unsurprisingly, the banks didn't oblige either. They didn't seem to understand what he was on about. They weren't sure if he was a competitor or not, after all, he was in the business of lending money, no matter how unorthodox his approach.

His choice of the name Unique Trust was not coincidental. Amoabeng genuinely wanted to 'listen to the people, solve their problems, get to know them, develop trust and make the loan'. He was actually attempting to build a business based almost entirely on trust.

> When I took the name Unique Trust I really thought we were going to do this business on special trust not on collateral and accounts. If we trust that you are a genuine person then we'd do it. It was a bit naïve

but that was the idea.

And what an idea. It was 1996 and the turmoil in the banking sector at the time hit his business plans hard. Banks were losing money and the government had to step in and restructure some banks. The government had created a non-performing assets recovery trust to recapitalise the banks who were failing in the delivery of credit. The general feeling coming from the banks was that; 'Ghanaians don't pay, so why should we give Kofi money?' But Amoabeng was still fired up about the opportunity that stared him in the face. Convinced his idea would work, he knew he needed to rethink his original strategy and forget the idea of looking for 'big time' money to fund his start-up.

> It hit me that my friends were failing me because they didn't want to risk 'big money', but they liked me enough to risk 'small money'. So one day I woke up and wrote a personalised letter to every one of my friends who I thought could afford small amounts like US$1 000 or US$2 000. I had a list of 55 names. I drove around and delivered all of the letters by hand and then started chasing them.

In all, about 40 of his targets said no, however, with the people who responded positively, he had exactly the amount for which he had budgeted. After a few months of trading, the Central Bank of Ghana came back to audit his books and they were not happy at all. They threatened to shut him down if he carried on doing business in this very unorthodox way. They could not believe that anyone would be foolhardy and naïve enough to lend money to people using none of the conventional tools that banks traditionally used.

In the first year he made a loss of US$100 000. But he was borrowing money at an interest rate of about 7% per month and lending it out at about 14–15% per month, half of what he believed the market could take – there was huge room for growth. Amoabeng grew Unique Trust organically. He attracted attention by consistently borrowing and returning investors' money on time and with interest. He recounts the story of the 'friend' who lent him US$50 000 at 42% for a six-month period, A day before the six months was up, he called his friend:

> 'Tomorrow is your due date, would you entertain rolling it over?' I asked my friend, who immediately replied: 'No, no, no. I will never

roll it over, I want my money.' So I wrote him a cheque. I was told that the moment he got back to his office he had asked if I had brought the cheque, then he told his office to go and clear it immediately to see if the money was there. He was surprised to find that it was. He called me back and asked if he could lend me the money again. I said not at 84%. I said I would take it at 60% and he agreed because he now had confidence in me that I would deliver his money back to him.

From there on, Amoabeng built his business on performance and delivery using money, initially from his friends. People came to trust him. The more consistent and reliable he became, the more people wanted to invest with him and the bigger the business grew. Investors came to him because he was reliable and much more profitable than the government bonds. Business people came to him because of his lightening quick response to their practical needs and of course they came for the money, which was delivered at the time they needed it.

At this point, his staff count was four, by the end of the first year he had six staff. Ten years later Unique Trust employs more than 300 staff and its total assets sit at about US$75 million. Shareholders' funds are worth about US$7.9 million. And if the company were to be valued on the local stock exchange it would be worth in the region of US$65 million. Unique Trust is a well-established indigenous company that has won the respect and trust of the banks, provident and pension funds, which now make up 40% of the company's funding. The institutions now view Unique Trust as a low- or no-risk investment.

Company philosophy

Modestly, Amoabeng puts his business success down to something that Aretha Franklin sang about in the 1967 Motown classic, *Respect*.

I find that most companies collapse because the owners don't show much respect to their staff or their customers. What really matters is having respect for everybody. Everything we do is about people; our actions are intended to benefit our stakeholders and if it's clean and clear, you'll get it right.

Although he believes in respect, it is not at the cost of performance. Amoabeng readily sacked his own brother for non-performance, as well as his best friend's son. 'The rules are clear and apply to everybody exactly the same,' he says firmly. The extent to which he believes that everybody is exactly the same is borne out by the fact that he is very much a part of the business. Amoabeng's direct mobile phone number – which he really does answer – is on display in each of the branches of his company.

> I do get calls and I take all the calls. I am only interested in the dissatisfied clients. I still see clients and usually the ones who are more complex. There are many loans I do based on sentiments and emotions, and they always go bad. I do them sometimes because the world is not always about money.

He cites the example of one of his staff members who motivated for a number of loans, all of which he strongly suspected would end up defaulting. But Amoabeng went ahead and approved one of them and, as he suspected, the loan was never repaid.

> I did it for his own ego and to teach him a lesson. I wanted him to have first-hand experience. Let him learn the hard way, even though we'll lose a bit now, the company will benefit in the long run.

His business strategy is simple: 'Business will thrive if you keep the needs of your clients in focus all the time.' Unique Trust's growth has been entirely dependent on this strategy. His decision to open their first additional branch in the port of Tema, east of Accra, to help importers who were having to travel between the capital and Tema to clear their goods, was a direct result of this. 'It just didn't make sense to me. We were not providing them with a good service on time, so we set up an office in Tema to take care of them,' he says matter-of-factly, explaining that his decision was based entirely on servicing his clients. Unique Trust even built a car showroom where customers who purchased cars overseas to sell locally could display the vehicles. The idea was to help the clients sell their cars quickly, eliminating the need to store them at a warehouse. That way, Unique Trust loaned clients the money and got the money back quickly. Unique Trust also set up a logistics company to help customers with clearing and warehousing, collateral management and trucking. Amoabeng describes his actions as realistic: 'It's not that I have the vision. The need comes and then we figure out how we respond to the needs of our customers.'

Politics, corruption and lifestyle

Amoabeng could not have chosen a better business, judging from his attitude to politics and politicians.

> I don't have time for politics. I know it's very important but I don't have time for it. All I do is borrow money and lend money and make sure the money comes back so I can pay back the investors. I don't need politicians to help me do that. With almost every business you must dine with the politicians so they can give you some juicy contract – with this one you don't.

Although, according to Amoabeng, the Ghanaian political and economic climate is very much in his favour and he admits that he has the government to thank for it.

> The currency is stable, interest rates have come down, and the govern-ment has introduced fast-track courts to deal with commercial cases quickly. They passed a credit rating bill and are working on an ID card system to make it easier to track people down. Although they seem to be resisting the urge to name the roads and number the streets!

With regards to the ID card system, Amoabeng logically points out: 'If you can't locate someone, what is the use of identifying the person?' It is the bold vocalising of this type of logical reasoning that has earned Amoabeng a bit of a reputation. Not the most diplomatic of characters, Amoabeng shoots straight from the hip. He is outspoken on his views on Ghana's economy and the state of the nation in general. People who know him say he is 'straightforward', a plain-spoken man who has very strong opinions. His take on corruption is sympathetic in a sense, in that he believes it is inherent to African culture, but despite that he has a zero tolerance approach to it.

> The problem with corruption is that it's part of our culture, so we don't see anything wrong with it. It's in our culture to send gifts to thank

people and it's very difficult to get away from that. If you take a gift – not even a bribe – you are compromised, which is why one of the unshakeable rules of engagement at Unique Trust is that no member of staff is allowed, in any circumstances whatsoever, to accept a gift.

He admires Donald Trump and Richard Branson because they are both not only successful but also controversial. 'I like business people who take on the norm, turn it around and succeed,' he explains. Something he has managed to do with Unique Trust. Amoabeng lives his life based on three basic philosophies: That nothing is permanent, which makes him look at things objectively; that humans are no more important than plants, and that while you are here on earth, you should be of some use to your creator. He's got life figured out and that is why he believes he is content.

His pleasures are simple. He reads *The Economist* every week, he drives himself everywhere, including to his village every weekend where he plays golf, swims and drinks with his friends. He has five children from two wives and is currently divorced. With his single-figure golf handicap, Amoabeng plays the game every single non-working day he has available. Apart from that, you'll find him in his office, with the door open, dealing with some of the more complex loan cases. Unique Trust is a business he loves and one which he takes personally. 'Through it,' he says, 'you can put smiles on people's faces.' And what a great reason to do business.

Mo Ibrahim – The Accidental Entrepreneur

VITAL STATISTICS

Born: 3 May 1946
Country: Sudan
Position/Title: Founder and chairman of Celtel; founder and chairman of the Mo Ibrahim Foundation and Satya Financial
Company turnover/assets: US$150 million in Satya Financial Private Equity Fund
Nationality: Sudanese (British citizen)
Industry: Telecommunications and private equity
Highest education qualification: Master of Science in electronics and electrical engineering and a doctorate in mobile communications

If it wasn't for an unassuming Sudanese engineer, the world of mobile communications as we know it would not exist. Back in the early 70s, Mo Ibrahim left his native Sudan to attend an International Telecommunications Union (ITU) training programme at its headquarters in Geneva. It was during a journey in a taxi through the city's busy centre that he experienced a moment that must have been comparable to Sir Isaac Newton's 'discovery' of gravity. Ibrahim's falling apple moment came when he noticed his taxi driver using a public radio system in his car. Nothing unusual to the untrained eye, but to Ibrahim the engineer, the fact that the taxi driver was using his radio in a built-up area without being in direct sight of a satellite was a significant observation. His mind went into overdrive as he realised that he could actually apply what he had just seen to a new technology which he was working on. Ibrahim had been calculating transmission paths and planning a mobile phone network that would allow people to communicate literally anywhere in the world. It was a complex mathematical problem that appealed to his engineer's mind and he was determined to solve it.

In January 1985 Mo Ibrahim made history when he led the team that invented the first truly 'mobile' phone network. He was working for the state-owned telecoms operator, British Telecom, as an engineer at the time. The network he built was the only one in the world that was designed from the very beginning to support what were then called 'hand portables' – phones you could carry in your hand as opposed to mobile phones, which until then, were designed to be used solely in cars. Building the world's first mobile phone network may have seemed a difficult achievement to top, but Ibrahim was to go on and break even more records. In 2005 he sold the second business he had started from scratch; Celtel, the pan-African mobile phone operator, for a staggering US$3.4 billion, making it one of the most valuable corporate transactions on the African continent. And then, in 2006, he established a radical new initiative, the Mo Ibrahim Foundation, which offered the world's biggest prize – US$5 million and US$200 000 a year for life – to a different African president every year. The criteria were leadership, good governance and perhaps most important of all for Africa, a president who stepped down from power timeously. Through his various achievements, Ibrahim managed to make himself a multimillionaire, not once, but twice over.

The early days

To meet the man, you would never suspect that he had attained such heights in one lifetime. Ibrahim is one of the most modest, unassuming businessmen and distinguished academic-turned-philanthropist you will ever meet. As expected, he played his achievements down: 'I'm no hero myself; I'm just somebody who happened to be in the right place at the right time, with the right know-how.' The right place was Britain, the right time was back in the 70s, and the right know-how was mobile communications.

Mo Ibrahim was born in Eshket in northern Sudan in 1946 and was educated in Egypt. He was the son of a cotton trader and the second eldest of five siblings. At the time, Sudan was under joint Anglo-Egyptian rule and Sudan and Egypt were treated as one country with no borders until 1956. Ibrahim was an academically gifted child who excelled at school and was often top of his class. He enjoyed maths and physics and it was no real surprise that he ended up at Alexandria University in Egypt studying electrical engineering. His ambition back then was to be a 'a top engineer' and to win the Nobel Prize in physics.

In 1968, after university, Ibrahim went to work for the Sudanese fixed-line operator as an executive engineer. The International Telecommunications Union (ITU) had just opened a telecoms training centre in Khartoum, Sudan's capital, where Ibrahim worked as a counterpart. This meant that he provided support to foreign experts while being trained by the centre. During his time there, Ibrahim travelled extensively around Europe and it was on one of these trips to Geneva that the seed for a new way of planning a mobile phone network was sown.

Keen to develop his career as an engineer, at 28 and recently married, Ibrahim left Sudan with his wife to do a Masters degree in electronics and electrical engineering at Bradford University in the UK. From there he went on to Birmingham University to do a PhD in mobile communications. He was undoubtedly a brilliant student and it was clear in which direction he was headed.

> It just fascinated me. Mobile communications was a complex, new mode of communications with very little knowledge (available) about how to effectively plan or manage it. I made a real breakthrough, but of course nobody could predict at the time that mobile communications would

be so universal today. At that time it was a very small industry.

His breakthrough was to produce one of the first acknowledged mathematic models for prediction, which was how mobile networks were planned. The model was named after him and is still in use today. Although a life in the hallowed halls of academia beckoned, Ibrahim really wanted to get his hands dirty and implement his ideas in the real world. His research work for his PhD had brought him into contact with the commercial world and the corporate world beckoned. Ibrahim tries to justify himself:

> I actually enjoyed working with networks and engineering. It's fun and it's a very creative job. I never intended to really stay long in academia because I've always been an engineer and I really wanted to play with the big train set and you cannot do that in academia.

And he couldn't have asked for a bigger train set. BT (British Telecoms), one of his research project clients, invited him to join them as a technical director to work on building a mobile phone network. And the rest, as they say, is history.

The making of an entrepreneur

After launching Britain's first truly mobile network in January 1985, Ibrahim stayed with the organisation (BT) for some time but soon got frustrated with the company's lacklustre support for his passion:

> I didn't see BT as an agile organisation and at the time they were not focused on mobile communications. The management failed to see the future of that industry so the support we were getting from the company was very lukewarm.

So he left, with the intention of starting out on his own: 'I really wanted to have my own freedom and that essentially was my motivation, it was not to try to make money, I just wanted to have peace of mind and to enjoy what I was doing,' he explains. Many people did not understand his decision. In those days, leaving a solid dependable organisation like BT to work for yourself was just plain crazy, particularly as he had a wife and young children to look after.

Yes, of course, a lot of people thought I was crazy. I had a very cushy, good job. I had a big company car. I had all my telecommunications for free, but I increasingly became unhappy and I really wanted to enjoy what I was doing – there was no point.

BT's loss became the mobile communication world's gain. In 1989, five years after the launch of BT's mobile network, Ibrahim decided to do what every dissatisfied executive does: 'You go home and you take over the dining room and say "This is my office, I'm going to be a consultant." So I decided to go home and declare myself a consultant!' His family supported his decision. Ibrahim's wife, a medical doctor who was working part time, agreed that if things went terribly wrong she would go back to full employment to provide the family with a safety net. But she never needed to work full time ever again. Within four weeks of setting up his first business, Mobile Systems International (MSI), Ibrahim sold all his time upfront for the next three years. He was easily earning more than the CEO of the company he had just left.

It was immediately clear to him that there was much demand for his skills. There were an increasing number of firms worldwide with GSM (Global System for Mobile) licences but very little idea of how to design networks to support them. Short of cloning himself, Ibrahim decided he was going to have to employ staff. This was the beginning of the meteoric growth of MSI. Ibrahim had no problem recruiting staff because, as he explains, 'almost every single person wanted to leave BT with me – I had tremendous loyalty among my people. I had trained them all'. The following year, Ibrahim moved into offices in the Docklands in London with a team of four people and by the time he sold the business 11 years later the staff complement at MSI had reached 900. His business growth was phenomenal. Ibrahim had stumbled on a cash cow and he was milking it for all it was worth. The business was launched at a time when the developed world was building its first mobile networks and he found himself designing networks literally all over the world

There is no major country where we have not at least designed one network. It was great. Clearly we had some very valuable and scarce know-how which was how to design and build GSM networks. MSI was a great success from day one and we made profits from the first year onwards. I mean it was just like selling hot cakes!

In the first year of business, MSI made a profit of around £200 000; in the second year their profit had leapfrogged to £900 000. The following year it went up to £1.5 million, a year later £2.5 million, a year after that, £5 million, then £9 million, and so it went on. By the time the company was sold to Marconi in 2000 it was valued at US$900 million. At the time, Ibrahim and at least 50 of his staff became instant millionaires. The significance of his achievements and the enormity of the financial success of the business he had started the day he walked across his hall into his dining room seemed to have escaped him.

> Maybe because I didn't have the disadvantage of going to business school I never appreciated that it was successful at all, so I always thought we were not doing that well, actually.

This ex-academic-cum-engineer may have seemed a little naïve at the time, but dig a little deeper and you'll find that he actually was very naïve.

> I couldn't even read the balance sheet of the company when I started because I had no financial training whatsoever, so I managed the company using cash. I managed it by common sense and good advice from people I knew. It becomes so simple when you do it this way; you don't get trapped into business models. This was a company run completely by common sense.

It was 'common sense' not to have a sales and marketing department for more than six years because, as Ibrahim explains, 'we didn't need to market or to sell anything'. It was also common sense not to have a human resources department because they had full employment all the time and seemingly no problems with recruiting and keeping staff.

One thing which Ibrahim did which must have helped tremendously and which was still fairly novel in the UK market in the early 1990s, was to offer shares to all his employees. This was long before the dot-com boom and by the time he sold the business, 35% of the company was in the hands of the staff, 25% in his hands and the balance in the hands of investors. It was also common sense for him to change the business halfway through its life, from a consulting company to a software house, to deliver what the market demanded. Reflecting on the MSI days, he says:

> It was interesting because I went into business unintentionally; I just wanted my freedom and nothing was planned. I look at the financial performance of this company, now that I know what I know and it was incredible. To start a company without funding and no loans – we never borrowed money for the first six years – we got tremendous value. The company started with capital of £50 000 and we sold it for US$914 million. That's incredible, exceptional performance. I did not appreciate it at the time, maybe now I do.

Despite the amazing growth, Ibrahim was not a risk-taker, although he did take a few gambles in the way he allowed some of his clients to pay for his firm's services. Over the course of the years, MSI came to own minority stakes in three mobile phone operations; in Hong Kong, India and Uganda, valued at US$11 million. It was the new investors who came on board in 1996 – a firm of venture capitalists – who pointed out a potential conflict of interest between his current business of building networks, which later changed to providing software to build networks, and his informal 'licence acquisitions' business. This inadvertently led to the start of what is today one of Africa's largest mobile phone operators.

Two years before selling his first business, MSI, the three minority stakes he owned in mobile phone operations were 'placed' in an Amsterdam holding company by his investors. The holding company was called MSI Cellular Investments, a subsidiary of MSI, and this became the foundation for a new business focus that Ibrahim had been toying with. After years of designing mobile phone networks for operators across the world, he decided to become a mobile phone operator himself. His timing was impeccable. Countries across Africa were liberalising their telecoms regulations – governments were offering affordable mobile phone operating licences. Most foreign mobile phone operators were scared to go near Africa, yet the continent was hungry for telecommunications services as governments lacked the ability to meet demand. Perhaps most important of all, there was investment money available for Africa – lots of it – and it was looking for a safe way in. Many of the funds were after much of the same sort of investment opportunities and there simply weren't enough of them to go around.

Ibrahim knew he needed large amounts of financing upfront to bid for licences on the continent and to operate the mobile networks he planned to build. If his business was to be successful, he needed to raise capital – large amounts of it – and to do this he needed investors. In March 1998, Ibrahim began building his second business from scratch. This time he started with five key players, including his long-standing personal assistant. The new business already had US$11 million in assets in the form of three mobile phone operating licences owned by its parent company, MSI, and a very exciting idea to put into action.

Next, Ibrahim cleverly assembled an executive board – one that shared his vision, but more importantly, one that would reassure the investment community that good corporate governance was a given within his business. His carefully selected board was made up of some of the best brains in the mobile phone industry at the time and high-level politicians from across Europe and Africa. It included a former UK Secretary of State, a former African prime minster and an ex-CEO of a UK-based mobile phone operator. He then courted a variety of investors and embarked on a series of debt and equity financing rounds to fund the purchase of the mobile phone operating licences, the equipment and the people needed to run a pan-African telecommunications network. He raised funds from development groups like Actis Capital, the International Finance Corporation (the private banking arm of the World Bank), and financial players such as Citigroup Venture Capital.

In its first year, Celtel successfully raised US$16 million through debt and equity financing and acquired GSM licences in Zambia, Malawi, Sierra Leone and Congo Brazzaville to add to its existing Ugandan licence. From nowhere, MSI was fast becoming a major player in African telecoms. The next year Ibrahim raised a further US$35 million and again licences were acquired and businesses opened up in Gabon, Chad, the Democratic Republic of Congo (DRC) and Guinea. In another two years, a further US$216 million was raised in two separate rounds to finance more acquisitions in Burkina Faso, Niger, Sudan and Tanzania. MSI, which changed its name to Celtel in January 2004, seemed to be living up to its reputation as a 'very sophisticated investment bank with telecom assets'. Growth was rapid because demand was huge. The continent had a seemingly insatiable appetite for telecommunications services and Celtel could barely meet it. Its very presence in some of the toughest and most investment-unfriendly countries in Africa had sparked a need that required increasing funding to satisfy. It was a simple equation. If they didn't grow they would lose the market. So grow they did, and by the time Ibrahim sold the business in 2005, just seven years later, to MTC, a Kuwaiti-based operator, for US$3.4 billion, Celtel boasted mobile phone operations in 15 countries with more than 8 000 staff and 20 million subscribers.

Casting a superficial eye across the business, it was the high-profile world of investment financing that grabbed headlines and raised Celtel's global profile. But it was the people for whom he created jobs that Ibrahim was most proud.

> When one visits an operation in a country and you see the energy and the large number of young men and women really working hard, I think these were the real moments for me.

But building businesses on the African continent was not without its challenges, and a profitable business like telecoms attracted more than its fair share of trying moments. Dealing with bureaucracy in general, and the industry regulator in particular, being perceived to be a foreign company even though all the company's assets were in Sudan itself, and being subjected to arbitrary taxation 'whenever the government was short of money', were the types of issues that Ibrahim dealt with continuously. They proved to be a source of irritation, amusement and irony. He recalls one particular situation in Chad at the height of tensions in the country:

> One minister would come and ask us to close down the network, usually the minister of defence or the minister of interior. Then the president would come and say, 'No, no, no, no! If you do that we'll throw your guys in jail. You cannot close down the networks.' And then another person would come and say, 'No, we'll close the network.' On the one hand we were really helping to develop an economy and build infrastructure but sometimes we had to convince people to do what was obvious and in their own interests.

Bureaucracy, political tension and governments who preferred to bite off their noses to spite their faces seemed to be part and parcel of the telecoms business in Africa, however, Celtel's primary goal was to initially connect their growing network and ultimately to build one continuous network across Africa. It was during this period that Ibrahim realised just how little regard some African governments seemed to have for their noses.

> We tried to abolish roaming charges, which is something Europeans would die for, because we had an international gateway and you can take traffic anywhere. African customers wanted it, yes, but not African governments. Most of them did not actually even try to understand what we were doing.

On the issue of corruption in government in particular, Ibrahim is unequivocal:

> Bribery is a crime committed by two consenting adults – and yet the onus has traditionally been placed on the African participant. I am convinced that much of the bribery that occurs is less the idea of the African than of the Westerner, who gets frustrated at the slow pace of negotiations, hotels he isn't used to, and unusual foods and smells, and decides to speed things along with a bribe.

Ibrahim's insights were interesting but managing the frustrations of dealing with governments was just one side of the business, managing his ever-widening base of shareholders was another. In addition to Ibrahim, there were 16 institutional investors and staff members with shares at Celtel. The downside to successfully raising money through equity funding was the fact that investors now had a say in the business. And in Ibrahim's case, nearly 60% of the business was in the hands of institutional investors and funds. He flirted extensively with the idea of an initial public offering (IPO) to provide an exit for the institutional investors:

> These investors were looking to realise their investment. They had already made a large return on their investment and they wanted to crystallise that because their funds have certain limits. After three or four years, they really wanted an exit.

The IPO, however, was not the perfect solution because Ibrahim was reluctant to put 60% of the shares of the company on the market. So when an offer to buy that was about 30% higher than the IPO

price came in, the shareholders opted for the inevitable. And so
Ibrahim sold his second business and became a multimillionaire
for the second time.

> In fairness, I really had to support my shareholders and that's why I
> had to sell. I have to respect the people who came and supported me
> with their money and accepted the risk. If they decided it was fine for
> them to crystallise their gain, I think it was fair.

At US$3.4 billion you could argue that 'fair' was an inadequate
description for one of the largest telecommunications transactions
on the African continent.

For Ibrahim, deciding what to do next must have been extremely
difficult. He could have done anything. And anything turned
out to be quite an unexpected move. For the next chapter in his
alarmingly successful life, Ibrahim was about to create something
radical, something that had never been done before – anywhere
in the world. And in true Ibrahim style, he first consulted those
around him – from Clinton to Mandela, to Kofi Annan and Tony
Blair. This was going to be big.

> Before we launched, I talked to over 400 people. This included
> presidents, chief executives, friends. Not one of them said, 'This stupid
> thing, Mo, why? Save your money and save your time.' The reaction
> was always favourable. I think the idea was absolutely correct.

The idea was to create a US$5 million prize for African leaders
who left their presidency unaided and who had demonstrated the
greatest commitment to democracy and good governance. This
innovative solution was Ibrahim's way of addressing what he saw
as the fundamental problem facing Africa and its people:

> Travelling around in Africa, I was amazed at the natural beauty and
> the wealth of Africa. And of course you ask yourself the question,
> 'Why are we poor? What's the difference between Switzerland and
> Malawi?' You look at the landscape, you look at the country. You can
> see immediately that really without good governance and effective
> leadership, our countries will go nowhere.

In October 2007, the Mo Ibrahim Foundation made its inaugural award to President Joaquim Chissano, the former president of Mozambique. Chissano received US$5 million, to be paid out over 10 years, plus a further US$200 000 every year for life. Not bad going for doing what Ibrahim referred to as the 'right thing'.

> The important thing here is that we are African and this is an African foundation with African money. This is Africa taking care of its own business. We cannot just sit there and expect the world to do things for us.

Ibrahim knows there is no instant recipe for fixing Africa – he believes the effect of his leadership prize and the fund will only come into effect in 10 years' time. But his passion is clear and no one could argue that he has not put his money where his mouth is.

> There's no magic wand to change things. What we hope to do is enrich an already ongoing process. There are changes happening in Africa; there is a new crop of leadership coming forward. We need to have clean and effective government, and that, for sure, is the first step towards really rebuilding and developing Africa.

Supporting the prize is an index which measures and benchmarks good governance on the continent. In 2007, Mauritius was ranked number one on the Mo Ibrahim Index for African Governance, scoring the highest rating for the index's criteria, which includes rule of law, transparency and corruption, safety and security, and sustainable economic opportunity.

Ever the businessman, Ibrahim the philanthropist was not merely content with trying to change a continent through the foundation. He started a US$150 million private equity fund to invest in African businesses. Today, he divides his time between the fund and the foundation. Looking back on more than 18 years in business, Ibrahim fondly remembers the biggest challenges he faced:

> We had huge arguments trying to convince people that things can work in Africa and it was always a pleasure to meet them after we sold the business ... that made me laugh – all the way to the bank!

And he is still laughing, while he appreciates a few other things in his life. 'I'm an old man now, so I deserve a little bit of rest,' he says. At 62, Ibrahim plays golf, although he admits to having a terrible handicap. He takes the occasional holiday in Barbados or Mauritius. He listens to jazz from time to time and he reads a little – but never business books. He has no real interest in politics, 'It's a field which I don't think I have any skills to justify me going into and I think really what we're trying to do here will probably have more effect than me trying to run as a politician,' he explains firmly. And although he respects Nelson Mandela as a leader, he has no heroes in the business world and is honestly irritated by what he calls the 'idolising' of business leaders, particularly in America:

> I wish people were a little bit more humble than that because behind any one of those figures there's a great team of people who really work together in an efficient manner to deliver whatever was delivered. So I really don't think of business people in terms of heroes.

His leadership style has been entirely of his own making and displays the hallmarks of his personality – open, simple and straightforward. 'You cannot ask your people to work 12 hours a day when you only work two hours a day. You cannot ask your people to do things which you're not doing yourself.' However, the one thing that Ibrahim attributes to his success above all else is something so glaringly obvious and freely available that most business books forget to recommend it. He explains: 'It is called common sense. Forget about all those Harvard books and business schools. It's just common sense. If that prevails in what you do, you'll always be safe.' And 'safe is what he is now – a multimillionaire twice over, Ibrahim has the satisfaction of knowing that he has realised his dreams, both business and personal, and along the way he has made, and is making, a difference to the lives of Africans.

Sources:

1. The Mo Ibrahim Foundation website: www.moibrahimfoundation.org.
2. Hardymon, F and Leamon, A (2005). *Celtel International BV.* January. Boston: Harvard Business School. Available at: http://papers.ssrn.com/sol3/papers. cfm?abstract_id=954254.
3. Scheen, T (2007). 'Mohammed Ibrahim – Connection for Africa'. *Frankfurter Allgemeine Zeitung*, 11 August. Available at: http://berufundchance.fazjob. net/s/Rub2309A3DB4F3C4474B93AA8610A24AE0A/Doc~E2F9AAC4A64 5640E79E33D7C077CB0939~ATpl~Ecommon~Scontent.html.

Kwabena Adjei – The Traditional Entrepreneur

VITAL STATISTICS

Name: Kwabena Adjei
Country: Ghana
Born: 24 May 1954
Position/Title: CEO Kasapreko Company Ltd
Company turnover: US$30 million
Nationality: Ghanaian
Industry: Alcoholic and non-alcoholic beverages
Highest educational qualification: GCE Advanced Level, Workers' College, Accra

I wanted to create a product that had the properties to cure malaria, act on sexual weakness in men, help with joint and bodily pains and increase appetite. I gave some to my workers. I said to them: 'You drink some and then give me feedback on whether it's working or not.' And the boys told me: 'Hey, it's working oh ... it's working! Oh!'

Then we started giving it away so we could get feedback. I began hearing stories, people were queuing up for it. It spread like wildfire! Everybody wanted to buy it, even women; those who were not giving birth, those with menstrual cramps. We were able to cure all these things because it's herbal! And that was the beginning of our success.

The product that had caused all this excitement and that stirred the loins of Ghanaians across the country is Alomo Bitters, a herbal alcoholic product made from plant extracts, researched by the World Health Organisation affiliate in Ghana, the Centre for Scientific Research into Plant Medicine (CSRPM). Today, Alomo Bitters is by far Ghana's best-selling herbal alcoholic drink and purports to protect drinkers against an eclectic range of ailments. The product has a 98% market share of drinking bars and pubs in Ghana, and at just less than US$20 for a 750ml bottle, it is easy to see where Kasapreko's US$30 million annual turnover comes from. Alomo Bitters is the first 'scientifically formulated, herbal-based beverage' in Ghana and the flagship product of Kasapreko Company, an alcoholic and non-alcoholic beverage manufacturer in Ghana which produces 11 drink brands – many of which are market leaders in their categories.

In 2004 Kasapreko was admitted into the prestigious and ex-clusive Ghana Club 100, an institution that recognises the best performing companies in Ghana. Kasapreko entered at number 37; the following year they had climbed to number 15 and secured second place as the most profitable entity on the club's elite list. In 2007 they moved up to number nine. The visionary behind Kasapreko is Kwabena Adjei, a self-made millionaire whose career is a testament to his belief that 'anybody is capable of succeeding in life, provided you have a dream and the desire'. It was this dream and desire that kept Adjei going through what can only be described as a very tough childhood, characterised by poverty, with literally no parental support. Adjei's journey to CEO of the privately owned Kasapreko, an entity he founded in 1989, is the quintessential rags-to-riches story. His incredulity at his success is evident, and also serves as an indicator of just how far in life he has travelled: 'I never thought I could be where I am today. I never, ever thought that,' he explains.

Today, Kasapreko, whose motto is 'a step beyond excellence', employs more than 120 permanent staff and about 90 contract workers in their state-of-the-art, fully automated bottling plant – the first of its kind in the country. The plant effortlessly substantiates the company's claim to be the most innovative drink manufacturer in Ghana. Kasapreko was also the first to collaborate with a research organisation – the CSRPM. It was the first company in Ghana to market a scientifically formulated drink, the legendary Alomo Bitters. With its focus on research and development, Kasapreko was also the first of the local manufacturers to establish a modern quality control and product development laboratory, and it was the first to install a wall-to-wall bottling-to-packaging production line. And it is more than likely that Kasapreko is the first to have invested in a 100-acre forestation project in the eastern region of Ghana, which will grow the medicinal plants it plans to use for the Alomo Bitters concentrate.

In addition to its 11 indigenous drink brands, which include home-grown gins, brandies, liqueurs, tonic wines, cordials and soda mixes, the company is also in partnership with UTO of the Netherlands, whose products it bottles for sale in Ghana under licence. Kasapreko's top three products after Alomo Bitters are Kasapreko Dry Gin, Opeimu Bitters and the uniquely named Ogidigidi Bitters. Its award-winning products are exported throughout West Africa and increasingly to the United States, Canada and Europe to service predominantly the Diaspora market. Although at 5%, exports still remain a small part of the business. There is even purported to be a Kasapreko appreciation club somewhere in Australia!

All of Adjei's successes, including being voted Marketing Man of the Year in 2002 and being nominated to the Ghana Club 100, his various directorships and his role as adviser on the Chartered Institute of Administrators of Ghana, would have been difficult to foresee given his background, which is what makes this story even more remarkable.

The early years

Born on 24 May 1954, Kwabena Adjei was brought up by his father after his parents divorced. His father was self-employed and was not in a financial position to contribute to his son's life. Financially at least, Adjei was pretty much on his own. According to Adjei, his education prospects were 'very, very, very bleak; my father was not able to take care of me so I didn't have much to learn from him'. However, at a young age Adjei proved to be both academically gifted and streetwise. He was top of his class in the school he attended in the Western Region of Ghana, Bonuama Catholic School, at worst, he came second. He excelled consistently in the regular inter-school exams held in his town in the Western Region. Adjei recognised the fact that he was good, but his situation seemed destined to determine his fate.

> I knew I was very clever but because of my circumstances there was nobody to help me attend school, so all my education has been on my own. I used to feel a bit embarrassed when my teachers kept telling me: 'Kwabena, you are very good.' When I was in Form 2 at secondary (school) I had to leave. I was shattered and I realised that this was the beginning of my challenge.

So Adjei rose to the challenge. He clearly had 'a will to succeed' in his education and at a time when most children were doing all they could do to get out of school, Adjei put all his energies into trying to get back in. It was, he says, 'the beginning of the fire that began burning in me':

> It was my wish to be a priest because of the difficulties I was facing at the time. I was looking for something like a scholarship but the only places I could look for this was from the clergy. So I wrote letters to the bishop, and then a Roman Catholic company in Accra to see if they could sponsor me.

When that didn't work he tried something else:

> I learnt that in Ghana people from the Northern Region had free access to secondary school if they passed the common entrance, so when I was in Form 3, I chose a school in the Upper Region, hoping that if I passed, I'd also get a free scholarship. I did not realise that they were only giving it to the northerners.

Needless to say, Adjei, being a southerner, didn't get the scholarship. On his own, and armed with little more that his internal fire and determination, Adjei left his village and moved to Ghana's capital city, Accra. He was a 23-year-old largely uneducated man with limited prospects. He had no choice but to start at the very bottom. 'When I came to Accra, I used to do manual jobs, mainly weeding on the roadside. I would work for two to three days and then I would be laid off,' he explains. His first proper job was as a labourer in the Department of Forestry, where he spent his time weeding in the state-owned plantations. Physically small, Adjei did not fare well in this demanding job, which usually attracted men of a larger build who could handle the heat, pace and demands of the job. He admits that he wasn't very good at the physical labour and he soon got fed up with the back-breaking outdoor life. He quit and moved in with his sister, who lived in Accra, and took a job as a house helper.

The Greek playwright Sophocles believed that 'there is no success without hardship', and in Adjei's case this proved to be very true. He was treated so badly by his employer that on one particular occasion, after a severe beating, Adjei ran away. But he didn't run far. He approached one of the neighbours in the area for a job, again as a household hand, and luckily, the neighbour took one look at Adjei and saw potential. He realised that Adjei was no ordinary servant. He could see that the young man was ambitious, so he gave him the address of the Accra Workers' College and the Institute of Adult Education, and with this, Adjei took his first steps towards gaining an adult education.

Going back to his village was not an alternative for Adjei – neither was failure. 'I wanted to prove to my hometown that when I came to Accra, I would not go back empty-handed – so that was the drive,' he explains. So began a journey which propelled Adjei from obscurity and poverty to recognition and fortune. Using the little money he had saved up as a household hand, Adjei enrolled at the Institute of Adult Education, registering for a correspondence course in mathematics, English, geography, history and accounts. At the time he wanted to join the air force as a pilot. In between lessons, Adjei found himself a job as a kitchen helper at an American aluminium smelting company, Barco, to help pay for his studies. His aim was to get into university and he put all his energy into achieving this goal. 'I didn't want to fail – at all,' he says firmly.

For two years, Adjei worked as an ordinary 'kitchen boy' by day and an extraordinary student by night, acquiring knowledge that would help him in the future. Throughout his double life he remained driven and focused, never losing sight of his goal. Although the urge to educate himself was strong, the need to make money to supplement his meagre wages soon took over. Spotting a potential business opportunity, Adjei decided to take his first tentative steps into business and put his night studying on hold.

The fledgling entrepreneur

It was the early 70s, and Ghana had been under the leadership of seven successive presidents, including Jerry Rawlings, who could not seem to pull the country out of its economic slump. Ghana had been suffering since the collapse of the price of cocoa, one of its largest exports, during Kwame Nkrumah's time in the 60s. The country was going through difficult times – almost everyone felt the impact of a failing economy. There was little to buy and even less with which to buy it. But in all this Adjei saw a perfect opportunity. Using the money he had saved up, he decided to invest in a small trading business. He started buying basic necessities; commodities like soap, toothpaste, cigarettes and underwear from neighbouring Togo and selling them to his colleagues at Barco. Where he got the products from and how he got them into Ghana was an adventure that clearly demonstrated Adjei's sheer determination and will to succeed. Introduced to the trading business by his sister, Adjei soon joined the growing, merry band of small-time traders, dabbling in informal imports across the Ghana-Togo border.

> During the military regime there was nothing in Ghana, so I was going to Togo. I would go by road and come back before I had to go to work, all in the same day. I would wake up at four o'clock in the morning and catch a taxi across the border. They often got into a lot of accidents on the way because of the fast speeds at which they were going – I was risking my life but that is where my capital started.

The government had imposed price controls which restricted traders like Adjei from selling commodities at black market prices. Anyone caught selling was likely to be detained and whipped. Like the true businessman he was fast becoming, Adjei realised that the potential to make money far outweighed the potential of a whipping and he soon left his day job to concentrate on the trading business. Despite the risks involved, with just two trips to Togo, Adjei worked out that he could make more than his current monthly salary working at Barco.

> I thought, why don't I just work for myself? I was going around like a hustler, going to houses and selling. In times of scarcity you don't have to be a good salesman because you if you have it – people will buy it!

And they did. For the next three years Adjei continued to bring in commodities from across the border. His product base expanded to include clothing; he began to make some real money and was able buy his first home. But Adjei was not content; he had tasted success, albeit in a small way, and he wanted more of it. 'I wanted money and I thought those gems would give me money.' The gems Adjei refers to was gold – Ghana's leading export commodity. Gold has been the country's principal export since 1992 and contributes to one tenth of the world's market. Needless to say, the sector was also highly regulated by the government, but once the administrative loopholes had been cleared, entry was not too difficult. Adjei registered as an agent and got a licence to become an accredited buying agent for the government's diamond- and gold-buying company. The licence allowed him to buy gold from small-scale dealers and sell it on to Diamond House, the government-owned buying house. At the same time he started operating a jewellery shop and workshop in which he hired a team of jewellers to make wedding bands and chains which he sold directly to the public. He laughs as he remembers his baby steps up the success ladder: 'I was now becoming a full-time, big time businessman – in a small way!'

The gold business became Adjei's main source of income, and although he couldn't determine exactly what his turnover or profit was, he knew he was doing well. His approach was rudimentary: 'The only thing I could judge was whether I was losing or not losing. I made sure that anything that I bought was sold. For example, if I bought let's say $1 000 worth of goods, I would go and sell it and get $3 000,' he explains, outlining his concept of making a profit. A 200% profit margin was not bad going at all, especially for a first-time businessman.

Adjei's next venture was a hardware store that sold cement, iron rods, padlocks, nails and anything concerning building. Ironically, he continued to run the jewellery shop while his wife ran the hardware store. At the time, Adjei was living in Nungua, a suburb of Accra, which boasted the dubious honour of housing the most distilleries in Accra, and most if not all of the local alcoholic drinks were being manufactured there. Nungua was affectionately known as the 'Scotland' of Ghana, because like Scotland, it was known for its numerous distilleries, which seemed to be very lucrative. Consequently, the area was home to some of the most successful and wealthy business people in Accra. Adjei saw their comings and goings and wanted more than anything to join their league.

The alcohol business

The alcohol business was indeed a lucrative industry in Ghana, but it was also highly competitive. This did not put off Adjei in the slightest; in fact, the very number of players in the market proved to him that there was money to be made and he was out to make it.

> As a curious entrepreneur at that time, I would look at those who were driving cars, their houses and I'd say: 'Whose house is this? What does he do?' They'd say: 'Oh, he's in the alcohol business.' 'Who's this young man?' 'He's also in the alcohol business.' I said 'Ok, why don't I also go into the alcohol business and see if I can make money there.'

Undaunted by the fact that he knew little or nothing about manufacturing alcohol, Adjei embarked on a project to start making his own gin. He started with four workers – one of whom was a gin maker from a competitor – along with a tank and a filter. He didn't need significant capital to start the business and his revenues from his two other businesses easily funded the start-up and initial operating costs. Adjei intended to start small, and he soon launched into the market with 60 bottles of his very own brand of gin. It was not an easy business, and he didn't expect to make any money at the time because he was simply 'curious to see if I could start something'. He was still running the hardware and the jewellery operations, and shuttled between the three businesses. Adjei soon realised that in order to hit the big time he needed a competitive edge in at least one of the businesses. He saw his opportunity with alcohol.

I got to know that the people who were making alcohol were mainly all using the same flavouring, which meant that most of the products tasted the same. I thought, 'No, that can't be right.'

One of his friends knew of a consultant in the UK who specialised in food and drink flavours. He encouraged Adjei to go to the UK and try out some of the flavours, with a view to creating a new taste for his gin. This was revolutionary thinking in a local, typically small-scale business sector.

So I went to Britain and looked for different types of flavour to bring back to make ours a bit different. The taste of our product became distinctive – different from what was on the market. People started tasting the difference.

Despite already having an advantage with his new distinctive flavouring, Adjei went even further and set his price below that of his competitors to convert consumers and encourage people to try it out. People tasted his product, they liked it and the reputation of his gin spread.

Adjei knew he was on to something when one day, a competitor of his came to ask him about the flavour he was using. The competitor had been in a local bar and had overheard someone asking specifically for Adjei's brand. It was at that moment that Adjei realised he could be on to something very big. 'I knew then that the trick was working,' he says smugly. The 'trick' that Adjei had used to blindside the competition was simple. It was more to do with a competitive approach to business than pulling a rabbit out of a hat. He explains: 'I always try to build on what is on the market; I try to create something new and not follow the norm.' And it was this simple approach to business – not following the norm – that eventually took Adjei to the top. Still basking in the glow of the success of his gin, Adjei started working on his next trick. He applied his magic to one of the oldest traditional drinks in Africa.

Our forefathers used to chop roots and put them in a bottle. They would put alcohol on it and do the extractions and we called it bitters. But I thought, 'Why can't I do that in a refined form, using herbs in a scientific way, to come up with a product?'

The thought sent him to the CSRPM in Mampong, a government-owned research institution that uses plants, as the name suggests, for scientific research into healing. Never before in the history of the organisation had anyone approached them with a request as bizarre as this. As could be expected, they resisted. However, Adjei persisted:

> 'I want to come up with a herbal product using alcohol,' I told them. They said: 'No, we're only a research company. You know we don't do large-scale production.' So for one year I was chasing them and eventually I was able to win them over.

Adjei's request for an all-in-one, general feel-good herb-based potion took more than a year to research and develop. Finally, in 1995, Adjei was given the concentrate to produce Alomo Bitters and this single brand started the meteoric rise of Kasapreko. 'People started testifying that this thing was good,' Adjei says. The excitement that surrounded the introduction of Alomo Bitters could be likened to the enthusiasm that greeted the launch of Prozac in the West. It was almost as if Alomo Bitters could make the blind see, the deaf hear and the lame walk. However, it was its claims of heightened sexual performance that seemed to propel the product's popularity. 'Everybody wanted to buy it. It was my own dream, my own creation and nobody had ever done it in Ghana,' Adjei says proudly.

In order to meet demand, Adjei needed to up production quickly from the initial 15 cartons with which he had started. He began hiring qualified workers, buying more machinery and negotiating with the CSRPM to produce more concentrate, more quickly. Soon, the company introduced several product lines, including gin, schnapps, aperitifs and a tonic wine. Adjei embarked on an aggressive marketing campaign, going house to house, door to door, taking his product straight to his customers. He bought a car on which he wrote: 'Buy the best and ignore the rest'. At the time, no one else in his industry was using the kind of marketing tactics he had adopted to promote and sell his brands. It was not surprising then that Adjei won an award for Marketing Man of the Year in 2002 in recognition of his brand-building strategies.

It wasn't just his approach to business; Adjei's distribution methods were also unique in the market place. While his competitors waited for bar owners to come and pick up stock, Adjei did the opposite. 'I would deliver my products to a bar or a retailer, leave it with them and come back in a week or two to get my money. No one was doing it at that time. I had a good product and I wanted to sell. It was a very hands-on business,' he explains. His hard work paid off:

> The company soon became a household name. You see, that's what competition is about. You must be able to create – grab market share. I look at the marketing strategy of my competitors and I try to improve on it.

His initial team of four staff grew as his business spread rapidly from Accra to the rest of the country. He acquired vans and developed his market in Kumasi, the second-biggest city in Ghana, then to Takrabe, then the Brong Ahafo region. Kasapreko soon had vans crisscrossing the country and the business took off. In 2008, Kasapreko vans were delivering more than 2 000 cases each of Alomo Bitters, dry gin and Opeimu Bittters to bars, markets and retailers across the country.

Education and leadership

Adjei's achievements in the business world and his intrinsic understanding of business strategy – particularly marketing – are all the more remarkable given his educational background. A very practical man, Adjei realised his shortcomings early on and made moves to fill the educational gaps while he was growing his business. He registered with an organisation called Empretec, an entrepreneurial development institution organised by UNCTAD (the United Nations Conference on Trade and Development), which offers short courses to entrepreneurs in order to promote the creation of sustainable small- and medium-sized enterprises. They gave him the valuable basic training he would need in business.

> When I started the business, I was doing about three courses every year, and that was apart from the social courses. I was working in the business and I was educating myself at the same time. Bit by bit I covered almost all the business subjects. We had to do public relations, financial management … I had to know something about economics, about commerce, about advertising and marketing. All this knowledge I

acquired, not through the formal education sector but through my own efforts. I knew I was handicapped and the only way I could do those things was to go on these short courses – (for) four days, one week – I have a lot of certificates!

Adjei was not just driven; he had a clear goal in mind and knew exactly where he wanted to take his business.

When I was with Empretec, they asked me this question: 'In three years' time, after you have left this school, where do you see yourself?', and I said to them: 'I will be the best or the biggest alcohol manufacturing company in Ghana.' So when I won the Marketing Man Award, a friend of mine called me and asked me: 'How come what you said has come true, just like that?' It was because I was working towards that. I wanted to be the best. It had always been my motivation, to lead not to follow. I can't just be following like that. I need to excel.

Adjei's business philosophy is simple and leaves little room for failure: 'You lead, follow, or forget about it. Your presence has to be felt.' And there is no doubt that Adjei's presence is felt not just by his competition – his brands are by far the market leader – but also by those who work for him.

I would say I'm a hands-on manager because at times even my workers tell me that I'm an MD who does not stay in his office – I believe in going to where the action is. I'm always there, so that has helped me a lot. I know most of the workers; I know their names. I call them and we converse and eat together. I tell them that I don't want to close my office, so I operate an open-door policy and it's practical. When you come to my office, you don't have to knock – the door is always open.

An amusing, but painful example of his hands-on management style resulted in an incident that led to a dislocated shoulder which put an end to his golfing days. Adjei laughs at the memory:

We were building this factory and there were some workers doing something on the roof. I said I wanted to go and check on it to see whether they were doing it right or not. So I climbed up the building and I fell down! I dislocated my shoulder and I had to go to the US for surgery!

Just as well that Adjei feels his continued value to the business is largely mental and not physical. 'I have the capacity to think, to create. I'm very creative. I think a lot – look at all this,' he says, pointing out his ever-growing product range. 'I'm developing a lot of new products, I'm thinking of them one by one.' Adjei is also highly patriotic and staunchly pro-African. He believes that anything that can be done in the West or the East can be done in Ghana – at least in the drinks manufacturing business.

> Let's introduce more products that are created in Ghana, using our own herbs, not using American herbs or those from China. We should be using our herbs – African herbs for Africans.

His pro-African stance does not stop there. Adjei is a man who is proud of his roots, so much so that he named his company, Kasapreko, after the name of the chief of the area from which he is from, the Wassa Amenfi traditional area.

> I went to him (the chief) and asked for the name, because I'm from that village and this is my way of exposing my pride in my area. I told him I wanted to christen my company and my drinks using his name and he said: 'Ok, my grandson. Use it.' So because of that he's also on our board.

The fact that Nana Kasapreko Kwama Bassanyin II, a renowned traditional ruler, is a non-executive board director of Kasapreko alludes not just to Adjei's traditional leanings, but also to his shrewd business acumen. The chief holds a double degree in economics and estate development, and is also trained as an industrial laboratory analyst. In addition to the chief, Adjei is also inspired by business leaders who have successfully created something huge from something small. He explains:

> Ted Turner, the owner of CNN – I had him in mind when I was young because he started something small and look at where CNN is now. I thought Honda was just a car, but later I got to know that it was a name, somebody's name, a human being! Things like that motivate me.

Being a self-taught man, Adjei is a voracious reader of business and particularly motivational books; he has read the whole Rich Dad,

Year and Marketing Person of the Year by the Institute of Marketing Management. In 2005 he received an honorary award from Unisa for Outstanding Entrepreneur and Leader in the Business Environment. But it is Black Like Me, one of the most successful black-owned hair and cosmetics companies in South Africa, for which Mashaba is most famous.

> I don't come from an educational background; I was never tested on the things I do. It is scary what I have achieved in the last few years; the beauty of this country is that there are so many opportunities.

But the South Africa in which Mashaba is now flourishing is a very different one from the South Africa in which he started.

The road to manhood

> One morning at 6am the army surrounded the campus and we were asked to leave the campus by noon that day. We were thrown out. We hadn't been going to classes for two weeks at the time and one morning, instead of responding positively to our demands, the university decided to send us all to our respective homes and then they would call us back. I decided not to go back.

It was in Mashaba's second year at the University of Limpopo, studying for a Bachelor of Arts degree in administration, majoring in political science and public administration, that his academic dreams were so dramatically shattered. His decision not to return to his studies was one he never regretted. It was the early 80s and South Africa was a politically charged place to be. It was a time of much civil unrest and there were many highly politicised and defiant youths – just like Mashaba – who had little to lose by challenging the apartheid system. It was not really surprising then that Mashaba harboured a secret passion to join the military and help fight for South Africa's freedom.

> I didn't go back to university because I had contacts that had promised to smuggle me out of the country for military training – to be part of the fight. At the time we were convinced there would be no way we would get our freedom without fighting and there was no point in subjecting ourselves to what our parents went through, because what

our parents went through didn't really make sense. Our belief was that we had nothing to lose, so why should we stick around and not do something?

While Mashaba was waiting for his turn to contribute to the struggle, his brother-in-law managed to get him a job as a dispatch clerk in the local Spar supermarket in Pretoria. It must have been a bit of an anti-climax for a wannabe freedom fighter. But it was his first job, and his first real experience of working with white people. In the days when he chose to stay back in the township and gamble, Mashaba would hear stories of what happened to the black workers in white suburbs: 'I used to listen to people, elders in my community and the kids, and every time they came back from their jobs they relayed the horror stories of how they were treated and how their dignity was taken away.' Mashaba was about to experience this for himself first-hand:

> You couldn't find ways to get into trouble with the whites because there was just no way one could avoid it. I came into direct contact with open racism. For the first time in my life I had to face it head on.

Notwithstanding the difficult working environment, Mashaba persevered with his job for seven months and tolerated daily humiliations, convinced that it was only a matter of time before he got the call that would take him out of the country for military training. In the meantime, he found another job, working once again as a dispatch clerk for an Indian furniture manufacturing company called Motali Industries. Although his situation greatly improved in terms of working in a less racist environment, there were no real prospects for Mashaba to develop himself. And by then it was dawning on him that the call to take up arms was probably not going to come. Mashaba was ambitious and wanted to make something of his life. When he realised that his job was no longer a means to an end, and was becoming the end in itself, he decided to take charge of his life.

> I wanted to be something one day. I could see that with the people in my community, some of them were good human beings yet they would tell tales of how they worked for a company for perhaps 30 or 40 years and one day (the employers) would decide their services were

not needed. The next day you wouldn't even have to blink, you would be out of a job. So then you ask yourself; what's the point? To wait 40 years hoping that it's going to happen in our next life? I wanted it to happen now; I was not prepared to waste my life.

So Mashaba decided to explore the little he knew about the world of business.

I thought definitely business would be the answer. You know, you buy papers every day and there were always companies looking for commission sales reps. The ads would ask if you want to make R1 million a day – we have products for you to sell (they said). I thought maybe this was something that could give me my independence.

There was only one small hitch. To take advantage of most of these commission-only sales jobs, Mashaba required a car, which presented an interesting dilemma.

On the weekends friends and I would go and party at different shebeens (pubs) and *stokvels* (savings clubs). I knew it would be dangerous to have a car with all these friends and I didn't want them to have the impression that my car would be a taxi for their use. I knew I could not go out and buy a car and run a business under these conditions, with all these friends around.

So he came up with a slightly unusual solution – he got married!

Before this idea came to my mind, 'marriage' was not in my vocabulary. Now there was a different reality. I was going to be in business and I needed a car for that business. I thought that to really get the protection and stability I needed, I had to get married before I bought a car, and it is the one decision of my life that I treasure most.

It may not have been the most romantic reason to get married but marriage nevertheless proved to be Mashaba's salvation. More than anything, it showed great maturity on his part and was the first tangible step the young man took down the path towards his goal. In 2008 Mashaba and Connie celebrated their 26th wedding anniversary. She is not only his wife, but over the years has become his business partner; at one stage the CEO of Black Like Me, the hair and cosmetics company that Mashaba founded in 1985.

From self-employed to entrepreneur

Being married didn't necessarily take Mashaba out of the gambling scene; it really just gave him a reason, and a good one, to duck out of his bad-boy antics. He was very focused and prepared to work hard; to this day he advocates discipline and stability as the key to success in life and in business. 'I could still go out with the boys but I had protection because I could say: "boys, I have to go home now!"' he laughs. Two months after his wedding, Mashaba finally bought the car, resigned from his dead-end job in the furniture factory and started working as an independent sales rep for a number of different companies.

> I sold insurance, but two months into it I decided this was not for me so I started selling exclusive dinner services by catalogue to ladies. I also sold bed linen, cutlery, fire detection systems and so on.

Mashaba loved his new life and he was undoubtedly an excellent sales person. The fact that he could consistently achieve high sales across such a diverse range of products proves that he knew the secret to selling. He understood the psyche of his customers and this innate skill would prove to be very useful later in his career.

> It was great, all of a sudden I was making two, three times what I was making working for an employer and I had total independence. I wasn't answerable to anyone, only to how much money I wanted to make. I did not have to be subjected to racism any longer. The companies I sold for, we respected one another and I would not deal with people I did not want to associate with.

All seemed well in Mashaba's new world, but he had not realised the impact South Africa's restrictive pass laws would have on his new found independence. Pass laws were implemented as far back as 1926 and were designed to restrict the movement of black people around the country.

> Once I resigned (from the job at the factory) I was a criminal because the pass laws required every black man and woman to work for a white

employer who signed your reference book every month to show that you were employed. I wasn't employed by anyone so I had no one to sign my pass book. So I decided I would rather live like a criminal and I lived like that for many years.

Living like a criminal meant keeping one step ahead of the police who were out to detain any black person found in the wrong place without a passbook. The challenge of not getting caught was even harder given the political instability that prevailed until the late 80s. These were dangerous times for black people – South Africa was on a knife edge and no one knew when or how it would explode. It was survival of the fittest.

> I became an expert in ducking and diving from the police. The chances of my going to jail were very high because I had to be in towns and able to move around in order to sell. The police were always around looking for passes. One thing I learnt that really helped me was to always look smart. I developed a habit of always wearing a suit and tie, so if the police stopped me they wouldn't think I was a criminal. I would negotiate my way out by claiming I had left my reference book in the office. Then I would phone an office not far from where we were and it would always be a big company so that they would be embarrassed to take me there. That was how I survived.

Mashaba did better than just survive, he prospered. Sales were good, in fact, very good, and he was earning more money than his friends who were bankers or doctors. It was an ongoing process though, because for the next three years he was constantly on the lookout for new companies whose products he could sell. But he was about to strike gold. Mashaba had stumbled on to a market that seemed too good to be true – the black hair products sector. And, he noticed, Super Kurl was the brand that seemed to dominate.

> It took me a few weeks to realise that I had found something quite exciting. Within two weeks I gave away all the other products I was selling and focused solely on hair products.

Mashaba's primary customers were the salons which were mushrooming all over the townships and in the cities. His new product had unlocked the secret that every successful salesman needs

– repeat business.

> When I sold you a dinner service how did I come back to you later to
> sell you another dinner service? But with hair products it was simpler.
> Deliver the products to a salon today and the following day the same
> salon wants more. These salons were based at a particular location so
> it made selling easier.

He meant easier in that the salons were in fixed locations, so once he
knew the police movements in the area, he could easily avoid them.
Mashaba was by far Super Kurl's top salesperson. His commissions
were high and life was good – but Mashaba wasn't satisfied. He was,
and still is, a very ambitious man who wanted more for himself
and knew exactly what he needed to do to get it.

> I decided I was going to try to make these products myself. I had no
> technical expertise, I had no financial muscle and I had no contacts to
> get premises in the first place, so putting this together was a nightmare,
> but I had set my mind to it.

Mashaba the entrepreneur

Mashaba was going into the haircare business. He was clever
enough to know that without a good product he had nothing. He
needed to find someone to help him create his product. It just so
happened the man he 'found' had been right under his nose all
along: Johan Kriel from Super Kurl.

> The owner of the business used to like me and he used to travel with
> me to different areas on my sales trips. On one of these trips he told me
> about his production manager, Johan Kriel, who had only been working
> for Super Kurl for a few months. Johan was an entrepreneur who had
> just come out of liquidation. He had always had his own business in
> the cosmetic line. I realised that he was not the type of guy who would
> stick around.

Mashaba bravely approached Kriel. Don't forget that this was
still apartheid South Africa and a black person instigating a con-
versa-tion with a white person, with a view to asking him to leave
secure employment and join a new business venture, was highly

implausible, if not preposterous. Mashaba explains:

> One day, I got the chance to talk to Johan. I told him that I was going
> to start my own business but I needed someone to manufacture, and
> that I would get the funding. Fortunately for me, Johan bought into my
> dream.

One down, one to go. Mashaba now had the technical expertise, but
he needed the funding to put the business in place. Interestingly, the
bank was the last place he planned to go: 'There was no way that
I was going to waste my time going to the bank. In 1984 the banks
would not listen to a black person – you had to be naïve to think
that way'. And naïve was something Mashaba was most definitely
not. Instead he kept his ear to the ground:

> I knew from talking to salon owners that there was this big businessman
> who used to be a distributor for one of the big American hair product
> companies in South Africa, and as the business was developing, I think
> he lost the agency. I immediately thought that he was someone who
> might be interested and who would have knowledge and interest in
> the industry.

Knowledge, interest in the industry and most important of all,
money. So, along with a friend and colleague from Super Kurl,
Joseph Moloantwa, whom he planned to recruit into the business
once it was up and running, Mashaba engineered a meeting with
the wealthy businessman, Walter Dube, and presented his dream
in the only way he knew how – with passion.

> I had my records to show my commission statements for every month,
> I had a list of all my customers all over the country. Johan gave me a
> list of the type of machinery and the budget. I had all that and I had
> an idea of the sales we could generate. Walter took a few meetings to
> be convinced but he eventually bought into the idea to finance me. He
> loaned me the R30 000 I needed to start the business.

That was the beginning of the realisation Mashaba's dream. The four
shareholders, Mashaba, Dube, Kriel and Moloantwa, all had a 25%
share in the business and all but Dube would actively participate
in the new entity. Dube also helped Mashaba find premises in an

area of Pretoria called Ga-Rankuwa which was considered to be part of the homelands – government-designated areas for black people to conduct business. It was 1985 and there were lots of hoops and hurdles to overcome for a black man wanting to do business in South Africa. Mashaba recalls:

> At the time we were not allowed to operate in white South Africa. We had to go to the homelands. Walter had contacts, so he managed to get us premises. We paid normal rent but to get premises as a black businessman was hard.

They ended up in a 200m^2 factory which was part of the Small Business Development Corporation (SBDC) a government-funded body that provided management assistance to small business owners. Mashaba and his production manager, Kriel, had already been selling and manufacturing a similar product – Mashaba for the last 19 months – so they knew all about the black haircare products industry.

> To come out with a range of what we wanted was easy and Johan came up with our own formulations, which we tested beforehand, so that we could really separate ourselves from Super Kurl. I did my own research on the product and the packaging and on what appealed – I knew exactly what the market wanted. We had sessions as shareholders and directors, and one evening after trying so many names Walter came up with the name Black Like Me; we decided that was it.

They had the name, they had the product and they knew the market. Mashaba was ready to fly.

The building of a brand

Mashaba and his wife, Connie, Kriel and Moloantwa worked tirelessly every evening to put everything in place. Mashaba finally resigned from Super Kurl in January 1985. On 14 February 1985 the first batch of Black Like Me haircare products hit the market. 'The market grew at a phenomenal rate,' Mashaba says. 'I knew who my customers were and I had already spoken to them before. By the time I went out to sell, people were waiting for me.' They were exciting days as Mashaba and his small team hit the ground running and tried to keep ahead of the demand.

> We would manufacture at night and the following day we would go
> out and sell. Joseph and I would sell and Johan would go and buy raw
> materials. For the first few months we used to buy all our raw materials
> on a cash basis because nobody knew who we were. Johan had to travel
> to Johannesburg from Ga-Rankuwa on a daily basis to buy materials,
> and he used to buy from six different suppliers because we didn't want
> anyone to figure out what our formula was. Connie stayed behind to
> look after the premises with no telephone.

They started selling to salons directly and from there the team
dealt with distributors in a particular area. By the late 80s and
early 90s the Black Like Me brand was available in most of the
major chains – the Jumbo Cash and Carrys, Diskom Discount
Stores, Shoprite Checkers and numerous independent wholesalers.
Mashaba was a marketing whiz; he knew exactly how to create a
buzz around his brand. Black Like Me sponsored many initiatives
in the townships and poured a lot of money in to the community,
all the while growing brand empathy which soon translated into
sales. Mashaba sponsored boxing tournaments: it was Black Like
Me that sponsored the SABC broadcast of the British boxer Chris
Eubank in South Africa, he sponsored beauty pageants and radio
shows. His objective was to excite his customers with entertainment
– and his strategy was working. The biggest challenge, and one he
could not market himself out of, was the political environment in
South Africa at the time:

> We were operating under one state of emergency after another and
> then the pass laws. You can imagine when we were operating in the
> townships there were all these riots. From time to time you could be
> in a township and suddenly you are in the middle of riots and you
> couldn't get out; you would just have to try deliver in the middle of it
> all. Those things were difficult to manage.

There was worse to come. The business soon outgrew the first
factory and by the late 80s, Mashaba had managed to build a new
factory in Mabopane a small town in the North West province
of the country, using what he describes as his 'own resources'.
At that stage, the Black Like Me business was one of the leading

black haircare product manufacturers in South Africa. His staff complement had grown from the initial four to 150, and he was turning over about R3.9 million every month. Mashaba was at the height of his career and having the time of his life running his own business, with the independence he had so craved.

> My products were being used all over the country. Coming from the township, it was really a fulfilling experience for me. But then unfortunately someone decided to torch it – that really was heartbreaking.

On 17 November 1993 a massive fire swept through Mashaba's factory and burnt it to the ground. It was 2am when his phone rang; Mashaba was fast asleep in bed. He was told the news of a fire at the factory and by 6am that morning there was nothing left. Mashaba watched eight years of hard work dissolve into a mass of smoke and black ash. He knew the fire was a case of arson, although to date there has never been a proper investigation and no conclusion to the case.

> When I realised that the factory was gone I also knew that the new South Africa was beginning to develop and that meant I had the opportunity to look for business premises outside of the homelands structure. I had the name, I had the brand, so I went out and looked for new premises to start again.

To hear Mashaba tell the story of the fire is to see a man who was so focused – his vision so clear – that he simply moved on, forever in pursuit of his clearly defined goal. 'I was even more determined to succeed because I had no choice. If I threw in the towel, who was going to employ me? My survival depended on my doing things on my own,' he explains. Although he was insured, Mashaba ended up getting back less than half what he lost in the fire. The damage to the business was immense and set Black Like Me back more than a year:

> That fire really affected our business very badly because you don't buy the type of machinery we used straight off the shelf. So we suffered badly in terms of market share. It took more than a year to get back (up and running) and during that time the consumer moves on. Because

we couldn't produce some of our key items our competitors cleaned us out.

Mashaba was down but he was definitely not out. He started trying to rebuild the business and soon realised he needed to bring in a partner to help return Black Like Me to its heydays. Over the years, he had had many overtures from various companies looking to buy him out. He had always passed them up. But that was before he had to contend with a fire that nearly wiped out his livelihood. Before long Mashaba had found a buyer in the form of the multinational, Colgate:

> I opted for the Colgate route because they were happy for me to keep a share. I didn't want to give this business away completely, as much as I needed some help. I wanted someone who could help me take it to the next level.

Mashaba ended up selling 75% of his business to Colgate, effective from July 1997, for an undisclosed amount. The new owners brought in new capital, new infrastructure, new distribution and new disciplines – Black Like Me was transforming itself into a large corporate. However, 18 months into the marriage, Mashaba realised it wasn't working.

> My business just refused to be part of a big corporate. Our decision-making process slowed quite dramatically. We couldn't move fast and this industry needs speed. We lacked speed.

His relationship with Colgate, surprisingly, was fine; it was just the businesses that didn't get on. Mashaba took a deep breath and told Colgate honestly that he couldn't work with them.

> Colgate was trying to help by putting discipline into the business but then we realised we were stifling it. I called my corporate advisers and said: 'This is not working and I am not continuing any longer. Please negotiate with Colgate to take me out.'

Mashaba was a pragmatic man. He was prepared to walk away from a dream that had taken him 12 years to create because he felt trapped in a corporate prison.

I thought my baby was gone but there are certain things you can change in life and there are certain things you can't. I accepted that I wasn't going to be able to afford to buy this business from Colgate because if I looked at what they had paid me for it, I was not prepared to pay that much to get it back. I accepted that as a fact. You move on in life.

But Mashaba didn't bank on the negotiation skills of his corporate adviser, Shane Ferguson, who later became his partner in the investment holding company he would establish.

I had a good corporate guy who came to me and said: 'Herman, there is an opportunity for you to buy the business.' I said: 'Shane, you must be joking if you think Colgate will sell.' But we started discussions with Colgate and six months down the line on 1 August 1999 I bought Colgate out – I bought the business back.

There is no mistaking the excitement and pride in Mashaba's voice as he tells of how his baby came home. Mashaba and a few shareholders produced the money to buy back the shares. Using his undisclosed payout from Colgate, Mashaba had started investing in small businesses – anything from R500 000 to R1 million a time. As a result he had grown a sizeable war chest, which had suddenly become very useful.

The Colgate guys moved out and I put in new management, got rid of people I did not need in the business, and brought back some of the people who used to work for me, who had resigned during the Colgate era, including my wife, Connie.

It was just like the old days. 'Very exciting times,' says Mashaba proudly. 'Fortunately, things worked for us. It was difficult and challenging but exciting. We had a great run.' Black Like Me had always been synonymous with haircare and at the outset of the business, that's all the company sold. Since then, the company has branched out into skincare products and hair colouring products. As well as Black Like Me, the product range now consists of Perfect Choice, the skincare range, and Colorissimo and Crazy Colour, the two hair colour ranges. And then in 2005 Mashaba sold 50% of Black Like Me to Amka Products, a South African health and beauty products manufacturing and marketing company. He shut down the manufacturing arm of Black Like Me which, as part of the deal, he outsourced to Amka. Mashaba is now chairman of the company and Connie, his wife, is still actively involved in the business.

From cosmetics to high finance

Mashaba would have kept on running had another opportunity not come and quite literally dragged him, kicking and screaming, into a new era of black business in South Africa. Fast forward to 2002, post-apartheid South Africa: Mandela had been released, the country had staged its first democratic elections eight years before, the landscape had changed and black people were being encouraged and helped, through government policies, to participate in the economy. There was a new style of black businessman emerging and there were lots of opportunities. Black economic empowerment (BEE) was the buzzword.

> In 2002 when the government started coming out with legislation to govern the Black Economic Empowerment Act, that's when I realised that with or without Herman Mashaba, BEE was a reality. I decided it was time for me to graduate; take my life to the next level.

The next level Mashaba had in mind was to establish an investment holding company that would buy equity stakes in predominantly white-owned companies.

> I had done a very big deal and I had a bit of money to invest. After I sold to Colgate I used to do investments while running Black Like Me, and had started to have some experience in making money.

Mashaba decided to focus on investments full time and promptly resigned from Black Like Me. He initially hired someone else as the chief operating officer, but two years later Connie took over. Mashaba started his first investment company, Leswikeng Minerals and Energy, and continued to operate from the Black Like Me premises, with Shane Ferguson, the man who had helped him buy back his company five years before, at his side. Once he was formally in the game, a whole new world opened up. 'I discovered a minefield of opportunities because when people knew that I was a BEE player they started talking to me about investments,' he says. Mashaba listened and today he has more than 18 investments worth billions of rands, covering mining, real estate, transport, retail, technology and tourism. He is either the chairman or a non-executive director on the boards of all 18 companies. He proudly explains some of the investments:

> At the moment in South Africa the construction industry is the flavour of the moment. We have a big investment in Stocks Building Africa and in Sea Kay Holdings. I own a share in one of the biggest quarries in Johannesburg and a big share in a brick-manufacturing factory in Gauteng.

So far, Mashaba's investments are all providing substantial returns and although he doesn't want to give specific figures, he is clearly happy with the type of returns he is seeing.

> Mogale Alloy has grown substantially for me and in four years I have never taken the cash out of it. If I were to dispose of it, I will get at least 15 times what I invested at least. It has been one of the best. (With) UG2 Platinum Trailers I got my money back in nine months – a great investment. Then I can tell you that the big one is a listed company, Phatsima Properties. I took 22 million shares. Obviously this is a long-term investment because I had to borrow over R12 million. Can I afford to pay it back in nine months? No, but the business is over-performing. In terms of profits I have profited by over R100 million.

For someone who sold shampoo just six years before, Mashaba sounds like he's been a player in the investment world all his life. You could argue that his early gambling days prepared him for the high-risk world of equity investments. But like any successful investor, Mashaba has honed his instincts and uses some key strategies to minimise his risk:

> I buy into companies where I believe in the management. If I get an opportunity and you come to me and say: 'Herman, we are looking for an investor in our business', the first thing I do is look at the chemistry. Do I feel comfortable with you enough to partner with you? That's the first thing I have to get past. Then I can go into the finances with you and then your strategy. What do you have in mind for the business going forward? I want to make sure that I am working with people who

have a reputation and integrity – I can't afford to mix with cowboys.

Clearly his methodology is working and if Mashaba were still a gambling man his money would be exactly where it is right now. But his success rate to date has not been entirely of his own making. There is no doubt that Mashaba has benefited tremendously from the South African government's BEE policies, which drove white companies to actively seek out black partners. Unfair advantage or not, BEE is something for which Mashaba does not apologise:

> For the last 300 years blacks were not allowed to be business people. That is why I think it is an insult to make black people feel bad about BEE. BEE not only empowers individuals, it empowers their kids and their families, because when one black man is successful he feeds many mouths. I think people; black South Africans in particular, should not feel bad around participation in BEE activities. We can't do without it.

Despite his support of BEE, Mashaba sees himself as a thoroughbred capitalist, openly driven by profit:

> I don't think we have to apologise for wanting to be capitalists and being business people for ourselves and for our families. We must not mislead people though – when we tell people we are in business because we have a good social conscience. You don't start a business because you want to help people. If you want to help people go into politics because then people understand your agenda. Why should I apologise for being a capitalist when I work in a capitalist environment created by the politicians? I am not breaking the law.

Despite his tough talk, Mashaba understands that his success gives him certain responsibilities towards those less advantaged than him. 'I went into business because I wanted to make money, but at the same time I know I have responsibilities, that is why I get involved in corporate social investments. But those are separate matters which I can only do if I have made the money,' he says firmly. Without a doubt, Mashaba has made enough money to divert some of it, along with his time, towards a social project which is very close to his heart. He is the current chairman of the Fieldbands Foundation, a skills foundation programme which he is passionate about:

> We start bands all over the country. We want to produce future leaders
> and we use music to achieve this objective. I have seen how we have
> impacted on the lives of these kids. We work with kids from difficult
> backgrounds with a big percentage of parents unemployed; some are
> from single parent homes, some don't even have parents. But we have
> given these kids hope. We are not a charity organisation but we are
> there to provide opportunities for these kids. I am quite pleased; we are
> reaching over 10 000 kids and I know with the type of funding we are
> putting in place, this will run forever. You will see that this foundation
> is the beneficiary of most of my investments.

By his definition Mashaba is successful, and he puts his success
down to integrity: 'I strongly believe I have managed to do what I
have done because I can always go back to people I have worked
with. I don't say I don't make mistakes, but I will never mislead
someone – in life things always come back.' In business Mashaba has
been inspired by political and business leaders alike: the founder
of the South African retail chain Pick 'n Pay, Raymond Ackerman,
and the outspoken cleric, Desmond Tutu. But perhaps the biggest
influence and something that has had the most significant impact
on his life, is a book called *The World On Fire* by Chinese-born
Yale law professor Amy Chua. She claims that when developing
world countries embrace First World democracy and free trade too
quickly, the results are nothing short of catastrophic, as Mashaba
explains.

> This book is about the economic disparities in different countries all
> over the world – the type of consequences you get in each situation.
> It made such an impact on my life because Africa in particular is one
> of the most conspicuous examples of economic disparity. I thought,
> 'Herman, if you are not going to help and be part of the solution, you are
> not going to have the future for your kids and future generations.'

With that in mind, Mashaba has always put his family first. In
addition to his wife Connie he has two children: a 14-year-old
daughter and an 11-year-old son. 'I want to succeed for my family,
for my country and for myself,' he explains firmly. This golf-playing,
BEE capitalist with a handicap of 14 can safely and unequivocally

say that he has achieved his life's ambition. To paraphrase the lyrics of 'Lets get it on', one of the greatest hits of his musical hero Marvin Gaye, Mashaba no longer 'needs to worry' and he 'doesn't have to push' – he's made it.

Strive Masiyiwa – The Spiritual Entrepreneur

VITAL STATISTICS

Name: Strive Masiyiwa
Country: Zimbabwe
Born: 29 January 1961
Position/Title: Founder and chairman of Econet Group
Nationality: Zimbabwean
Industry: Telecommunications
Highest education qualification: Bachelor of Science in
electrical and electronic engineering, University of Wales

I was in Boston at the time and we'd been waiting for something like six months for the final ruling to be issued. I go to bed and I have a dream that the judge just gave his ruling. I wake up, I look at my watch and it's two o'clock in the morning and I ring Zach Wazara in Zimbabwe, one of my directors, and I say: 'Zach, has the ruling come?' He says: 'No, no, it hasn't come.' I said: 'Can you check with the lawyers?' So he rings the lawyers, rings me back and says: 'Strive, go back to sleep. You and your dreams! The court is in recess – it's closed.'

I go back to bed. Zach rings me an hour later and he says: 'Guess what? The judge has ruled in our favour!

It must have been 4am, it was 31 of December 1997. It was snowing. I got up and I just wept! I talked to my wife on the phone, then I got dressed, I put on this trench coat and I went on to the streets of Boston and I was singing a hymn. It was so cold in the snow but I kept singing my hymn, it was a Shona hymn and I was singing it at the top of my voice, tears streaming down my face.

Strive Masiyiwa had just received news that he had finally been awarded a GSM (Global System for Mobile) licence to run a mobile phone network in Zimbabwe. It was to be the only mobile phone licence in the world to be issued by a court of law, rather than a government, and it marked the end of a gruelling five-year battle with the Zimbabwean government that literally changed Masiyiwa's life. He lost his business and much of his fortune. It was, without doubt, the bleakest period of his life:

I was retrenching staff, my business was on its knees and my construction arm – they'd smashed that too. I couldn't get any work for my company. We were expecting our second daughter, and you know, I was completely crushed. I was contemplating that the time had come for me to leave the country. I had debts everywhere.

Masiyiwa had lost everything that mattered to him but that was when he found his God.

Every Sunday morning I would drive my wife and daughter to church, leave them at the church gate and pick them up again after the service, and I would go off to my mates. On the one Sunday my wife said: 'Why don't you come in with us, you're just so miserable?' I said: 'No, no it's ok.' I can't remember exactly what happened but the next time

I went. I dropped her off but I sat at the back (of the church) and I listened to this guy, this white American preacher, preaching. There were maybe 3 000 people in the church, but I thought he was speaking to me. At the end of the service he made an altar call. I put my hand up, someone came up to me and said: 'You put your hand up, can you go to the front?' And I said: 'No, I didn't put up my hand!' and I left the church. I did this for three weeks and on the third week I went to the front. That day I left that place and I was an absolutely different person. I was at peace. It was a very remarkable experience.

From that moment onwards, Masiyiwa became intensely spiritual; he would pray over problematic issues and make his decisions. Even now that his future looks decidedly much brighter than it did back then, his life and that of his wife and six children still revolves around the church. He reads the Bible every morning before he does anything else and his Christian beliefs form the basis of his business values.

Nowadays, Zimbabwean-born Masiyiwa is the founder and chairman of Econet Group, a global telecommunications group with satellite, internet, mobile and fixed-line interests in 14 countries. The privately owned group is rumoured to be worth about US$3 billion, possibly US$4 billion if shareholding issues in Nigeria are resolved and the economic situation in Zimbabwe stabilises. Ironically, one of the group's primary assets and the one that started Masiyiwa's climb into the business hall of fame is Econet Wireless, the Zimbabwean mobile phone operation.

With a market share of 61% of the total mobile sector and more than 800 000 subscribers, Econet Wireless is the largest telecoms operator in Zimbabwe. Its parent company, Econet Wireless Holdings (EWH), is one of the biggest companies listed on the Zimbabwean Stock Exchange by market capitalisation. EWH is a diversified group in itself, with interests in telecoms, financial services, property, hotels, banking, bottling, finance and insurance. In 2001 the group in Zimbabwe was valued at US$400 million but today, because of the ever variable Zimbabwean exchange rate, its current value is more difficult to assess. Its 2007 annual report estimated the company's value at US$640 000 million.

In a bid to diversify revenue streams and to utilise the cash resources the group has generated, EWH has been investing in diverse listed and non-listed companies. In addition to being the largest shareholder in Zimbabwe's second-largest insurance and pensions group, First Mutual Life, EWH has also taken over the second-largest Coca-Cola bottling plant in Zimbabwe. It runs the largest internet service provider and community phone operator in Zimbabwe; Ecoweb and YourFone.

EWH is the single largest institutional shareholder in the financial services, hotel and retail group, Chanakira's Kingdom Meikles Africa. It also has a presence in property and in agro-industry. EWH is the largest institutional shareholder in Pearl Properties, the second-largest property group in Zimbabwe. It recently teamed up with a property group with assets in Angola, Nigeria, Mauritius, Kenya and Tanzania, to build a regional and continental property portfolio.

Masiyiwa runs the rest of his diversified empire from South Africa, with a small core team, after leaving his country of birth in 2000. Since then he has been involved in numerous acquisitions across the ICT spectrum and beyond. The first mobile phone network Masiyiwa launched was in Botswana in 1998, where he established what is now the country's biggest mobile operator, Mascom. Its launch was followed shortly afterwards by his Zimbabwean operation. In Lesotho, Masiyiwa runs a mobile and fixed-line network; in Nigeria he has a 5% shareholding in what is now Celtel Nigeria, an operation he started in 2001. The group's mobile phone licence in New Zealand was merged into a US telecoms investment group called Trilogy, which is rolling out a new network expected to be launched before the end of 2008.

The group has started rolling out a network in Kenya and is due to launch by the end of 2008. In 2007 Masiyiwa bought into a company called ST Cellular, which owns one of Burundi's largest mobile networks, which is being expanded. Their UK operation, called Liquid Telecoms, is a provider of wholesale international carrier services to fixed and mobile phone telecoms companies in Africa and the Indian subcontinent. Notwithstanding the fact that Masiyiwa has three mobile phone networks in operation, will launch another two in 2008, has a rather lucrative shareholding in Nigeria, and all the non-telecoms assets he is accumulating in Zimbabwe, he still feels that the company is nowhere near operating at its peak.

If our journey was the ocean, we've finally arrived at the coast and our toes are in the water. It's too early to judge whether we've been a success. I think that if we can get through the next 100 years, that will be a good time to review. You cannot build a great company in the generation of one man.

But Masiyiwa, it has to be said, is trying very hard to do just that.

The learning years

Masiyiwa is a third-generation entrepreneur who grew up in a family that ran and managed a number of businesses, including a farm, a number of shops, a taxi business and a few restaurants. Even as a child Masiyiwa took an active role in the family businesses:

> I was up by four o'clock in the morning when most kids would still be sleeping. By the time I got to school I'd have done everything: fed the pigs, gone to the fields, been to the shop. We didn't have Christmases; we didn't have holidays. My mother was really the entrepreneur so she drove everything. It was a very typical small African family business.

Masiyiwa's early days were spent in the north-eastern part of Zimbabwe where he was brought up by his grandmother. His parents had moved to Zambia's copper belt in 1964, leaving the four-year-old Masiyiwa behind with his grandmother. One of his earliest memories, and the catalyst for his parents to move him to Zambia, was when, aged seven, he experienced the reality of living in a constant near-war situation. Although Zimbabwe's Liberation War, which brought Mugabe to power in 1980, did not officially start until 1972, there were sporadic attempts throughout the 60s and Masiyiwa was about to get up close and personal with a war.

> It was the most dramatic recollection of my life. I remember the helicopters. One of them came over our village, there was a white man sitting with a machine gun on his lap and they ordered us out of the house, from the helicopter. We came out and I was absolutely frightened to death – we'd never seen anything like this. My grandmother said to me: 'Don't be scared, they're looking for terrorists', and then, within half an hour, there were these white soldiers *everywhere* through our

village. A few days after that I was taken to Zambia and that's where I did my primary school.

At primary school in Zambia, Masiyiwa admits he was good at 'everything except mathematics', and was 'extremely gifted in English and history'. The teacher told his parents to make sure he took every available opportunity. So, at great family sacrifice, they decided to send him, at age 12, to school in Scotland. They found a small private institution called the Holt School, which had 150 students, of which 15 were African – largely Nigerian. Even in Scotland, Masiyiwa continued to be involved in the family business and 'consulted' telephonically to his mother. Every holiday he went home and would put in his time in the shop.

> To be honest with you, when I worked in our family business, I worked on it because that's what paid our school fees; that's what fed the family, I was not doing it because I was an entrepreneur. When I was growing up, we didn't know about entrepreneurship. I was known at school purely as a hard-working kid from an African family business.

Masiyiwa spent five years at the school in Scotland and in 1977, armed with an expensive British education, he returned to Africa. Back in Zambia, he spent much of his time with a Zimbabwean uncle who lived in Zambia's capital, Lusaka. His uncle was a lawyer, a staunch nationalist and part of the Zimbabwean nationalist leadership. The young Masiyiwa was fascinated by the Liberation War effort, which was in full swing by then, and his uncle would give him regular updates on the activities and events. Masiyiwa made up his mind to join the fight:

> I didn't think it was worth going to school because so many kids of my age were in the war in Rhodesia, which had really intensified. I met a lot of guys, young guys my own age, who were leaving school to go to war and I said I wanted to go as well.

He went to Zanu, the party Mugabe would eventually lead, and told them he wanted to join the movement.

> They took us to the camps and then they turned around, much to my disappointment, and said to a group of us: 'We've seen your papers,

you're very bright kids. We're not sending you to the war. We've decided
that you should be given scholarships to go back to school because we
need people. It's not fighting we've got to prepare for now. We're going
to win this war; we've got to prepare now for the people who are going
to rebuild the country.'

As a result, Masiyiwa and his group were told to go to Germany
on scholarships to be trained as technicians – the first group to
be sent by Zanu. But in what was beginning to develop into an
irritatingly familiar pattern, 'they' changed their minds once again.
As Masiyiwa and the group of super-elite students were being taken
through the technical programme, the head of the Zanu mission
in Lusaka looked at Masiyiwa's papers and said: 'No, you're not
going. People like you don't go and become technicians; you have
to go to university.' Each change of heart seemed to provide him
with more educational opportunities. From Lusaka he went to
Liverpool, England, where he completed his A levels and then
went, finally, to university. Masiyiwa attended the University of
Wales and completed a degree in electric and electronic engineering.
Afterwards, he decided to stay on in the UK and get some experience
working for a computer company in Cambridge.

> I was just a techie, a young graduate trainee engineer. It wasn't a particu-
> larly big business and after a couple of weeks the owner realised that
> I wasn't that technical and that I was actually pretty entrepreneurial,
> and he started to invite me to do other tasks. I gave him ideas on sales
> strategy – how do we push our products and services. It was probably the
> first time that I became consciously aware of being entrepreneurial.

Despite his new-found business skills, Masiyiwa decided that he
actually wanted to go back to Zimbabwe and get a PhD in engineering.
By then, the War of Liberation had been won and Rhodesia was
called Zimbabwe, after gaining its independence in 1980. Mugabe
was in power and to the young African in Cambridge, Zimbabwe
was finally beginning to feel like home. Masiyiwa decided to go
back home and into academia. He was told that the University
of Zimbabwe was running a sponsored fellowship programme to
encourage Zimbabweans to return home. So in the early months
of 1985, Masiyiwa went back and became the first member of his
family to use Zimbabwe rather than Zambia as a base.

One afternoon while I was at the university enquiring about my programme and the things that I wanted to do, I bumped into this white guy. He was part of the group that had interviewed me and he said to me: 'Young man, don't go down the academic route. Go and get some sand in your shoes – go get a job!' I took the advice.

With those words, Masiyiwa changed track once again and abandoned academia to start looking for a job.

The working man

Masiyiwa originally wanted to join what was then known as the Central African Power Cooperation (CAPCO), but a personnel manager at the Zimbabwe Post & Telecommunications Corporation (PTC) whom he knew, asked him if he had thought about joining them instead. He hadn't. 'I wasn't into telecommunications; I was into power back then. But I was told that they were desperate for engineers so I ended up at the PTC,' Masiyiwa explains. Although it was after independence, the PTC was still an extremely white organisation. The vast majority of engineers were white, all the technicians were white, and blacks were just beginning to arrive from outside to join the company. Masiyiwa put in his application.

> The postmaster general, the very top guy, sees my CV and he summons me to his office and he said to me: 'You're one of the guys who has just joined us?' and I say, 'Yes' and he said: 'Go around this organisation and write down what you think you can do for us.' Isn't that amazing? I must have been 24 or 25 at the time. And I said, 'Ok'. I wandered around, I came back and I said I can do this and the other. He basically created a department around me.

And with that, Masiyiwa had made it to the first rung of the ladder. He was on his way to building his professional career in Zimbabwe and he was very happy. In his own words, he was an 'extremely preoccupied young bachelor in Harare, having lots of fun and with lots of independence'. He was working hard and playing hard. Life was good. One of the projects he was involved in was the building of an earth station, the land-based end of a communications link to a satellite. It was the country's first earth station and was being built in an area of Zimbabwe called Mazowe. One day on a routine inspection of the site, Masiyiwa and the two engineers he was travelling with were asked by the then minister of communications to investigate a potential security issue.

> There was this guy who had apparently built his own earth station and they suspected him of spying. They wanted us to jam his transmissions, so we take a detour to his home. We're now very excited as engineers to find out how this guy can be building his own earth station, so we look over the wall and there's this big dish in the guy's backyard. That's how I learned about CNN for the first time!

But he would recall the incident years later.

> The minister said he wanted the 'earth station' shut down and this guy goes all the way to the supreme court and the government lost. It's important because I was watching; I saw the whole saga. How the minister got embarrassed, how he lost, and 10 years later, the same battle was to take place over the cellphone licence and I was the guy at the centre.

The first business

But that battle was still 10 years away and in the meantime Masiyiwa would build himself the most spectacularly successful electrical construction company in Zimbabwe. It was called Retrofit and at its peak, Masiyiwa employed in excess of 2 000 staff. It was the only business in the industry run by a young black graduate and Masiyiwa had started it a time when there were very few black-owned businesses in the country. He literally had a monopoly and he was at the top of his game.

> I had the pick of the jobs, basically. I did all the largest construction work in Harare. I look at all buildings built in that period and I did the electrical work on most of them. My biggest job was the Zimbabwe Reserve Bank, I did all the military barracks that were being built, the schools, the hospitals – I picked what I wanted to do.

Many of the jobs were government projects and as a smart, black, capable businessman, who knew how to deliver, Masiyiwa was the poster boy of the post-independence government – they loved him. However, the decision to start the business that subsequently became Retrofit actually came out of his frustration with the system. In 1997 the city council of Harare was issuing plots for sale and Masiyiwa bought one with the intention of building his home. Armed with a company guarantee from his employers, the PTC, he went to the Central African Building Society (CABS) to secure a loan to build. They took his design to their evaluations department and told him that in order to build that home he would need a loan of Z$96 000. Unfortunately the guarantee based on his salary was only Z$42 000. They told him he had to build a smaller house, but Masiyiwa had his own solution.

> I said: 'Ok, let's do this. If I build the house, will you still give me the money?' They said: 'You have no experience. Get an experienced contractor to quote you Z$42 000 and you can have it.' So I put a group of my friends together and we decided to start a construction business. There were five of us and we each put in about Z$25 each. But we never got that far. It was all about discussing how to start a business, but basically, in the end, we started a little contracting business and we got a guy to go out and start selling for us.

Although Masiyiwa was the chairman of the small business he and his friends started, all the members, including Masiyiwa himself, still had their day jobs. The manager they hired wasn't really working out, so one day the friends decided to do it 'properly' and Masiyiwa wrote a business plan.

> My business plan was a thesis on the Zimbabwean construction industry – that's all it was – and all I wanted to do was to wire buildings. There were no computers back then and I did a 10-year projected business plan cash flow – by hand. There were no printers, so I had stencilled the whole thing. I still have it somewhere, I stencilled each one of the numbers – you should have seen this thing.

With his rather unique looking business plan in hand, Masiyiwa went to the bank and told them he needed a loan for Z$15 000. The branch manager took a liking to him and offered him a deal. She had seen him drive into the car park with a smart Golf and she asked him to leave that as security and advised him to buy a second-hand pick-up which he could use for the business.

> I was the real Elijah. If you read the Bible about how Elijah went into
> ministry, that's how I went into business. I was pretty decisive, I took
> the Golf sold it and I went and bought a second-hand pick-up. Then I
> fired the manager we had hired and then I resigned.

Unfortunately his employers didn't take his resignation quite as
seriously as he did. They didn't want him to leave until they heard
what he planned to do – then they laughed:

> I actually went to the PTC; I said: 'I'm leaving' and the deputy postmaster
> general summoned me to his office. He said: 'I heard you want to leave?'
> I said: 'Yes'. He said: 'You can't leave, the minister won't let it happen
> and we're going to be in big trouble. We're not supposed to lose people
> like you. If you stay you'll be the next postmaster general.'

In spite of the laughter, he stayed on a few more months and took
his business plan to a new institution which had been set up called
the Zimbabwe Development Bank. A few days later he received a
phone call at work:

> We've been through your business plan and we've just decided to make
> the biggest loan that we've ever done – Z$250 000 – it's yours! You go
> and bring your resignation from the PTC and you can have the money.
> I've gone out on a limb and you can't be part-time.

The man on the phone was the CEO of the bank, who, apart from
being impressed with Masiyiwa's stencilling, was blown away by
the potential of the business. Retrofit was in business.

Masiyiwa was cleaning up on all the electrical contracts
across Harare when he spotted another opportunity. At the time,
Zimbabwe was going through a period of liberalisation. In the late
80s, the World Bank had put structural adjustment programmes
in place, and the International Finance Corporation, its private
banking arm, was providing loans to businesses. Masiyiwa applied
for a loan, got it, and set up a factory that manufactured electrical
switchboards. Masiyiwa now had not one, but two, very lucrative
businesses. But electricity was not really his passion; it turned out to
be telecoms. Even though he had left the industry when he resigned

from the PTC, Masiyiwa hadn't left telecoms intellectually. He was still monitoring the industry and writing articles for technical journals.

> I'm seeing what's happening with cellphones and I'm beginning to take an interest. I'm thinking this would be great to have in Zimbabwe. I make a couple of visits to see people, but what really triggers my interest is a project which actually failed in the end, which was probably one of the largest telecommunications projects ever. It was called Iridium and it was built by Motorola for US$4 billion. And Iridium was looking for African investors.

Motorola was indeed looking for African investors for the Iridium project – a global satellite-based telecoms system that was unfortunately pipped at the post by mobile phone technology. They found their way to Masiyiwa. In deciding whether or not to invest in this huge project, Masiyiwa embarked on a fact-finding tour across the world to see who was doing what in telecoms. On his travels he paid a visit to the undisputed father of African telecommunications, Miko Rwayitare, who had launched Africa's first mobile phone network in the DRC.

The gathering of storm clouds

> I wanted to be an investor in cellular phones so I take a trip to the DRC which had the only cellphone network in Africa and I visit the now late Miko Rwayitare, the founder of Telecel, who sold his company for US$430 million – nobody had done that yet in Africa. I spent a couple of days there. We hit it off immediately.

Masiyiwa and his new friend Rwayitare took to the skies, criss-crossing the globe attending telecoms conferences and researching the potential that Iridium might offer. Masiyiwa soon spotted a trend: the future was going to be in mobile telecoms, not satellite telecoms, and not in Iridium. He immediately asked Rwayitare to partner him in the mobile phone network he planned to build in Zimbabwe. At the same time, Masiyiwa approached his old employers, the PTC, whom he resigned from seven years before.

> I made a proposal to them that we form a joint venture and that they

would be majority shareholder. I would manage it and I wanted the equity. They wrote me a letter saying that they did not see any real viability in what I was proposing, and at any rate, they weren't interested in the joint venture proposal. So I wrote back to them and I said, 'In that case, I am proceeding without you.'

It was the PTC's loss. The response he received from the PTC should have given Masiyiwa a taste of what was to come, but without the benefit of hindsight, he had no way of knowing what would unfold.

They wrote back a real nasty: 'In terms of section so and so of the Telecoms Act, the PTC has an exclusive monopoly to manage and operate telecommunications in the territory of Zimbabwe. If you should proceed with your venture, you will be prosecuted.' The letter was written by the head of their legal (department).

It was the first salvo in a war that almost destroyed Masiyiwa. Over the course of the next few days, Masiyiwa discussed the roadblock with his bankers. One of them was a former lawyer who pulled out the Telecoms Act and declared that the PTC could not possibly have a monopoly. He suggested that Masiyiwa go to the high court and get a declaratory order stating this. In any case, the lawyer informed him, and here was the crux for Masiyiwa, the monopoly could arguably cover a fixed network, but could not extend to a radio communication network. Masiyiwa, excited by the prospect, paid a visit to a firm of lawyers.

The first lawyer I go to gave me a legal opinion; he says, 'You're wasting your time, they do have a monopoly.' It was clear that these guys didn't understand telecommunications so they didn't know the difference between radio and fixed (networks). I needed to find a lawyer who understood telecommunications. I knew that in the US people are specialised, so I investigated and somebody from Motorola suggested an American lady called Dr Judith O'Neill. I called her.

Unfortunately, Dr O'Neill's view was as disheartening as the first lawyer's opinion. She claimed that most of the African telecommunications networks were monopolies and that Masiyiwa would be wasting his time to try and fight it. She hadn't reckoned on the stubborn determination of her soon-to-be newest client.

> She said: 'Send me a cheque for Z$20 000 and I'll look at the Act (and)
> give you an opinion on it, but you're wasting your money.' So I sent
> her the cheque, sent her the Act. She comes back to me after two days
> and she says: 'Wow! I've just looked at this thing – it's different! It's
> not the same as the other Acts that I have ever seen. There's a window
> here. I think you can win!'

Those words must have resonated through Masiyiwa's head many,
many times over the next five years, because that is how long it
would take for O'Neill's prediction to come true. 'If somebody had
told me it was going to take five years, I wouldn't have touched
it and I guess that's how God does these things,' says Masiyiwa
ruefully. Masiyiwa and O'Neill ended up making the application
and in 1993 Masiyiwa went to court to battle his former employers
for the rights to start a mobile telecoms network in Zimbabwe.

Then, shortly afterwards, while on a business trip in Johannesburg, Masiyiwa got a phone call from his lawyer: 'Congratulations!
You just won – you can now start your business!' They were
prematurely optimistic words from his lawyer which turned out to
be totally inaccurate, because the PTC immediately filed an appeal
to the supreme court and suddenly the government was involved
and Masiyiwa's political network was about to come crashing
down. 'I was that golden boy who could do nothing wrong, who
could go to anybody, see anybody. Now I was a really, really bad
boy. I was daring to challenge the system,' Masiyiwa explains. His
one-time friends – the government – were now his enemies and
were determined to beat him.

> They drove me to the ground – simple as that. I was banned from all
> government work, and if you were a black contractor, most of your
> work came from government and state-owned institutions. I was kicked
> off all government sites. I was owed money, they didn't pay. The word
> was out: 'Don't give him any' because they thought I would abandon
> the case (if things got too tough). I was effectively shut down.

Between January and June of 1994, the Zimbabwean government
managed to bring Masiyiwa to his knees. He was persona non
grata in the system and just when he thought that things couldn't

possibly get worse, they did. The appeals court ruled against him and he was told that as a result, he could never bring the case back to court. His electrical construction company, Retrofit, had to retrench staff, he was up to his armpits in debt and he considered leaving the country. The only part of his business that was going well was Retrofit. It was during this period that Masiyiwa followed his wife into church for the first time and discovered God. And his religious beliefs helped him survive. He likened the emotional state brought on by his new relationship with God, at a time when his world was crumbling, to the magical place elite athletes enter, where mind and body work in perfect synch and movements flow without conscious effort. 'I got into this zone where you could just see so clearly what was going to happen, to the point where you become clear about your vision,' Masiyiwa tried to explain.

His vision was to focus all his energies on winning the court case. He decided to sell his once-successful but now struggling business, Retrofit. He approached one of the largest companies in Zimbabwe, TA Holdings, which was a supplier to the construction industry. TA Holdings said no, believing it would be a conflict of interest for it to purchase Retrofit. It didn't end there, however, because Masiyiwa had a premonition that TA Holdings would buy his business after all:

> Two weeks went by and I had a dream that I had gone back to TA Holdings and the CEO of the company agreed to see me and offered to buy my company. Now, you wake up in the morning and you kind of think, you know, this is really weird. This is wishful thinking! That morning as I got into the office the CEO called me and said to me in Shona: 'My young brother, can you come and see me?' So I said, 'Yes' and went to see him.
>
> He said: 'You know, you used to be a very good customer of ours, and now you owe us a lot of money. I had a meeting this morning with my management and I hear you once came to talk to us about buying this business. We can't afford to have this business collapse and fail; it's an icon to black business. So how about I convert all your debt to us to equity?'

The birth of Econet

It turned out to be as easy as that. After a series of meetings, and when all the due diligence had been done, the deal was concluded with one small proviso. TA Holdings wanted Masiyiwa to withdraw from the licence litigation which was in the name of Retrofit, the company that TA Holdings was about to purchase. Masiyiwa didn't even hesitate.

> I created Econet, transferred the legal case to the company, signed the transaction documents and left the country. I had been left with a 23% shareholding in Retrofit after they had converted the debt to equity and I went back to them and I said: 'Can I donate my 23% to you?' I wanted a clean break. They said, 'Sure'. I donated my 23% to them and took my court case with me.

Masiyiwa walked away from his business and from the country of his birth with nothing – apart from a court case. He explains why:

> At that point in time I had become intensely spiritual in my perspective and I would pray over issues. I would make decisions and I said that I wanted a clean break so I separated myself. I sold all the assets that I could sell and auctioned what I could auction. I decided I wanted to be in it (the court case) at any cost.

He went to say goodbye to his staff at the Retrofit head office. By this time the headcount had shrunk from 2 000 in the company's heyday under Masiyiwa to about 500, following the massive retrenchments. Masiyiwa took two employees – his personal assistant and the messenger – with him and rented a small office which was to be the headquarters of the newly formed Econet. Econet would be a company with few staff, no assets and only a hint of a mobile phone operating licence. But something was about to happen that would change the direction of the court case. It started with a phone call from a source that Masiyiwa will only refer to as his 'deep throat':

> I got a phone call from a very senior member of the party (Zanu). He said: 'You know, I was at Lancaster House and I was involved in the writing of the constitution. Go and look at section 20 of the constitution.'

Masiyiwa immediately dropped the phone and went and bought a copy of the new Zimbabwean constitution. It had been created under the 1979 Lancaster House agreement which ended white rule in Zimbabwe. Masiyiwa went straight to section 20, read it, and called Judith O'Neill. Section 20 of the Zimbabwean constitution says: 'Every Zimbabwean has a right to receive and impart information without hindrance.' Masiyiwa and his legal team were about to challenge the very basis of their government – the constitution. It was a daring move and one of his lawyers likened it to Masiyiwa 'breaking into the KG6 military barracks, stealing a tank and driving it into Harare's Unity Square, because that's how the government is going to react if you take them to court!' The lawyer suggested instead that Masiyiwa take his advice and leave: 'You've sold your assets; you really don't have anything more. You're a great professional engineer. Apply for a job, go back to England, do whatever you have to do.' But Masiyiwa ignored the advice: 'The Lord said I shouldn't; that's the simple truth. As I prayed about it, my convictions became stronger and stronger. I just never hesitated.'

Masiyiwa instructed his lawyers to prepare the papers to take the Zimbabwean government to court, and the rest, as they say, is history. He planned to ask the supreme court to form a constitutional court to look at the legality of the Telecoms Act and effectively strike it down. The legal challenge was based on the premise that the Telecommunications Act, with which the PTC had argued and used to defeat Masiyiwa, in fact breached the freedom of expression clause in the Zimbabwean constitution. It was a brave and radical move. Some would say it was foolhardy and short-sighted, but regardless, Masiyiwa was in for the long run, and he never took his eye off the ball. He was one step ahead of the government at every turn.

Politics and telecoms

In 1996 the Zimbabwean government launched its own mobile telecommunications service, NetOne, and shortly after, issued a tender for a private mobile phone licence. Masiyiwa submitted a bid. He was one of six bidders, along with his old friend, Miko Rwayitare of Telecel, who subsequently won the tender. Rwayitare's consortium was backed by a number of political heavyweights.

Suspecting foul play and collusion in the tender decision, Masiyiwa used the 30-day window allocated to bidders to inspect each other's submissions, to discover that the Telecel bid did not meet the licence conditions. He went back to the high court in an attempt to overturn the decision. But in the meantime, Telecel started to roll out its network. By July 1997 Telecel was operational.

Masiyiwa was now fighting two battles on two fronts for a third mobile telecoms licence in Zimbabwe. Through the courts, he managed to get the Telecel bid suspended, but shortly afterwards it was reinstated by the telecommunications minister. It was rumoured that the minister was linked to one of the Telecel shareholders. Following a Cabinet reshuffle two months later, Telecel's bid was cancelled once again and the courts issued a telecoms licence to Econet, making it the first time in global history that a telecoms licence had ever been issued by a court of law. In other words, Masiyiwa had won. It was about this time that he took to the streets in the early hours of 31 December 1997, in the middle of winter, in the middle of Boston, singing Shona hymns and crying out loud. He had just proved that it was possible to start a high-profile business in Africa without political connections.

The launching of a telecoms business

Masiyiwa never realised his dream to set up the first mobile telecoms operation in Zimbabwe because by the time he got the operating licence in 1997, the government's own service, NetOne, and Telecel were already in operation. Undeterred, Masiyiwa established his company in Zimbabwe and because of the much-publicised run-up to the award of the licence, Econet became a raging success from day one, despite two other established players in the market. At the time, Masiyiwa was much more than a businessman with a mobile telecommunications licence; he was a local hero and an icon to most Zimbabweans, who showed their support by digging deep into their pockets. The Econet network was launched in July 1998, and within a week of starting operations, Masiyiwa's company had no fewer than 10 000 customers. Two months after its launch, Econet controlled 45% of the market share and before the third month was out, they had listed on the Zimbabwe Stock Exchange and the shares were heavily oversubscribed.

Econet became bigger than NetOne in just three months! The reason was because thousands of Zimbabweans had boycotted NetOne because of what they saw as persecution, so we were overwhelmed. We just continued to add on customers.

The network grew rapidly, spurred on by what Masiyiwa calls the 'emotional capital' his case had generated, but once there, the customers stayed because Econet gave them good reason to. Econet had a better quality network than its competition, better distribution, the only 24-hour customer care service in the country and a much better marketing campaign. Essentially, Econet offered better packages, more innovative services, including a news-on-demand service to mobile handsets, and they were the first operator to introduce a dual-numbered SIM card in Zimbabwe in 1998.

Econet Zimbabwe was not Masiyiwa's first network. In March 1998, just four months before his Zimbabwean operation launched, he launched Mascom in Botswana and broke an African record by rolling out his network just six weeks after the awarding of the licence. With its current subscriber base of more than 720 000 and a 72% market share, Mascom holds the record of the highest penetration ever achieved in Africa. Mascom was one of two companies awarded mobile licences on the same day in Botswana – the other being France Telecom. However, it was only Mascom that didn't underestimate the potential in the deceptively small Botswana market, and they entered it accordingly – with scale. Today, Masiyiwa's Mascom – a name formed from the first three letters of Masiyiwa's own surname and the word 'communications' – continues to be the market leader in Botswana by a long way. Sadly, Masiyiwa only ran the business in Zimbabwe for just over a year, because in January 2000, he got up, packed his bags, and did something he should have done much earlier.

I left Zimbabwe just after the referendum (held in 1999, when the government proposed a new constitution). The government accused me of mobilising the 'no' vote against the constitutional amendment. So I got on a plane and came to South Africa. I lived out of a hotel for two months and never set foot in Zimbabwe again.

His departure followed accusations that during the country's 1999 referendum to adopt the controversial constitutional reforms, which, among others, granted more power to the presidency, Masiyiwa's network was used to drum up support for the opposition. His shareholding and financing of the anti-government newspaper *The Daily News*, made him even more unpopular with the government, which eventually shut down the paper in September 2003. Masiyiwa was no longer welcome in Zimbabwe. He moved to South Africa and back into a small office with only a few employees, but this time he had more than just a hint of a telecoms licence and a very big plan.

Building a global telecoms business

Flush from his successes in Botswana and in Zimbabwe, Masiyiwa began to focus on building himself a global telecoms business. In 2001, he bid for and won a licence to run a fixed and mobile phone network in Lesotho. The following year, he went into Nigeria as a 5% shareholder and vice chairman of the board of Econet Nigeria with a contract to build and manage a mobile phone network. In August 2001, he launched Econet Wireless Nigeria which achieved market leadership during its first year of operation. Around the same time he was awarded a licence in New Zealand, which he merged with US-based telecoms investment company Trilogy. That year, 2001, was also the year in which Masiyiwa diversified his business outside Africa and outside mobile telecoms for the first time. He identified the need for an African carrier services company to operate out of Europe, combining 'knowledge and experience of operations in Africa with leading European technology and practices'. Econet made the strategic decision to compete in an aggressive but severely underserviced carrier market for Africa. It purchased two satellite antennas, which were installed at a facility north of London. Two satellite transponders and switching equipment followed, along with a management team of 25 professionals, and Econet Satellite Services (ESS) was born. The company has since changed its name to Liquid Telecoms and continues to operate out of the UK.

In 2003, Masiyiwa won the hotly contested third mobile operator licence in Kenya, and was soon in court fighting to retain it after it was suspended by the government. In 2007, the licence was returned to Econet, and in order to raise the finance needed to build the network, Econet went into partnership with the Indian family-owned group, Essa, a huge player in telecoms, power, construction and oil on the subcontinent. With Essa's financial support, Econet is in the process of rolling out a network in Kenya. In May 2006, Masiyiwa acquired a controlling interest in ST Cellular, formerly Spacetel Burundi, one of the four licensed operators in Burundi. He plans to start operating that network by the end of 2008.

But Masiyiwa's road since 2000 has not been smooth. Some analysts argue that since his heydays in the late 90s, Masiyiwa's star is now beginning to wane; there is no disputing the fact that he spends a fair amount of time battling business issues in the legal arena. This, coupled with the claims from unhappy ex-partners of a lack of funding, has given him a reputation for non-delivery and for being litigious. But as they say, there are two sides to every story. In Nigeria, two years into the business, Econet was stripped of his management contract worth 3% of the company's revenue, his 5% shareholding and the vice chairmanship of the board by the Nigerian shareholders amid allegations of cronyism and lack of funds. At the height of the standoff, the shareholders approached Vodacom South Africa and brought them in on a management contract, ostensibly to rebrand the network, but they were looking for a buyout. Masiyiwa invoked the arbitration clause; he went to court, effectively trying to stop his shareholders from selling their shares. During the highly publicised legal process, the Nigerian shareholders tried to bring in Virgin Mobile. But ultimately it was a team of ex-Vodacom managers who resigned and set up their own management company that kept the Nigerian network afloat for the next three years while shareholders battled it out. In 2006, Celtel International, which had been eyeing Nigeria for some time, stepped up and paid a cool US$1 billion for a 65% share in the operation, despite Masiyiwa's attempts, which are still ongoing, to stop the sale.

Masiyiwa is still in arbitration as this is being written, with the intention of buying back the same shares that Celtel now own, which, according to Masiyiwa, they should not have been allowed to purchase in the first place. The reason for Masiyiwa's refusal to let this issue go is obvious when you understand the size of the market and the amount of money that is at stake in Nigeria. To give an idea of the value of his 5% shareholding, in 2006, Celtel paid US$1 billion for its 65% stake in the operation in Nigeria. Econet had a subscriber base of one million. In 2008 Celtel had nearly 15 million subscribers and is growing rapidly, as is the value of their shareholding. According to Nigerian Communications Commission figures, active subscriber numbers in the country are expected to reach 55 million before the end of 2008, and with three major players to share the market, Nigeria, in anyone's opinion, is well worth fighting for.

The Kenyan licence process was equally fraught. In 2003, Econet had to legally defend itself against a losing bidder who contested the award of the licence to Econet via the courts. Shortly afterwards, one of the partners in the consortium, a Kenyan group, pulled out on the grounds that it was not allocated enough shares. As a result, the government suspended Econet's operating licence, which is when Masiyiwa went to court to fight for it. After a four-year dispute with the government, Econet eventually settled out of court in 2007.

Even a planned sell-off of 50% of Econet Group in South Africa ended up in court. In November 2004 the South African-based Altech Group paid US$70 million for the stake, which included joint management of Econet's interests in Botswana, the UK and New Zealand. Zimbabwe, Kenya and Nigeria were not in included in the deal, although it is rumoured that these were the assets that Altech really wanted access to. The deal was called off less than a year later when Altech filed a suit in the Botswana high court, asking for the winding down of its joint venture with Econet after the relationship between the two companies broke down irrevocably over a racist human resources issue. The merger was described by one insider as a 'case of the rabbit and the porcupine sharing the same hole'.

The man behind it all

Regardless of the many controversies he faces, and there will no doubt be more in the future, it is Masiyiwa's entrepreneurial daring that has brought him the recognition he has today. In 2003 he was chosen as one of the 15 Global Influentials of the Year in a CNN/*Time* magazine poll. Over the years, his growing profile has seen him serve on many international boards and foundations, and he has been involved in numerous initiatives to promote entrepreneurship and social development in Africa. He speaks regularly on African business at international business gatherings and to groups of future entrepreneurs.

When I lecture young people one of my favourite opening lines is to ask them which is the most successful business one can be in? Supermarkets? IT? Telecommunications? Oil? And the kids will jump up and they'll say: 'Software – look at Microsoft!' or 'Telecommunications!' Then I say 'No, they're all exactly the same. Go and do the one you have a passion for.'

You see so many people when they saw Bill Gates make money in software, they went in there and they lost their shirts. God has put it in such a way that a guy with no education and bow legs called David Beckham makes huge amounts of money and his wife boasts that she's never read a book that was more than 20 pages and she's making money! Does that mean now if we all stop reading, we'll make money? Or if we all slim down to size zero, we'll make money?

As well as being a great raconteur, Masiyiwa has proved many times that for him, it is not entirely about the money – he is undoubtedly one of the biggest risk-takers still in business today. He risked, quite literally, his family and his fortune for a mobile licence: 'Yes! I'm the biggest risk-taker that you'll find! They don't come bigger than me,' he boasts proudly. And despite all the risks he has taken, both in those instances that he has won and when he has lost, Masiyiwa has absolutely no regrets about any of the choices he has made in business. 'I have never regretted a decision. I can regret a mistake, but I can't regret a wilful decision. If I'm comfortable that this is the right decision, with all the information in front of me, that's ok.'

Masiyiwa's success has been built on what he calls 'insight', which he describes as 'when you see something there that others don't'. It was his insight that caused him to back a mobile operating system and bid for a licence in Zimbabwe, not Iridium's much-flaunted satellite system. Way back then his instinct told him mobile phones would have an impact long before other industry players realised it.

I remember when we negotiated with SBC and MTN (to buy my business). We negotiated for three months and they said the business in Zimbabwe was going to have 100 000 subscribers. They said: 'There's 12 million people, how can you have 100 000 subscribers? These are cellphones, not Coca-Cola!'. We go to Botswana, the government almost refuses to give us the licence because they said I'd over-exaggerated the projections. 'How can you, you an African operator with no experience, come to tell the Swedish consultants that Botswana, with a population of 1.2 million is going to have 100 000 subscribers in five years? It's going to be 30 000 max!' Do you know how many subscribers we have now? 720 000!

As well as his insight, Masiyiwa's success in business is also due to his leadership style, which over his 20 years in business, has evolved around his personality, his Christian values and his passions. 'I'm not a quiet leader. If I'm sitting with my management, I'm not sitting quietly like this while they talk. Hey, we talk! We argue,' he laughs. 'They tell me I don't know what I'm talking about. I'm more that kind of leader – of course in a disciplined way – but I'm very comfortable with people.' Indeed he is comfortable with people, essentially because he is a compassionate man who handles his team with total respect. This is the reason why many of his staff have remained loyal to him and stayed with the business over the years.

> They get paid but they're volunteers, because they can be somewhere else. When you're dealing with a professional engineer, a highly skilled technician, an accountant, if I call him in here and I humiliate him in front of you, his resignation will be on my desk in the morning – that's what makes him a volunteer. Therefore how I relate to him must relate to his own aspirations.

When Masiyiwa is not battling in the boardroom or the courtroom, the family man and staunch Christian can be found reading. He is currently reading a book on Mao, a biography on Milton Friedman, a book by respected geneticist Francis Collins on faith and beliefs, and of course the Bible. 'I don't read poetry, I don't read fiction, but otherwise everything else I read. I read about four books at the same time. You'll not find me reading an engineering book or a book on telecommunications at home, but I will read them at the office,' he explains.

Masiyiwa is first and foremost a family man: 'I've got six kids, I look at these guys (and) I feel staggered at how different they all are, the kids of one man. This is what I tell my children: we are all born originals, there's no one who looks like you, talks like you, has your fingerprints, has your eyes, has your hair, has your personality.' The same could be said for Masiyiwa himself – and the Zimbabwean government is probably the first to be thankful.

Although he is nowhere near to retiring and has no intention of seeing the end of Econet, the 48-year-old Masiyiwa has nonetheless given himself an estimated time of retirement: 'I've set myself a date to leave professional business at the age of 56, so I've got eight years left, and then I'm going to go away and do something else so that I can watch this company over the next 30 years from outside.'

It is written in the Bible that to 'whom much is given, much is expected'. Masiyiwa believes he has been blessed with much. But what is also important, he says, is 'did I meet the expectations?' And for Masiyiwa, it's too early to tell.

Sources:

1. Lock, Alison. 'Chasing the thrill of the deal' IN *African Investor Magazine,* 1 September 2007.
2. Ochieng, Z (2007). 'Econet wins reprieve from government' Biz-Community.com, 20 July. Available at: http://www.bizcommunity.com/Article/111/78/16427.html.
3. Powers, J (2001). 'Zimbabwe's liberation war'. Available at: http://www.suite101.com/article.cfm/african_history/61056/1.

Kagiso Mmusi – The Systematic Entrepreneur

VITAL STATISTICS

Name: Kagiso Mmusi
Country: Botswana
Born: 25 October 1965
Position/Title: Founder, executive chairman of Pula Holdings
Total Assets: 170 million pula
Nationality: Motswana*
Industry: Diversified holding company, including energy, transport
Highest education qualification: Management Development Programme; University of Cape Town Business School

---

* A person from Botswana is Motswana; the plural form is Batswana.

I wake up at 3.30am every morning. I have a quick shower and then I am on the road and I go for my 8 km run. If I am going to run 8 km every day, I need some help. So I do a lot of praying early in the day before I run so I can ask for the strength in the day. I enjoy running; I run early in the morning and enjoy the fresh air. It's a good breeze, you see the stars – not many people see the stars.

Then its gym for an hour or so, then a bath, and I probably shave my head. I enjoy coming into the office at 7am in the morning and leaving at 7pm in the evening. After 7pm I get tired because I've woken up at 3am in the morning. I'm quite disciplined because I believe that if you are going to do something in this world you need to build your strength to achieve your goals and my biggest strength is my commitment. What ever I decide to do, I commit to it.

Kagiso Mmusi is not just a highly disciplined and very committed man; at the age of 42, he is also one of the youngest and most successful entrepreneurs in Botswana. From a single filling station 19 years ago to running one of Botswana's largest home-grown and diversified companies, with more than 20 subsidiaries covering energy, transport, distribution, technology, education, trading, advertising, real estate and financial services, Mmusi has come far. He is the founder and executive chairman of the privately owned Pula Holdings, which he named after Botswana's national currency. The group has an asset base of 170 million pula (US$25 million), employs in excess of 400 people and is the only company in the country to have sought and secured an investment grade rating. Mmusi has aggressive growth plans for his business; he aims to achieve a growth rate of 20% every year, and he plans to do it, not by acquisition, which isn't his style, but organically. He started every single one of his 20 companies, bar two, from scratch.

Mmusi was described by a leading national newspaper as one of Botswana's 'most ambitious crop of young entrepreneurs who has done away with the country's tradition of aversion towards risk'. In a country known more for its cattle and farmers than its entrepreneurs, the accolade is even more pertinent. Interestingly, all of Mmusi's businesses have been funded by the businesses within the group or through bank loans – he is the sole shareholder. He has no intention, at this stage anyway, of listing his company on the highly liquid Botswana Stock Exchange, which in 2007 provided happy investors with a 75% return. He explains how Pula Holdings operates:

In Pula I don't have any shareholders, this probably makes business
sense because the companies are all growing substantially. In 1988
when it started each company was separate. In 1994 we formalised
it and all the shares were transferred to the holding company, which
today operates through a trust. Basically this is what has become Pula
Holdings.

What is even more unique about Mmusi's success is the fact that
he has achieved his success on the scale he has, in one of Africa's
smallest markets; Botswana has a population of just 1.8 million.

Botswana was one of those lucky African countries which, when
it discovered diamonds and other lucrative minerals on its lands, put
in place a responsible government that could manage the resources
properly and run the economy well. As a result, it has become one
of the richest countries on the continent. Since independence in
1966, Botswana boasts the highest average economic growth rate
in the world – thanks to its diamond mining industry, which is
the country's biggest employer and largest contributor to its tax
revenues. What's more, Botswana is one of the easier places in
Africa in which to do business. There are no exchange control
rules, the tax regime is one of the most relaxed in Southern Africa
and the government has many schemes and incentives aimed at
growing local business and attracting foreign investment. Mmusi
acknowledges these benefits but points out the downside:

Things in Botswana have been quite easy because the government is
wealthy. I would say it is easy to start a business here but it is not easy
to maintain it and to sustain it. It's small, with a small population, so
it's very competitive and you need to work for it.

Small population or not, there isn't anywhere else that Mmusi
would rather be.

Botswana has the same potential as South Africa; the economy is good.
Yes, we have one small disadvantage in the population, but there are
a lot of resources here which make up for it. We have a lot of mining
opportunities coming up. I don't want to be in mining but there are a
lot of supporting businesses which one can do here. In the end I was
born in this country, I have family here and I believe that I have to
always give back to my family.

Growing up

The family to whom he wants to give back is actually one of the most well-known families in Botswana. His father, Peter Mmusi, was vice president to Sir Ketumile Masire, for nine years between 1983 and 1992. Mmusi was 18 when his father took on the role and 27 when he stepped down. He remembers it as a privileged but challenging time for himself and his five siblings, who suddenly by default became public figures. He tries to describe what it was like: 'People look up to you; you are in the public domain. You need to be careful because it could make you or destroy you.' Mmusi chose not to let it destroy him: 'It did help me,' he confesses. 'It gave me a lot of exposure and it opened doors. It also made me a very serious person.'

From the moment he left Maru-a-Pula School in Gaborone at 18, Mmusi had already decided not to go to university. 'I was not a top student, I was average at school, but towards the end I knew what I wanted to do. I wanted to be an entrepreneur,' he explains confidently. Mmusi was ambitious and way before he knew how or what he would do, he would tell his friends that he wanted to be a millionaire. 'I wasn't driven by money,' he recalls. 'It wasn't about having money to splash around. You set goals in life and that's what I wanted to achieve.' Even now, although he could easily splash around his money if he wanted to, the young millionaire doesn't – it's just not his style. He is known in Botswana as one of the 'shy boys' and there is not an ounce of arrogance in him. Mmusi has been quietly and systematically getting on with building his empire and staying under the radar. 'I am very humble, very down to earth. My biggest extravagance is hard work – I enjoy it'.

For one still so young, Mmusi's attitude to entrepreneurism and business is old-fashioned. In today's fast-paced world of instant gratification, he still believes that the only route to success is long and paved with lots of hard work. 'There are no shortcuts in business,' he says firmly. 'It has taken me 18 years to get where I am and I believe that without discipline and patience you can't succeed. You have to start small and expand, and that will give you the necessary experience.'

Mmusi got his real-life experience and exposure when he started working, first for his father, then for an Indian family. He was 18 at the time. While his father was dealing with matters of state,

Mmusi took on the responsibility of looking after his father's cattle. From there he worked on and off for an Indian family who ran a cash-and-carry wholesale outfit. 'I took any job they gave me; I did deliveries, I was a cashier … I wanted to touch and feel everything. I knew what I wanted from day one.'

But Mmusi's real break came when he took a job working for the well-known Indian entrepreneur Satar Dada at his motor dealership. Naledi Motors, which is still in business, is one of the oldest and most successful motor dealerships in Botswana. It was started by Abdul Satar Dada, the primary school dropout who kicked off his career as a salesman in a small business and is today one of the best-known and wealthiest Asian entrepreneurs in Botswana.

> I really wanted practical experience so I worked all over the business. I worked in sales, in accounts, in stock control – I wanted to get experience of the business. I learned all my management and operational skills from Naledi.

Despite the fact he chose to go straight into the workplace after school, Mmusi has never let his lack of further education stand in his way, and has more than made up for it since.

> I did make sure I read a lot of books and I did a lot of management development programmes. I still do that now. I go to the London Business School to make sure that I still understand what is happening in today's business world.

The making of an entrepreneur

In 1989, armed with a little knowledge and a little experience, Mmusi ventured into the world of business – he started small. He had done his homework and had decided that starting a filling station was the way to go.

He secured a loan of 120 000 pula (US$18 000) from the Bank of Credit and Commerce and bought a piece of land in a good location. He negotiated with Total and soon started operating a Total garage and filling station. The station where it all began still exists today and is still owned by Mmusi. He admits that being the vice president's son certainly helped him raise the initial capital; he was no stranger to the people at the bank.

They knew me. They gave me the money because I persisted. I was very lucky because one of the bank managers believed in me – there has to be someone who believes in you. Also, Mr Dada spoke very highly of me; he knew I had put in the hours at Naledi.

Armed with his start-up capital, Mmusi began his one-man journey into the world of entrepreneurism.

I started the filling station from nothing. It was bare land. I had to come up with the designs, do everything from scratch. It was very small – a two-post filling station. At that time, the city (Gaborone) was nothing really.

Not only did Mmusi design the filling station, he was also actively involved in the daily operations of the business. He was there every day to meet and greet customers and fill up their tanks – personally. Nothing was beneath him. The filling station was profitable; Mmusi was moving about 700 000 litres of petrol a month. It took him five years to finally pay off the loan and he was left with a piece of land which he owned outright and which he could use for future collateral. Being part of the fuel retailing sector gave Mmusi insights into the downstream side of the business. He soon spotted an opportunity linked to fuel retailing that he thought he could leverage – fuel trucking. From the proceeds of his first filling station, he bought his first tanker, a 17 000-litre Mercedes Benz 2624 Long Nose, which he purchased for R70 000 (about US$9 000) in South Africa. It was the beginning of his transport business, Pula Carriers. 'I started off with one little tanker which I drove up from Johannesburg. It took me four days to drive a 3 000 km round trip,' he recalls. It turned out that driving big tankers was something Mmusi actually enjoyed, and what started off as a pure business necessity became a bit of a hobby.

I used to drive once in a while when we didn't have a driver or the driver didn't turn up. I'd jump into the truck and just drive – it was fun. The furthest I have driven is probably a 3 000 km round trip in two days – I had to do that because I wanted to make sure I could do it whenever I needed to.

The timing of his entry into the business was impeccable.

There was a big boom in Botswana. We were involved in transporting food for the UN for Angolan refugees. We were involved in building the Western Bypass (highway) – providing the trucks. We used to get contracts all over for transport, and today it is one of our core businesses.

Pula Carriers is now a logistics company with a fleet of 20 tankers, each one fitted with state-of-the-art technology, cameras, computers and satellite tracking, bringing the value of each truck to about 1.5 million pula. Pula Carriers is also involved in cross-border petroleum trucking and the distribution of petrol, diesel and paraffin, mainly for Total and Engen in Botswana.

At around the same time Mmusi started Pula Carriers in 1990, he began a small trading company which specialised initially in a product used for oil and chemical spills. Today, the company, TK Trading, trades just about anything in the industrial sector, including the supply of safety tools and tyres for plant machinery in the mining and heavy machinery sectors.

TK has always been a trading company. We got a contract to supply electrical poles to Botswana Telecommunications, we've been to Korea to source fibre-optic cables, then we got into the mines. We now do quite a lot of work with the mines.

It didn't stop there, Mmusi felt compelled to keep looking for new opportunities, citing Botswana's size as the reason.

Because Botswana is a small country, for you to grow or to increase turnover you have to do a lot of things. You could only grow so much in certain businesses. I used to take opportunities which fell in front of me; it wasn't because I liked these businesses.

A few years later, Mmusi introduced another business into his growing conglomerate. He diversified his transport business away from its dependency on oil into a completely new area – distribution mainly for the breweries. He called it Smart Investments, which it was, and in 2008 it had an annual turnover of 20 million pula. Smart Investments also receives just less than one million pula in rental income from industrial land that it owns and develops. Smart Investments started off with a distribution contract from

Botswana Breweries and now transports for Kgalagadi Breweries and Capital Tobacco products. It recently secured a wholesale liquor licence and has built a new warehouse from which it will sell liquor wholesale to retailers.

The next business in which Mmusi got involved was one that had nothing whatsoever to do with oil or transport. It was also a business that his mother, Louisa Mmusi, started.

> My mother put in money from her savings account. She said this is my money; I want to build two classrooms. It started as nothing, just one block and 30 or 40 students. Thereafter, the school built itself.

The school, which was built in 1996, is called St Mary's and is one of the leading educational institutions in Botswana. Louisa Mmusi, one of Botswana's pioneering teachers, is the headmistress of the 1 000-strong catholic school which she started from scratch. Although the school falls under the Pula Group, it is for management purposes only and Louisa essentially runs what has become a real family business. Mmusi explains.

> Two sisters-in-law work here as teachers and my younger sister helps in the admin here. My elder sister, who is the overall boss, is very strict and she won't allow anyone to come in just because they're family.

And that includes Mmusi himself, who has little operational influence at the school – he would have to get past his mother and sisters first. Nevertheless, the school is a profitable business concern and easily holds its place in the group alongside another unexpected business which 'snuck' into the Pula family.

> I didn't know anything about advertising. A friend of mine had a newspaper and he was also involved in an advertising agency. One day he came to me and said he had this business he would like me to put some money into, so I put some in. After a little while, he wanted more, so I put in some more.

The friend was an elderly man who has since retired to Australia. It seems that this friend wasn't so much looking for a generous financial partner, but rather, he was looking for a successor, which he found in the form of Mmusi.

After some time he said to me: 'I have taken so much money out of your pocket on this business, I think you better take it.' So I took the business and turned it around. It was struggling, it was a nightmare – it still is. It is a very tough business, even though there are lots of advertisers in Botswana. A lot of people in this country don't understand brand building and marketing. I like it; I got involved and found a passion for it.

Despite it being a bit of a nightmare, Optimum Mccann-Erickson, an affiliate of the global advertising group McCann-Erickson Worldwide, is now the market leader in Botswana. Since 1998 it has offered the full service of marketing communications, including web design, media planning and buying, and design. Apart from securing all the other Pula businesses as clients, it also handles the Botswana Telecommunications Authority, Mascom, Standard Chartered Bank and the Botswana Stock Exchange.

From moving fuel across borders to transporting beer, educating young minds and branding big businesses, Mmusi just seemed to have a knack for making money. There certainly seemed to be enough of it around because he started buying up real estate in and around Botswana. One of Mmusi's first developments was the house in which he grew up. 'My parents gave me the rights to the property. I bought it from them – and I paid a premium,' he laughs. 'I had to give them back two houses for it.' He soon demolished the original family home: 'It was only a small house; we didn't have any bedrooms. It's now been let out for the last five years to the Botswana government's Ministry of Presidential Affairs.'

Mmusi eventually consolidated his numerous commercial and industrial property interests under Pula Real Estate in 2005. Its portfolio was valued at 60 million pula in mid 2008 and he is currently working on a 30 million pula project to build a residential complex for his senior management in Gabarone. But the business which he is most excited about and the one that is being touted as the flagship company of the group is Pula Energy. It is Mmusi's liquid petroleum gas (LPG) and liquid fuels distribution company, which owns two gas bottling plants and 35 depots across the country, through which it distributes domestic gas. The fuels division also resells bulk fuel to customers. Pula Energy, along with the advertising agency, is the second company within the group that Mmusi purchased as a going concern. Currently it houses

Pula Holdings' most significant project – the building of an US$18 million energy terminal in neighbouring Walvis Bay in Namibia.

> I didn't know about advertising but energy I had a passion for. I've always thought energy was the thing, so we bought the company. It was a very small company then, and the guy said he wanted to retire; we paid a premium for it. I think Pula Energy is exciting and it will make us a lot of money, maybe not now, because of the huge investment, but soon.

The 2 000-ton LPG terminal he is building in Walvis Bay is part of his bold plan to take Pula Energy global. It will put the company in a position to import LPG from world markets to service at least three other Southern African Development Community countries and take advantage of the global energy crisis.

> Three years ago, there was a shortage of gas in Botswana, immediately after we got into this business, and one morning I thought, 'There is big potential for LPG here.' And then I thought there must be somewhere else apart from South Africa where I could buy from. I decided to go to Dubai and see. I realised there was an opportunity to buy LPG from there. Botswana is a landlocked country and the only way to bring it in is by ship.

The obvious route for a Motswana company would have been to ship it via South Africa but Mmusi realised that it would not be easy to build his own terminal in the highly competitive South African market, so he went to Namibia.

> We decided to approach NamPort (the Namibian Ports Authority) for a piece of land. They were excited but it has not been an easy process because of the environmental impact assessment. But we are now building a port where ships will deposit the gas, then we will load the gas into Pula-owned tankers which will then be transported into Namibia, where we have our bottling plants.
>
> We procure it, we bottle it, we distribute. We now have our own cylinders – previously we were tied to one company and now we can dictate our price. LPG is a highly consumed commodity and we are building the market here. We can now buy from whoever gives us the best price.

Mmusi's enthusiasm is obvious: 'The potential of energy is so big, it gives me the opportunity to become a worldwide company. If you go for these LPG international seminars, you see that there is so much money and so much wealth there. It's quite exciting,' he explains. What is potentially just as exciting for Mmusi is an opportunity he stumbled on while researching LPG, and he has moved into it very swiftly.

> When we were doing the LPG we realised there was an opportunity in oxygen – medical and industrial oxygen – and other elements like helium. We are now setting up a plant to produce those and our own cylinders. This is very exciting because we are the only 100% Botswana-owned company that will produce self-branded products of this nature.

Mmusi's other business ventures include two technology companies, Foneworx, an SMS and IVR platform company, which he started at the same time as St Mary's opened its doors in 1996, and Pula Tecor, a hardware, software and network services company. And linked to these, in 1998 Mmusi set up a company called Airtime, which sells prepaid airtime scratch cards for mobile operators.

Mmusi also has a number of personal investments that are held outside Pula Holdings. He set up Citizen Investment in 2004 with a partner and through it acquired a 20% stake in Mascom – the country's leading mobile phone operator owned by Strive Masiyiwa – which he diluted to enable the company to meet its financial obligations. He owns two commercial farms in the Kweneng District Council at Sekgwa sa Tholo and Mokgalwana, with about 750 head of cattle and also has a stake in Kalahari Energy, a gas exploration and development company with a mining project in Botswana. Success and fear have been the motivating forces behind Mmusi's continuous growth and accumulation of wealth.

> Fear is what drives me. I fear being a poor person, someone who can't maintain himself, who can't put food on the table and feed my children. I worry a lot. Worry to me is about making sure that things go right.

Establishing a corporation

Things are certainly going right for Mmusi. His mind is constantly ticking and always on the lookout for the next business opportunity. He is exploring more openings in the mining sector – Botswana's main economic driver – and plans to start a diamond cutting and polishing business. He is also looking at other projects in the energy and infrastructure sectors. The ideas never seem to stop flowing.

> Most of the times I will be sitting with someone and they'll be talking about something and I'll pick it up and will go and try to develop it. But we don't want to overcommit ourselves, that is why we carry out serious investigations before venturing into new businesses.

And he isn't exaggerating when he says 'serious investigations'.

> We have a committee which is called the Business Development Organisation, which will come up with an idea. We give each other tasks and form an agenda. If you have to travel to the UK to do research then you come back and report to the committee. We sell it to everybody and then we formalise it. Then we also have guys who do the research, who don't sit on the committee. Then we have a legal committee which sits outside of this and they do their own research.

Mmusi's thorough and methodical approach to new business is a reflection of a highly logical and systematic mind, which is constantly on the lookout for structure. He is not just trying to milk money out of a series of businesses he owns; he is trying to build nothing less than a corporation, a world-class multinational in Botswana.

The country's finance minister, Baledzi Gaolathe, also the guest of honour at the official opening of the new Pula headquarters in December 2006, said this about Pula: 'There is no reason it cannot be a multinational and raise the Botswana flag. Look at the Netherlands: with its small population it was able to produce Philips, and Sweden has Ericsson and Scania. We can do it in Botswana, this is what Pula is about to do.' The minister could very well be right. But Mmusi calls attention to some of the key differences between working for Pula and working for other multinationals operating in Botswana:

> It is very different working for a company like Pula, which was started from nothing, compared to working for someone like Standard

Chartered. If you look at them, they have international backing; things can be monitored by somebody sitting in London. They can afford to bring in people very quickly. We here are still developing our own internal systems day to day, we are developing everything. It's not even about the making of the money; it's about making sure the systems are in place.

His systems seem to revolve around centralising key administrative functions within the business. So far he has set up three companies within the group – including Pula Treasury – which all deal with the financial management of the group. Pula Treasury was established in 2004 and all the group's financial transactions go through it. Mmusi continually re-invests the group's profits back in to the now cash-rich Pula Treasury, which in turn invests in outside projects and other financial institutions. Pula Treasury also helps the group negotiate the best financial packages across multiple businesses; Mmusi calls it a 'sort of internal bank'.

As well as Pula Treasury, Mmusi has created a division called Pula Mission, whose function it is to handle major medium- and long-term projects until they become fully fledged businesses. Pula International is another separate division which handles all of the group's international trading. It's not just the companies that he tries to structure; it's also the organisation itself. He puts proper systems in place to help with people management issues.

There are a lot of systems that have to be developed if you really want to see this company still in operation in 100 years from now without me. There need to be systems that make the company self-operating. That is why it is totally impossible for me at this time to say I can back off or take it easy.

Mmusi has no intention of doing either. He is like a proud parent hovering over a child to whom he has given birth.

I am continuously working at 110%. If I were to reduce my pace by just 5%, it would be like flying in a plane and the pilot dropping the altitude – everyone feels the change.

It has taken me 18 years of hard work to build up these businesses and it's not been easy. A lot of pain, but you tend to get used to it. Life is about pain, life is about hard work. For me, life is not about having fun and being at parties, life is about commitment, being dedicated, working hard and delivering.

He has little to say about the businessmen who become successful on the back of a single deal or a government contract. He believes such businesses are unsustainable.

> There is a lot of money in Botswana but one has to be careful. There are a lot of things which you have to follow through, otherwise easy come, easy go. But to get to the point where you do a deal with Barclays, for example, for 50 million pula, you have to do a lot to gain their confidence. It takes a lot of preparation to get there.

It is this type of dedicated and detailed preparation that creates the hard work to which Mmusi refers. But after hard work comes the reward.

> I think I am happy when I do these things. Sometimes I think I could just run a little transport business – fewer headaches. But then I say, no, I am wrong. Go create employment for close on 500 people, pay taxes. I create a lot of things and I give to the community, so these things give me the drive, they excite me. I really enjoy that.

With the shell of Pula Holdings put in place with the launch of his new headquarters in 2006, Mmusi's main focus currently is to work on the soul of Pula Holdings – the 400-strong staff component. Like a well-oiled multinational, the entire group has been condensed into a page-long organigram with clear reporting lines for all the divisions and companies, leading directly into Mmusi.

> I'm quite involved. I'm in the office, I'm out there. I visit these operations. I put in six days a week of work, close to 12 hours a day. I am monitoring, analysing, but I don't get involved in doing the operations. I am guiding. I get to use people, I tell people what to do, guide them, and basically I try and plan forward.

He is a tough taskmaster who expects nothing less than he is prepared to give. He is aware that many of his staff talk about too much work and too much pressure in their work environment, but again he has put structures and systems in place to help them share his passion for Pula.

Mmusi runs an open book: even though he is the sole share-holder, he publishes an annual report-style corporate profile which details the vision and the assets of the company for staff and other stakeholders to appreciate. In the 2007 edition, he opens his executive chairman's statement with the following words: 'Hard work, commitment, a desire for success, passion, integrity, strong values, a strong belief in oneself, in systems, in people and most importantly in God – this is the bedrock that holds Pula holdings together.' Every quarter, there is a newsletter which keeps the group informed of where and what Pula Holdings is doing, be it corporate developments or social programmes. He has put in a number of new staff training initiatives and incentives and he recently established a housing loan scheme for all staff and a medical insurance scheme for the low-income workers in the operations.

Mmusi is a strong leader but sees his main weakness as his lack of ability to always fully engage his team.

> Sometimes I take quick decisions because I should have taken more time and consulted others. Maybe it was because I used to take decisions by myself. I believe I am a forceful person, particularly when it's about getting proposals through. I sell it very hard but I don't mind being defeated as well. I will always confess to mistakes.

But being such a disciplined person, he does try to minimise on his quota of mistakes.

> If at the last minute I realise that something is not right with a project, I'm not shy about pulling away. It doesn't matter how many people, how many commitments, how much money is involved, because if I go ahead with it, I'll lose more. The most important thing is that if I realise something is not right, I pull out of it immediately.

With so much responsibility on his shoulders, it is easy to believe that Mmusi is a very stressed individual. In fact the opposite is true:

> I don't get stressed – I take it as part of living. There are issues that crop up which have to be solved. There are matters which have to be resolved so I have to find a solution. Stress is when you don't want to

face your problems and you try to avoid them. My belief is that if you put a lot of rubbish under the carpet it gets you later on, and that is what creates the stress.

The country man

They say the Batswana are farmers. Each will have a farm or a cattle post and if not, then at least some cattle back in the village. Mmusi is no different. On the one day of the week he gives himself off, he heads out to his farm in his home village of Mmakgodi, just 20 minutes outside Gaborone. He goes there not so much to de-stress but to regenerate.

I like going there, it's quite relaxing. You hear the water, feel the breeze. For me the corporate world is from Monday to Saturday, then I come here to recuperate. My mind works there all the time (but the farm) is the place where I restore my energies for the week.

He actually does a little more than just relax on his farm. The farm is a 30-hectare holding with 67 goats and 80 sheep which Mmusi calls an 'expensive hobby'. But it is nothing compared to his two massive commercial farms. This smaller farm is more of a small business than an expensive hobby as it comes complete with a farm manager and a handful of farm hands who tend to the goats and the sheep, and plant the crops he grows. Mmusi plans to build his country retreat there but his secret goal is to plant and grow olives – in Africa! 'I just had the idea that there is a big demand for olives. We start ploughing in April, so by the end of the year there will be an olive farm there,' he explains. With that type of confidence you can only assume that in 2009 the first crop of olives from Botswana will be on the market! Mmusi's strong convictions in life are built on his even stronger conviction in God.

I believe that without faith you wouldn't achieve a lot. A lot of my achievements are there because of my faith. I go to mass every Sunday. Whenever the church needs my services right now, for example, I sit in the finance committee for the bishop – I go and help.

Mmusi takes a very active role in his church, and outside of work, his farm and a chairmanship of the America Business Council, a non-profit organisation that promotes investment between the US and Botswana, Mmusi has little time for anything else. 'I am not the type of person who wants to have friends and go out. I come home on a Friday and I rarely go out,' he explains. This does not necessarily mean that Mmusi spends a lot of time with his family. His two children from his first marriage live in South Africa and spend limited time with him, while his one-year-old daughter from his second marriage gets more attention. He leaves his older children to decide on their own careers and future ambitions.

> I'm not going to put a lot of pressure on them to be in business. If one of them or all of them would like to, I'd like to create a situation where they would have to go through the process of developing themselves and really wanting to take it to the next level. I believe I would like to build a business that would have an executive to run it – a trust that would run whether or not I am there.

Mmusi seems to be creating an escape for himself with his references to his business continuing without him. It soon becomes apparent that he has some political ambition for himself. Growing up in a political family, with a father who had the number-two job in the country, and being so close to the seat of power must have give him an inside track that appeals to him.

> You meet a lot of people who tell you that you've done well, this is what you need to do. So if the opportunity comes up, then I would go into politics. I'd never rule it out. I've been in business for 19 years; I'd probably do it (politics) for 10 to 20 years.

Politics aside, Mmusi will have to retire one day, or the more likely scenario; be carried out of the boardroom on a stretcher, and it is unlikely he would want to see 19 years of hard work disappear with him. He wants to leave behind a legacy, a testament to his hard work and entrepreneurial spirit. 'I would like to achieve growth and continuity in what I have started. I want to see it develop. It won't be smooth – things never go smoothly – but as long as there is continuity, I'll be happy.'

Sources:

1. Gabotlale, B (2004). 'Monarch of all he surveys'. *Mmegi Business Week*, 10 September. Available at: http://www.mmegi.bw/2004/September/ Friday10/210877979777.html.
2. Mokgoabone, K (2006). 'Pula Holdings can be multinational – Gabotlale'. *Mmegi Business Week*, 4 December. Available at: http://www.mmegi. bw/2006/December/Monday4/9402003461606.html.
3. Pula Holdings. *Pula News*. Botswana, March 2007.
4. Pula Holdings. *Pula News*. Botswana, August 2007.
5. Pula Holdings. *Pula News*. Botswana, March 2008.
6. Pula Holdings. Corporate Profile.

Miko Rwayitare – The Trailblazing Entrepreneur

VITAL STATISTICS

Name: Miko Rwayitare
Country: Democratic Republic of Congo
2 December 1942 – 25 September 2007
Position/Title: Owner and founder of Telecel, chairman
of Telecel, MIH and GTS
Nationality: Born in Rwanda (Congolese and South
African citizenships)
Industry: Telecommunications /ICT
Highest education qualification: Electrical engineering
degree from Karlsruhe University in Germany

Sadly, Miko Rwayitare died on 27 September 2007. His story is told here by one of his closest friends, Dr Gabriel Twagira:

> An American friend of his called Joe Gatt, who used to run the Intercontinental Hotel and Air Zaire in Kinshasa, told him that there was a military technology called AMPS, which was declassified in 1975 and now open to civilians. Miko saw an opportunity because the telecoms infrastructure was so poor in Congo. He went to the US and applied for a permit to use this technology in Africa and he got it. It wasn't even in commercial use in Europe or the US at that time.
>
> Miko loves to tell the story of how he struggled ... People thought he was crazy. Banks did not have the culture back then of loaning money and no one believed in the project – it was an unknown technology. He had gone everywhere looking for money; he approached many organisations. He came to see and asked me to put money into his project. I told him that he was crazy that I wouldn't risk my money. I said to him: 'You're selling wind!' and he said: 'I think it will work.' Many people reacted like me, even big business refused to put in money – everyone refused. But it didn't stop him looking. He started with US$35 000 from his pocket and raised a US$200 000 interest-free loan from a Canadian fund to buy equipment from the US.
>
> That's how he created Telecel with Joe Gatt. It was a 50/50 partnership, and by doing so, he became the first person in Africa to make a mobile phone call.

Dr Gabriel Twagira, who tells the story of how the visionary, entrepreneur and telecoms legend Miko Rwayitare built the first pan-African mobile operation on the continent, was friends with Rwayitare for more than 50 years – they were 'school mates' and 'beer mates'. Twagira was part of the team of family and close friends who prepared the moving eulogy read by Rwayitare's close friend, Mr Djamboleka, to shocked mourners on 4 October 2007 at a packed funeral service in Johannesburg, South Africa, Rwayitare's home for the last 11 years of his life. On 26 September 2007, the Rwanda News Agency (RNA) in Kigali filed the following report that shocked the business world:

> Rwandan-South African telecoms tycoon Miko Alexis Rwayitare died yesterday in a Brussels clinic after an intestinal operation, RNA has established. From different friends and officials contacted in Kigali,

RNA has learnt that Mr Miko – as he is hugely known among all sections
of Rwandan society – died after bleeding non-stop.

The news came as a complete shock to the many people who knew
Rwayitare. At 64, by all accounts he was fit and healthy, and was
in the throes of rolling out an exciting new broadband project in
which he was heavily invested. Goal Technology Solutions (GTS)
was Rwayitare's vision for the future, just as Telecel, the mobile
operation he started in 1986, had been. Speaking about his new
project Rwayitare had said:

> This is not the first big opportunity we want to achieve; the past has
> shown us we can do it. We have the financial means to invest and we
> have experience in human resources and management, and we have
> all the ingredients not to fail.

To Rwayitare, broadband, like telecoms was something we would
all soon find impossible to live without. 'We all need broadband to
run a modern lifestyle. It's essential, like water and electricity,' he
said. Rwayitare's plan was to deliver what he called a 'triple play'
of services: high-speed data, voice and video to homes in South
Africa using the already existing electricity grid infrastructure.
His vision, like his plan to build a communication network using
old military equipment, was fresh and exciting. When he passed
away he had already started the roll-out, and was well on his way
to providing broadband services to more than one million homes
in South Africa. In his mind, the future was clear and broadband
was everything:

> Voice has no more future; video is the future and for that you need a
> 20 MB broadband line. My dream is that by 2010, South Africa will
> get real broadband. I am looking forward to watching Brazil (playing in
> the 2010 World Cup) in high-resolution broadband, which will be 40
> times faster than today's internet services. We have no legacy system
> to overcome in this country, so we can use the best technology on the
> market to make this dream come true.

Sadly, Rwayitare would not personally see that dream come true.
Nor would he live to see his dream of building an African academy
of excellence, a world-class university that would develop and nur-

ture the next generation of future leaders and thinkers on the African continent, realised. Twagira explains the legacy his friend wanted to leave behind: 'The academy highlighted Miko's deep commitment to investing in the youth. Through the high-tech school, the students would have been trained and shaped into leaders in the key fields of development in Africa.' Rwayitare's dream was rooted in the opportunities that had been afforded him.

The early days

Rwayitare was extremely talented and lucky enough to have been trained at one of the most prestigious technical universities in the world. Karlsruhe University in Germany is today still recognised as one of the leading research universities with a focus on the natural and technical sciences – particularly mathematics and electrical engineering. Electrical engineering was the subject of choice for Rwayitare when he was selected as one of an elite group of top students from Rwanda, Burundi and the Democratic Republic of Congo to win scholarships to Europe. Twagira remembers when Rwayitare won the exclusive scholarship:

> It was in the 60s, Africa did not have good technical universities. Miko got a scholarship for Switzerland and spent a year in Zurich and then left for Germany. He went for engineering; he was a brilliant student.

In 1970 Rwayitare graduated with a degree in electrical engineering and a love for Germany. He loved the German discipline and the German precision; in fact, Rwayitare loved all things German, including the language which he spoke flawlessly. A native French speaker, Rwayitare was born in 1942 in Kisenyi, a town in the west of Rwanda, into a strict Catholic family. His upbringing, according to Twagira, was 'hard and tough', which was to be expected as he was the eldest of six siblings. His parents, particularly his father, who worked as a government administrator, were tough disciplinarians. When he was 12, Rwayitare was sent to boarding school in neighbouring Bujumbura, the capital of Burundi. He spent four years at Saint Esprit College, a school run by Jesuit priests. There seemed to be a strong focus on Greek and Latin, which were subjects that did not appeal to Rwayitare's logical mind. 'Greek was very hard for him,' explains Twagira. 'A word would have a different meaning according to the context and he had a problem with that. He was good at maths and science, so he left that school to go to another one where there was a scientific department.'

Rwayitare didn't choose just any other school, he choose a school in another country. It was the College Notre-Dame de la Victoire in Bukavu, a city in the eastern DRC which had a strong scientific department, also run by Jesuit priests. The college was not a boarding school so the 16-year-old Rwayitare lived with a family and would cycle to school every day. It was here that he met his lifelong friend, ally, and ultimately, his business partner, Gabriel Twagira. 'Miko was very friendly – he was a very good friend to me, he had compassion, Twagira remembers. 'He was very naughty, very intelligent though, and he was always in the top 10.' In fact all the children at the College Notre-Dame de la Victoire were academically gifted, including Twagira himself, so for Rwayitare to consistently come within the top 10 in a school full of smart kids, was quite an achievement. Twagira explains:

> To be admitted to the Jesuit school one had to pass an exam and they would only take three people in each primary school from three countries across the region: Burundi, DRC and Rwanda. It was quite an elitist school, full of very smart kids. Not a lot of people generally went to university – it was a rare thing – but most of these kids would have gone on to university.

It was during his university days in Germany that Rwayitare became politically aware. His formative years had been spent in the DRC and it was inevitable that he would identify more with Congo than his country of birth, Rwanda? which he had left at a very young age. In Germany, Rwayitare adopted Congolese citizenship and became involved in politics. He joined the youth wing of the Popular Movement of the Revolution (MPR), the only political party in Mobutu Sese Seko's Zaire. Mobutu was the president of Zaire (the DRC) from 1965 until his overthrow in 1997. He came to power following a turbulent period after the Congo's independence in 1960 and soon assumed sweeping powers. In 1967, after banning all other parties, Mobutu launched his political party, the MPR, which Rwayitare joined while he was still in Germany. The MPR espoused nationalism, revolution, and authenticity. Membership was obligatory for all citizens of Zaire.

In Germany, through the MPR, Rwayitare closely followed the events happening in Congo. In 1971, Mobutu changed the Congo's name to Zaire and embarked on a campaign of 'pro-African cultural awareness' or authenticity, which must have appealed to the young Rwayitare, as he was an African in Europe. One of the practices the new campaign discouraged was the use of European names by Zaireans. They were also forced to abandon Western suits and ties, seen by Mobutu as un-African.

After spending a year working as a technical manager in an engineering business venture, 3S System Software, in Germany, Rwayitare decided to return home. The Zaire he returned to under Mobutu was beginning to suffer an economic slump. The businesses that had been nationalised were being pillaged and run to the ground, and Mobutu was forced to start wooing investors back into the country. Rwayitare, with his foreign experience, stepped into a good job as technical manager at the Republic of Zaire Data Processing Centre in the president's office, and was tasked with setting up a national information database to assist potential investors.

From there he moved to the country's largest mining conglomerate, the state-owned Gécamines, which was the third-largest producer of copper and cobalt in the world. As marketing vice president, Rwayitare's role involved a lot of travel around the world. It was this travel that gave him the exposure to global international technology trends and his first inkling of the need to work for himself. As an engineer, Rwayitare was excited by the technical advances he saw playing out in Europe and the US. He saw the potential impact such technology could have on the way business was conducted on his continent and he saw no reason why Africa could not be a part of the technical revolution. This insight was the impetus he needed to venture into the business world.

'His sense for business started around this time,' remembers Twagira. 'He was looking for opportunities; he wanted to leave and start his own business. He started small, using his own money – his salary.' In 1978 Rwayitare set up his very first company: Computing Industrial Engineering (CIE), and secured the tender to distribute Hewlett-Packard and Rank Xerox products in the DRC. The business was so successful that he soon started selling computer hardware and office equipment to the neighbouring countries of Gabon, Rwanda, Cote d'Ivoire and Ethiopia. CIE was largely a distribution company but it was also involved in the maintenance of the products it sold. Rwayitare clearly enjoyed technology and made a point of keeping up with the latest trends and products; he sent his engineers to the US for training. But CIE remained a small operation and at the company's peak, there were just 10 sales and technical staff. Despite this, the business was very lucrative. Rwayitare had filled a gap in the market at a time when technology was beginning to wake up Africa.

Rwayitare was overwhelmed by his initial success with CIE and would joke: 'In the end, we replaced nearly every IBM computer on the continent with HP.' He ran CIE for several years until computers became commonplace. It wasn't long before he spotted his next opportunity and this one was going to be huge.

The birth of Telecel

Rumour has it that one particular day Rwayitare was struggling to transfer data between computer terminals because of the poor quality of the cables. His frustrations with the existing technology led him into a conversation with Joe Gatt, his soon-to-be partner. Then followed a trip to the US and a short while later, Telecel, the continent's first pan-African mobile phone operator, was born. But it wasn't quite that easy. Rwayitare first needed a licence from the government to enable him to run the mobile phone network he envisioned.

In 1985, the telecoms sector in Zaire (DRC), like most of the rest of Africa, was highly regulated and even more inadequate. At that time in most African countries, telecommunications was usually run as an inefficient state-owned monopoly. In trying to start up his own network, Rwayitare had to ask for permission for a private individual to operate in a space that had usually been the preserve of the government – it was unheard of. In fact, through his various negotiations for licences, first in the DRC and then in the region, Rwayitare played an instrumental role in opening up the path for the privatisation of telecommunications in Africa. With the global privatisation of the telecoms sector today, it is difficult to believe how hard it was for Rwayitare to get his first licence. He couldn't simply submit a bid to purchase one, as is common practice today. He had to be very clever about it: 'I hired an army of lawyers to find me a gap in the law,' explained Rwayitare. But rather than take the legal route, and because he was totally convinced of the success of his new offering, he did something that had never been done before – then or since – in the history of mobile telecommunications. It was a once in a lifetime offer:

> The first 12 months we offered free of charge. Just to show that it was feasible. And the people fell in love with the cellular phone. Our first handheld phones, which were Motorolas, had about 30 minutes of talk time, had no memory, and they could only recall the last number called. They weighed as much as a bottle of wine, yet they were a huge success.

The 12-month free trial period was, unsurprisingly, not initially in Rwayitare's roll-out plan. But he saw it as a strategic marketing tool and decided to offer phones exclusively to the people who could influence the granting of his licence. 'He gave the handsets to government for a six-month trial, saying they should return (the phone) if they didn't want it. After another six months they gave him the licence,' smiles Twagira.

The licence came with a price tag: US$1.5 million, which is laughable today, when mobile phone licences are being snapped up at hundreds of millions of US dollars. Still, this was 1986, and within the first year of his licence, Rwayitare had secured 3 000 contract subscribers and was on his way. Despite the size of the phone and the costs involved – a mobile phone could set a subscriber back US$5 000 – being on the mobile network became a very prestigious thing in Zaire. Rwayitare's entry strategy had worked. Telecel, the company he registered to run and manage the network in the DRC, took off. The man whom everyone thought was crazy had been vindicated.

His success didn't stop with just Zaire either. By 1991, five years after his launch in 1986, Rwayitare was operating in four other African countries: Burundi, Guinea, Madagascar and Central African Republic. By 1998 he was in eight countries, adding Ivory Coast, Zambia and Zimbabwe to the list. By the time he sold 80% of Telecel to Orascom, the Egyptian-owned mobile operator, for US$413 million in 2000, Telecel was a household name in 11 countries.

Rwayitare sold for various reasons, mainly to access more funds to enable him to further grow the network to the target of

20 countries he envisaged and, by linking up with Orascom, to provide the technical strength he needed to keep Telecel ahead of the competition. At the time of the sale to Orascom, Rwayitare had said: 'The future in telecommunications is to develop synergy, and with Orascom Telecom we will have access to resources that will enable us to expand and be a dominant force in the industry.' Rwayitare truly believed in developing synergies with other operators. A few years later, he joined forces with Orascom and the German operator, Detecon, to buy a majority shareholding in the newly privatised Uganda Telecom (UTL). In November 1999, he created another joint venture with the US-based Titan Corporation to provide satellite-based rural telephone services in the countries where Telecel was operating. He truly believed that technology was the solution for Africa and he planned to be at the forefront of this revolution.

The new South African

Rwayitare had been running his pan-African empire from Kinshasa, the capital of the DRC (Zaire), since its launch. However, in 1996, he was forced to leave the DRC following the aftermath of the 1994 Rwandan genocide, when Tutsis like Rwayitare were being threatened and forced out of the country. He moved to South Africa and continued to run Telecel's operations from there. He explained why he chose South Africa:

> When Telecel reached 12 countries it became difficult to manage from Kinshasa. Business works well in Johannesburg, so I relocated there, but I do miss the glamour of Central Africa. Johannesburg is not as cosmopolitan as one might like. It is empty by 10pm.

That sentence was the essence of Rwayitare: he worked hard but loved to enjoy life as well. He loved to live well. Johannesburg may not have had the glamour of Central Africa, but Rwayitare did his best to recreate it. The house Rwayitare bought in Johannesburg was grand and opulent, and oozed the glamour he craved. It was also the object of media interest and many reports focused on the sheer extravagance of the building. 'He recently splashed out over R50 million to build his lavish 10 000m² home in Oxford Avenue, now valued at an estimated R100 million. Estate agents say Rwayitare's home leaves in the dust the R30 million mansion belonging to controversial entrepreneur Dave King,' said one property report. Another described the home as a 'hilltop mansion of Versailles-like proportions'. It wasn't too far from the truth.

Rwayitare had amassed a small fortune building his business. He was the first African telecoms mogul to become a millionaire and although he lived comfortably, he also knew how to simultaneously invest and enjoy his money. A year after he sold to Orascom, Rwayitare decided to consolidate his love for wine and fine living with his requirement for good financial returns. He snapped up an 82-acre wine farm in Cape Town's Franschhoek for US$3 million. His immediate plan was to invest in updating its production facilities and building up its export base:

> A farm in St Emilion, France, would cost three times as much as one in Franschhoek and the results are not always better. We are a boutique wine farm at Mont Rochelle and I want to reduce the production and improve the quality.

Mount Rochelle still produces Cabernet Sauvignon, Chardonnay, Merlot and Shiraz wines, and bottled its first vintage in 1994. Along with his partner in the business, Erwin Schnitzler, the estate produces in excess of 14 000 cases a year. In 2006, Rwayitare bought up the adjoining 28-room boutique hotel, creating the Mont Rochelle Hotel and Mountain Vineyards. Even though he referred to it as 'not a big thing', it clearly was in South Africa. Rwayitare will forever hold the record of being the first black person in the country to own a wine farm. And, according to a review that appeared in *The Citizen* newspaper in 2008, Rwayitare's wine farm was not just any old wine farm:

> The location of Mont Rochelle reminds one that South Africa is filled with corners so beautiful that there isn't a plane ticket on sale that will take you to a better place ... This is the perfect place to fall in love; with the person sitting opposite you, the food, the wine or just with life itself ... With the Mediterranean-inspired Country Kitchen, the fine dining restaurant Mange Tout, a Colonial Cigar bar, library, rolling lawns and wine tasting venue, the hotel never feels crowded and in fact the only time one notices that there are other guests is at breakfast, a situation ideal for honeymooners and escapees of the rat race ... If

food is your passion then a tall glass of Mont Rochelle's premier Miko Chardonnay *sur lie* 2006, the tumbling notes of Bolero played on the piano by Alfio (a Mont Rochelle institution worth experiencing) and the elegantly prepared cuisine of Executive Chef Ryan Smith, makes the Mange Tout Restaurant an ideal place to lose a little time.

In the same year he bought the wine farm, Rwayitare retired to Franschhoek to become a part-time wine maker. At the time he claimed the wine farm was something he was just 'doing for pleasure'. But the pleasure didn't last too long. 'When I sold Telecel, I tried to retire, so I tasted wine for six months. But I got bored and came back to the office,' laughed Rwayitare. Forgoing the good life, he fled back to Johannesburg and resumed the role of a telecoms tycoon and hard-nosed investor.

Back to the future

In 2002, Rwayitare was forced to step up a gear when Orascom Telecoms, which had purchased Telecel only two years before, decided to disengage from sub-Saharan Africa. This meant they were effectively pulling out of Telecel. In its announcement of the demerger, Orascom said it wanted to place its emphasis on larger markets like their newly acquired licence in Algeria and other interests in the Middle East. Within two years, Orascom restructured and sold off all 12 operations it had acquired under Telecel. Rwayitare bought back four of the mobile phone operations: in Burundi, Central African Republic, Uganda and Zambia. He was back in business. Although building and operating Global System for Mobile communications (GSM) networks was where Rwayitare had made his money, ironically, his real passion was for the competitive mobile technology called Code Division Multiple Access (CDMA). Like the argument between Sony's Betamax and JVC's VHS tape format back in the 80s, the jury is still out on which is the better technology, although GSM has a much larger global market share.

Essentially, Rwayitare felt that GSM was expensive, particularly for Africa, and therefore unaffordable for most Africans. As a result, he created another company called Global Vision Telecom (GV Telecom) which used CDMA technology exclusively to build networks. GV Telecom acquired CDMA licences in Uganda, Burundi,

Nigeria and the DRC, and was in negotiations with the governments of Senegal, Tanzania and the Ivory Coast. To Rwayitare, CDMA was the way forward for telecoms in Africa. But he was soon about to come face to face with what he believed would be the ultimate technology of the future.

In 2004 Rwayitare was approached by entrepreneurs Adrian Maguire and Patrice Lasserre to invest in a new business they had started. It was called Goal Technology Solutions (GTS) and they had stumbled on a way to deliver fast, reliable and, most importantly, affordable broadband to almost every home in South Africa. Their revolutionary plan was to implement it over existing power line infrastructure. Rwayitare was so impressed with the vision and the possibilities GTS presented that, like Victor Kiam, the CEO of the US company Remington, who regularly starred in adverts proclaiming why he bought into Remington, he must surely have uttered the words: 'I liked it so much, I bought the company.' Rwayitare ended up purchasing 80% of the business and became a major investor and its chairman. He completely believed in broadband and in GTS. Twagira, who had once refused to give Rwayitare start-up capital for Telecel, didn't want to get left behind this time around. Today, he is an investor in GTS and like his friend Rwayitare, he too was totally sold on the concept of affordable broadband for African homes.

> Broadband is like water or energy, something everyone must have at home. Imagine a world where every power socket in your home is a broadband communication point without need for separate cabling, where internet telephony is of high quality and does not require you to have a computer. A world where high-quality surveillance and security systems are cheap and flexible, and easy to implement, and video streaming and video-on-demand though IPTV (Internet Protocol Television) becomes affordable and available to more communities that previously could not afford or access it. This is the vision for which Miko started GTS.

Twagira confirmed that Rwayitare's passion for GTS and its aims was instant:

> From Miko's very first contact with the founders of GTS, he saw it was the cornerstone of the next communications giant. Over the next two

years he drove the acquisition of what was to form a complete chain of broadband communication services to individuals. More than his finance, Miko provided GTS with unequalled leadership and business expertise.

Under Rwayitare's two-and-a-half-year association with the business, GTS completed a 130-home pilot in Pretoria which achieved speeds of 30 megabits per second, more than five times the speed required by the commissioning municipality. In addition, GTS secured a concession with three South African municipalities to provide broadband services to over a million homes and this was just the beginning. To realise Rwayitare's dream of high-definition TV via broadband, GTS was one of 15 bidders that submitted a tender to operate a pay-television licence in South Africa. The announcement of the five winners in September 2007, days before Rwayitare's death, unfortunately did not include GTS. Despite Rwayitare's death, GTS is still very much on track and investors are determined to see the realisation of his vision and goals: 'commitment in financing this project and providing human resources and strong management to lead South Africa in a new telephonic convergence to bridge the digital divide'. The founders of GTS are currently trying to find a new home for Rwayitare's shareholding in the business.

Building a diversified portfolio

Rwayitare wasn't only invested in technology projects; his portfolio was diverse and included hotels, financial services, medical research and real estate. The purchase of an 89% stake in the Hôtel des Mille Collines for US$3.2 million marked Rwayitare's first significant investment in Rwanda, the country of his birth. He had confessed to a 'growing interest' in hotels and was keen to grow his portfolio: 'Whether it be Mont Rochelle or the Hôtel Mille Collines in Rwanda – or even new projects in Kenya, Mozambique and Zanzibar – my interest is in core, iconic African hospitality at its best.' The 112-roomed, four-star Hôtel Mille Collines in Rwanda's capital, Kigali, is the same hotel that was the subject of the film *Hotel Rwanda*, which documents a hotel that became a refuge for more than 1 200 Tutsis and moderate Hutus during the infamous 100-day massacre. Ironically, the hotel itself was never actually featured in the film.

In a handover ceremony held on the hotel's grounds in September 2005, Rwayitare said: 'My priority will be building capacity, rehabilitating rooms, refurbishing the entrance and improving services.' He was in the process of delivering on that commitment when he passed away. Not long before his death, he had secured a US$2.5 million loan from the International Finance Corporation, part of the World Bank, to embark on a major refurbishment for the hotel.

It was a source of great irritation to Rwayitare that he never owned a telecoms operation in his country of birth, Rwanda, and it wasn't for lack of trying. On one occasion he tried to bring Telecel to Rwanda but was denied a licence, which subsequently went to MTN. 'Really, I don't understand it,' he said, shaking his head. 'They wanted to give only one licence and claimed that my technology was older than what MTN had offered. Yet mine was Siemens and theirs was Ericsson, so I really could not see why,' said a frustrated Rwayitare.

A few years later, in 2006, he would try again when GV Telecoms purchased an IT company called Terracom, which had taken over Rwanda's fixed-line operator, Rwandatel, for US$20 million. The government subsequently blocked the deal. It seems Rwayitare may have finally given up on owning a telecoms operation in Rwanda; he didn't bother to submit a bid when the government eventually put up 70% of Rwandatel for sale in 2007.

Mr Miko

Rwayitare often said: 'To succeed in life, you have three components. Chance 60%, work 20%, and 20% is imagination and ideas.' He had all three when he conceptualised Telecel. He has been described as a business visionary, a risk-taker and a hard worker who was humble and who inspired loyalty and respect among those he led. Twagira confirms this: 'He was a good leader; he wanted his staff to feel comfortable. From the cleaner to his partners – you didn't need protocol with Miko.'

But despite his business successes, Rwayitare somehow seemed to have dodged the class that taught sales and administrative skills. According to Twagira, he just wasn't very good at either: 'He didn't want to spend time selling things – he would appoint people to sell. He preferred to spend time thinking strategically.' And in a manner that only a great friend could get away with, Twagira continues his friendly onslaught: 'His day-to-day managing of the business was weak – he didn't look at the details.' He may not have had a passion for business detail, but Rwayitare was passionate about many other things: good living, fine wines, Formula One, architecture, classical music and jazz, Elton John and Pavarotti, fine hotels and technology. But perhaps most of all, according to Twagira, Rwayitare had a passion for Africa.

> Miko was a pan-Africanist; he believed in the continent. He thought that for Africa to be developed, it needed people with drive. He believed it was possible to achieve development if we worked hard, if there was passion.

Perhaps the person who influenced him the most in life was Cuban revolutionary leader Ernesto 'Che' Guevara, the Argentine doctor who abandoned his profession and his country to pursue the emancipation of the poor. 'Miko admired Che Guevara,' remembers Twagira. 'He had a big picture of him at his home. He considered Che a man for others, who left everything behind to fight for freedom and liberty.' Like Che, Rwayitare had a deep compassion for the world's poor – Africa's in particular. He stated proudly that he was an 'avid participant in anti-poverty initiatives'. He gave much of his time to finding ways to solve poverty issues and was on a poverty alleviation committee created by Kofi Annan to meet the millennium objectives. Rwayitare believed poverty was the result of the lack of certain essentials:

> Basic infrastructure such as transport and telecommunications could play a fundamental role in providing a platform that alleviate poverty because such basics make way for the enhancement of trade, human resources development, protection of the environment and promotion of education.

Through his trailblazing and revolutionary work in driving change in the telecoms sector across the African continent, Rwayitare touched millions of people's lives and put in place some of the telecommunication infrastructure he believed contributed to the advancement of Africa. The freedom of communication and the world-class telecoms technology which we take for granted today in Africa would simply not have been there without his fight to set up Telecel. 'Don't ever dream big, dream huge, and then you'll achieve big,' Rwayitare once said. Of the hundreds of messages on the online condolence book hosted on the African Heritage website to mark Rwayitare's death, there was one in particular that stood out in its summation of Rwayitare as a leader, a businessman and, most of all, a humanitarian:

> Miko has been a great inspiration for the young entrepreneurs of Africa. I grew up in Kinshasa where I saw Telecel growing from there to many other countries in Africa. I personally remember Miko who saved the lives of his employees of Rwandan Descent in 2006. He helped them migrate to Brazzaville and, later on, by freight on an airplane to Uganda. I was in that airplane; young, lost and wondering what the future will be. Since then many things have happened and I always promised myself one day to meet him and thank him for saving my life and the lives of many other people. – Jean-Claude N (USA)

Rwayitare once said: 'There is a French expression that translates as "without a struggle there is no glory" and I have always regarded challenge as the most exciting part of life.' Unfortunately Twayitare's life ended just as he was embarking on another exciting challenge, which, like his African telecoms revolution 22 years before, would have probably provided a struggle, but would have undoubtedly ended in glory.

Sources:

1. Bayne, A (2008). 'Fall in Love' in *The Citizen*, 25 April. Available at: www.citizen.co.za.
2. Orascom Telecom official website, available at: www.otelecom.com.
3. Africa Heritage Society online condolence book for Miko Rwayitare, available at www.africaheritage.com/mikorwayitare.php.

Nigel Chanakira – The Wonder Boy Entrepreneur

VITAL STATISTICS

Name: Nigel Chanakira
Country: Zimbabwe
Born: 11 July 1966
Position/Title: Group CEO Kingdom Meikles Africa Ltd
Market Capitalisation on Zimbabwe Stock Exchange:
US$600 million
Nationality: Zimbabwean
Industry: Key sectors include financial services, tourism,
and retail
Highest education qualification: Master of Sciences in
economics at the University of Zimbabwe

Then I got into trouble with the authorities. Our TV programme was taken off the air. I had begun to comment adversely on the monetary and economic policies in Zimbabwe. Clearly, from our perspective, what was happening in the country was not conducive to the development of financial markets. So some businessmen and some politicians targeted me and I was arrested twice and detained for two days each time in 2000. It was like my empire was crumbling because imagine: it was a new bank and I was being arrested with allegations of fraud!

It was a frightening thing because you would hear all these morbid stories about what happened to other people who were detained. I had to go to court twice; the state had no proof of any wrongdoing on my part. They were just trumped up charges. What made it worse was that come 2001, I had a third arrest pending. That meant they would have taken away my passport, which means you can't travel, you're in the courts and you are no longer the 'high-flyer' you were because you are being labelled by the press as a crook. I was tipped off and I decided it was time to leave Zimbabwe.

Nigel Chanakira, the wonder boy of the investment banking world, the high-profile economic analyst, entrepreneur and media personality had crash-landed. He had no choice but to leave Zimbabwe, his country of birth, and flee to South Africa, leaving behind his business, Kingdom Financial Holdings (KFH), the financial services group he and four friends had started seven years before in December 1994. Chanakira left at the peak of the bank's performance – KFH was making its presence felt and was blazing a trail in the market. It was different to any of the other indigenous and foreign banking operations in Zimbabwe, and at every turn, Chanakira seemed to have a new initiative up his sleeve to blindside the competition.

In 1997 KFH was the first to introduce unit trusts and make them accessible to the masses. The stockbroking business was doing phenomenally well, 'making lots of money' for their customers. KFH was the first to introduce banks into supermarkets through an in-store banking partnership with the country's leading supermarket chain. It was also the first to introduce a debit card, which could be applied for, issued and used, all within 20 minutes. Chanakira laughs:

Now that just drove the market topsy-turvy. The international banking groups with operations in Zimbabwe were not doing that yet. We had an edge over our competitors – we were exploiting technology. We were flying high and I personally won a number of business awards at the time.

Chanakira's frequent media appearances and his own popular TV show, which demystified financial jargon and the money markets, were serving him well – and people noticed. He was nominated as a World Economic Forum Global Leader of Tomorrow, he was the Zimbabwean Institute of Management's Manager of the Year and his company was so successful that it featured on the top-10 quoted companies in Zimbabwe by market capitalisation. It was on this career high that Chanakira fled from Zimbabwe to figure out why it went wrong and how he could come back and reclaim his crown. It would take him four years to get back to Zimbabwe and even then it wasn't under the circumstances he would have liked. Believe it or not, things got worse.

The early days

Chanakira was not destined to become a fugitive from the law – albeit unjust and unfair laws. On the contrary, as the product of a hard-working, middle-class Zimbabwean family, he was expected to live well within them. His academic and professional career would have been mapped out for him from an early age and renegade was definitely not one of the career options. From his early twenties he had been focused on what he wanted to do with his life. When he was much younger he flirted with the idea of a career in driving taxis, but his mother soon put paid to that, he remembers, laughing:

> When I was four years old I wanted to be a taxi driver. I was fascinated with cars. There was a Renault 8 car which I loved; it was a taxi that operated around my area. I was absolutely fascinated by it and I told my mother I was going to be a taxi driver. She slapped me hard, which fortunately put aside that dream!

Chanakira soon came round to his mother's way of thinking and went for a more acceptable career choice. 'I told her I was going to be a doctor and that thrilled her. But when I was 12 she took me to a hospital where I observed doctors and dentists at work and I realised

I didn't want to be a doctor either.' Given his family background, it would have not have been much of a surprise if he had told his mother that he wanted to be a businessman; his uncle was one of the first black businessmen of the 40s and 50s in Zimbabwe. His father was a grocer who ran a number of supermarkets for Chanakira's businessman uncle who owned a chain of them. His mother was the educationalist and disciplinarian in the family, and had worked as a nurse. She was the one who pushed her children to make something of themselves. Chanakira, the eldest of four siblings, was not particularly academically gifted, but he was very competitive.

> I struggled in school, in fact my sister was much brighter than I was and it was a source of great irritation (to me). I was middle of the class, not particularly bright or particularly dumb. I never got any academic prizes but I got prizes for being the best-groomed child in class. I was a very polite boy; I was the first black head of my school hostel at Churchill Boys High School (in Harare).

Under the influence of his mother, and the inspiring headmistress of his Catholic school, Sister Rosina, Chanakira's competitive spirit drove him to improve his grades. 'They made me take my studies very seriously so I started working hard; when I got to high school I became very good. I wanted to be top of my class,' he recalls. Chanakira's hard work paid off and he got himself into the economics course at the University of Zimbabwe – no mean feat. The University of Zimbabwe was the only university in the country and as such, places on the courses were highly contested. Apart from that, it was one of the few universities in Africa into which money and resources had been poured. It was evidence of Mugabe's heavy investment in education during the early years of his rule. Although economics was not Chanakira's first choice for a degree, it ended up becoming his calling:

> During my university holidays I spent a lot of my time reading the *Wall Street Journal*, *Financial Times* and *The Economist*. I absolutely loved those magazines. It was through reading them that I found out that top economists like Adam Smith also invested on the stock markets. I realised then that I had found my calling in the financial services. So I decided to pursue that.

He soon found a dream job for a young graduate with a passion for economics; he started work at the Central Bank of Zimbabwe as an assistant economist. He loved it, but while he was there, he stumbled on a potential opportunity and the beginning of a vision started to form. They say timing is everything.

The start of a vision

> The governor of the Zimbabwean Reserve Bank was in the process of opening up the country's economy and freeing up the markets. Banking licences were being issued for the first time to qualifying black people. I decided then that I wanted to have my own bank.

Chanakira was only 22 at the time, fresh out of university and in his first job, and it was highly unlikely that he would be given even a whiff of a chance to apply for a licence. But he displayed a maturity and patience way beyond his years. He decided to get himself trained in the intricacies of banking by finding a job in the private sector and building up his CV and his credibility, so that he could position himself for a banking licence. He just needed to find that job.

> There was an advert for an investment analyst. I had never heard of such a thing but because of my reading of the business journals I understood the job description and I knew it was perfect for me, so I applied. (It was competitive –) 400 people applied for that job and I got it. I had a deep sense that this was my job. The very fact that I was the one person who was chosen out of 400 applicants developed my confidence significantly. I realised I had my destiny carved out for me.

The company Chanakira had applied to work for was called Bard Discount House and it sold treasury bills and discounted financial assets. He soon became one of the company's top analysts and from there, a media commentator. Two years into the job, he started to develop a reputation as a smart, well-spoken young economist. He became president of the Zimbabwe Economics Society and was often sought out by the media for his opinions. The thought of owning his own bank one day, however, remained at the back of Chanakira's mind.

It was at around this time that Chanakira became a strong Christian. His faith would become the single most powerful influence in his life and came to provide the platform on which he would build his success. It wasn't just one thing that influenced his shift to faith; it was a series of different events that brought him to the realisation that 'God is real':

> My wife had started going to church and I used to stay behind and play soccer and drink beer with my friends in the 'Boozers League' in Harare. My wife was born again and she would often talk to me about 'my ways'.

But it took a child dying in his arms to finally get him into the church.

> I had a car accident in which a child died in my arms on the road. I had to go to court where I had a charge of culpable homicide laid against me. The impact of that was significant in my life. I would question life itself. It was this searching, along with my wife's influence, that made me curious to go into church and I have been a strong Christian ever since.

From the day he walked through the doors for the first time, the church has played a huge role in Chanakira's life. It was the church and a particular pastor, Tom Deuschle, that finally made him start thinking again about his five-year-old dream to run his own bank.

> Pastor Tom Deuschle preached in a compelling way about 'kingdom companies'; these were companies formed by Christians. I already wanted to run my own bank and the more he spoke about kingdom companies the more it became real to me. In Matthew 6 verse 33 it says: 'But seek ye first the kingdom of God, and his righteousness; and all these things shall be added unto you'.

Chanakira was particularly interested in the part of the verse that spoke of the things that would be added. So, he started to prepare himself for the day he would one day run his own bank. He enrolled in Empretec, the international organisation that runs entrepreneurial courses for businessmen, and took their two-week

course. Two women he met there were instrumental in giving him
the final push he needed.

> One of my lecturers, Busi Bango, impressed me greatly and the lady
> who ran Empretec, Tsitsi Masiyiwa, pushed me to set up my business.
> She said: 'You keep talking about this bank, when are you going to set it
> up?' I knew I didn't have the start-up capital and that was my reason for
> not starting my bank but she said: 'If you really want start-up capital,
> why don't you sell your house?

Chanakira had recently moved into a new house with his wife
and young family, and life was very comfortable. The Chanakiras
were living very well, with all the usual trappings of a successful
middle-class couple – a good car, a nice house. The suggestion to
sell his home, once he got over the shock, and realised it was the
only way forward, had to be broached very carefully with his wife.
'I told my wife at the time: "I will build you your dream house when
my business succeeds".' Chanakira's wife, Caroline, must have had
great faith in her husband because not only did she agree to sell
her new home, she also agreed to move back in with her in-laws.
Chanakira went straight to work: 'I took a leap of faith and I sold
my house,' he says proudly. At the time, a banking licence cost
US$500 000 and from the sale of his home, Chanakira managed to
raise US$120 000. He was US$380 000 short so he went to church
to get the rest.

> Malachite 3 verse 10 says: 'Bring ye all the tithes into the storehouse,
> that there may be meat in mine house, and prove me now herewith,
> saith the Lord of hosts, if I will not open you the windows of heaven,
> and pour you out a blessing, that there shall not be room enough to
> receive it.'
>   So that Sunday I went to church, I stood up in the service and said:
> 'I am going to give US$17 000 to the church in order to sow the seed in
> the Lord's house that I will have my own bank.' People told me I was
> stupid – I had sold my house, I was giving my money to the church,
> what was I doing?

With the US$17 000 pledge, Chanakira was even further away from
his target, but he was a man with a God-given vision, and four
partners who believed in him. 'I had a dream that told me to go to

the Karigamombe Centre and rent an office, but when we got there we ended up renting a boardroom as we simply could not afford the office,' he explains. A boardroom, four partners, desks and a computer were all he started with.

> I knew I had sales skills and I knew I understood economics. Within months, we all resigned and set up shop in this one boardroom. We were going to run a money market bucket shop and then apply for a banking licence.

Chanakira's team started with a stockbroking firm, largely because they did not need a licence to operate. In November 1994, the five partners sat at their boardroom table and started working. They wrote a business plan and put systems in place – the idea was to make enough money to pay for the balance needed for the banking licence. And that was the beginning of Kingdom Securities Holdings. The following month they officially opened up for business and things just took off: 'It went so well,' says Chanakira, 'that every day, for the next nine months we got a new client.'

> On 27 August 1995 we officially got the banking licence, and two insurance companies, Zimnat Life and First Mutual, became institutional investors and took 20% of the business. The first nine months were tough; we worked furiously – 20-hour days, five of us, all in the same boardroom.

In the first year, they did well. In the second year they lost money – the country's interest rate was high as a result of the aftermath of a drought which hit Zimbabwe's agricultural sector hard. Chanakira and his partners needed to kick-start the business. They had all risked a lot to start the company and were determined to make it work. In need of new ideas, Chanakira booked himself on to what would turn out to be a life-changing leadership course. It was a 12-week programme called the Dynamics of Successful Management, run by the Success Motivation Institute, a US-based motivation and leadership company. The course gave him a completely new insight into life, business and success.

> Don't forget, as black people, we were the first generation of business people to run public companies in Zimbabwe and we didn't have

mentors as such to look up to. This course changed my way of thinking
– it helped me set my goals and execute them.

Spurred on by what he now knew about setting goals and self-
motivation, Chanakira attended another entrepreneurial programme
which involved a six-week visit to the US courtesy of the United
States Agency for International Development (USAID). During the
course, he met top CEOs of US firms and got real exposure into
how businesses were run and managed. Chanakira was totally fired
up. 'My paradigm had changed; I could see what was possible,' he
explains. One of the first things he set out to do was to raise his
profile, a strategic move to bring attention to his business:

> I began to write a column on the back page of the leading financial
> newspaper, *The Financial Gazette*, which is our 'Pink Paper'. Then I
> went to the national TV station and said I was going to assist local
> people to understand financial markets. I simplified it for them and in
> the process I built up a phenomenal profile for myself and my company.
> Then I became an analyst, providing financial commentary. I would
> analyse the budget, its implications on the financial markets – all these
> were ideas I had picked up from CNN. Then we started a programme
> called 'Making Money Make Sense', which I presented.

Apart from building a media profile, Chanakira was also bubbling
with new ideas on how to grow the business. It was at around this
time that he started offering unit trusts and through them got a
lucky break which propelled the business forward:

> Old Mutual demutualised and the only stockbroking firm most local
> people knew was Kingdom Stockbrokers. So we had 10 000 or 20 000
> of these newly empowered black individuals who suddenly had share
> certificates and all they ever knew what to do with share certificates
> was to take them to Kingdom. Before we knew it we had a customer
> base of 20 000 clients. It was an absolute delight.

The stockbroking business had created millionaires out of a new
breed of financially savvy consumers. 'We were making lots of
money for our customers so everyone knew who we were,' says
Chanakira proudly.

In 1999 Kingdom Securities Holdings merged with the biggest

competitor of the company he used to work for, The Discount Company, an old established financial institution with old systems. 'We did a reverse listing and merged the two entities under Kingdom Financial Holdings, so now we had a securities company, stockbroking, asset management, a discount house (a financial institution that borrows and invests largely short-term funds, often by buying Treasurey bills at a discount from the government) and we wanted to go into traditional banking,' he explains. In the middle of this whirlwind of high visibility and growth Chanakira found time to go out fishing for more ideas and inspiration in international waters. He went to the International Banking Summer School held in Luxembourg, and came back with two new ideas for his business; one for microfinance and the other for a new concept – in-store banking.

> We started a company called MicroKing, which is now the biggest microfinance business in Zimbabwe. Then the in-store banking was going to be our way into banking. I knew we didn't have the money to compete against the big established banks which had the bank branches. Our capital base would never have matched theirs. We had to be clever about it.

He approached the Meikles Group, one of the oldest and most successful white-owned listed companies in Zimbabwe. They had interests in hotels and, among other things, owned a chain of supermarkets across Zimbabwe. Chanakira knew they were keen to go into banking but were looking for a partner.

> They had been looking for an established bank and I said to them: 'Guys, there is a cheaper way to do this. We'll use your supermarkets as our banking halls.' So I presented this concept of in-store banking which was at that time just being done in the UK with Sainsbury's and so forth. It hadn't even started here. So we decided to sell 25% of Kingdom Financial Holdings to Meikles, this was in December 1999, and we started to build in-store branches.

But the popularity of the in-store branches was, in a way, the concept's downfall. The supermarket simply didn't have room to cater for the banking needs of Kingdom's huge customer base and they were forced to invest in building 'brick and mortar' branches.

By 2001, Kingdom had opened up its first standalone branch.

Chanakira's business now had what he called 'serious share-holders', which made him a heavyweight in business terms. Added to his first two institutional investors, Zimnat and First Mutual, who had invested when Kingdom had first opened its doors, he could now boast the former Discount Company, institutional shareholders and the Meikles Group as shareholders. Everything seemed to be going well for the wonder boy.

Chanakira's fast-moving dynamic business and his high-profile media career were beginning to attract attention. The government didn't like the fact that he was paying some of the legal bills for his good friend Strive Masiyiwa of Econet, who was suing the state in an attempt to secure a mobile licence. At one stage the government newspaper had six different charges for six different crimes lined up against Chanakira. Eventually his empire began to crumble and he decided it was 'time to leave Zimbabwe'. In 2002 Chanakira took a sabbatical to Cape Town, South Africa, to avoid harassment and detention by the Zimbabwean government.

Saving Kingdom

Before he left for Cape Town, Chanakira appointed one of his partners to run the Kingdom business in Zimbabwe while he focused on trying to grow the business regionally from Cape Town. During his sabbatical, he travelled extensively and successfully built additional Kingdom Financial Holdings businesses in Zambia, Malawi and Botswana. In Zambia, Kingdom bought into an existing bank called Investrust Bank; in Malawi, he started a greenfields operation called First Discount House. In Botswana, Kingdom launched Kingdom Bank Africa, an offshore bank on the continent. During that period Chanakira also focused on developing some of the banks' value-added services and spent time in Nigeria working on a mobile banking product. Although he wasn't in the thick of things, he nevertheless had a handle on what was going on, but it wasn't the same as actually being there. And it wasn't long before the Zimbabwean banking crisis of 2003, which threatened to topple the empire he had left behind, forced him back into the driving seat.

In one sense, the Zimbabwean government had created the banking crisis. In 2003 it had appointed a new governor of the Reserve Bank of Zimbabwe called Gideon Gono. Gono introduced much-needed new policies designed to shake up the sector, but as well as hiking interest rates, he started scrutinising corporate governance within the indigenous banks. Many banks were deemed to be using depositors' money recklessly and conducting foreign exchange transactions that contravened the banking laws. Directors' shareholdings were also an issue and under the new regulations that Gono implemented, executive directors who sat on the board of a bank were not permitted to hold more than a 10% shareholding in that bank. As a result, many directors had to cut back their shareholdings and/or resign from the boards on which they sat. The subsequent investigations and ensuing publicity into the various banks' activities caused a run-on from the indigenous banks. Depositors panicked and started to withdraw their money in droves. Chanakira's bank, along with the other indigenous banks, took a hammering. In 2004, Kingdom Financial Holdings, with very little capital and next to no deposits, was on the brink of closure.

> It was the most traumatic time for me – I felt the pain. I felt the testimony was being destroyed because I believe this business was founded on the word of God. If it had collapsed, what would the story be?

That is when Chanakira decided to leave South Africa and go back to Zimbabwe to recapitalise the business. He spent most of 2004 and the early part of 2005 fundraising to save his bank. He had built up a fairly substantial personal asset base, which included a shareholding in Inter Fresh, a listed agricultural company. He also owned a small aircraft leasing company and shares in a Zimbabwean newspaper, *The Daily News*, in which he had invested a substantial sum just before he left Zimbabwe in 2001.

> When the bank was teetering on the brink of closure I sold everything and poured it back into Kingdom and bought out my partners. I said: 'Let me sort out the bank's problems because I can raise the capital.' So I did a share swap with them. They took the shares in the other companies and I stayed with the bank.

But it wasn't just Chanakira's assets that saved the bank – his friend and fellow enemy of the state, Strive Masiyiwa, stepped up with a fistful of dollars and bought a 25% stake in the business. The Meikles Group, which already owned 25%, injected more cash into Kingdom and raised its shareholding to 33%. The company also underwent the first of two rights issues and successfully raised US$100 million. Fully optimistic for the future of his bank, Chanakira was quoted as saying: 'We now have a dream team of institutional shareholders in Meikles, Old Mutual and now Econet, who between them hold 55% of the issued share capital of Kingdom. They have the financial muscle to help us in these challenging times.' However, not everyone agreed with Chanakira's reference to the crisis as merely 'challenging times', and fewer of his friends thought he was doing the right thing by risking his life and returning to Zimbabwe.

> Some called it stupidity; some called it fearlessness. But that's me, because I had 1 000 staff and I couldn't contemplate them losing their jobs. I couldn't contemplate our 40 000 loyal customers losing their money. The other 10 banks had gone bust and people had lost their savings. I couldn't live with myself. I thought, even if I get arrested on arrival I am not going to accept that.

He didn't, and in any case, he wasn't arrested. Chanakira checked his status with the attorney general's office and the police. He found that the case against the Econet directors, which had included him, had been dropped. He was, it seemed, no longer at risk of arrest in Zimbabwe. Chanakira leapt straight back into the business and started the process of trying to turn his bank around. The fact that he had been out of Zimbabwe for four years had helped him tremendously and his approach to banking was different. More significantly, most of his direct competition – at least 10 banks – had been wiped out in the banking crisis.

> When the indigenous bankers disappeared, the market was left to the old, traditional players. When I got back, I was one of a few black entrepreneurial bankers left. I had a different mindset from those other bankers – we were viewed to be pioneering.

With Chanakira visibly at the helm and seen to be trying to save the bank, the confidence of his customer base returned and profitability shot up. In a short space of time the bank's market share quadrupled as customers started to bring their money back to Kingdom. To give an idea of his success, when Chanakira first returned to Zimbabwe, the bank had recorded losses of Z$14 billion in the first quarter of 2005. With the recapitalisation exercise and the growing confidence, he managed to turn that loss into a profit after tax of Z$21 billion in just six months. And from there he sailed higher. He explains proudly:

> In the last two and a half years, after recapitalising twice and two rights issues, we have the fastest-growing share price in the world. Our share price went up 3 100% in one year in US dollar terms. You can check out Microsoft, GE – none of them have ever experienced such capital appreciation in dollar terms. Talk of Africa and the opportunities it has.

A new challenge

Kingdom Financial Holdings was back on its feet and so was the inimitable Nigel Chanakira. He had successfully brought his business back from the brink of certain death to a stage where he could now sit back and pat himself on the back. But he didn't do that for long; he had goals to meet, new ideas to implement and new partnerships to form to take his business to the next level. In 2007, he decided to merge Kingdom Financial Holdings with the Meikles Group. The timing couldn't be better; the government had introduced a controversial new empowerment or indigenisation bill which required all white-owned companies to have a 51% black shareholding. It would have been a win-win situation for Kingdom and the Meikles Group. Both companies had been involved with each other for more than eight years since the first in-store Kingdom bank was opened in a Meikles supermarket. The Meikles Group was a well-respected listed entity on the Zimbabwean and London stock exchanges. The diversified group had interests in retail, luxury hotels in Zimbabwe and South Africa, tea manufacturing and cotton printing and processing. It was not all plain sailing though; Chanakira had to fight for the merger to happen in a battle against the largest minority shareholder in the Meikles Group.

The insurance giant Old Mutual challenged the merger on the grounds that Kingdom Financial Holdings had been overvalued and that the Meikles Group was therefore paying far too much for it. The merger valuation of Kingdom had come in at US$90 million and the payout was in the form of a share swap between the two companies. In his explanation of the share swap to Kingdom shareholders, Chanakira likened it to 'trading a large slice of Madeira cake for a more modest slice of a richer fruit cake'. The battle raged over the course of a number of weeks, with various hearings and representations made by both sides. In the end, when it came to voting, the majority of the shareholders on both sides agreed with Chanakira and 52% of them voted in favour of the merger, which went through. Moments afterwards, a triumphant Chanakira was back in business mode. He was quoted as saying: 'Thank God we have won the battle. I am now going into the banking halls to see what is going on as far as the currency is concerned. We need to move fast as we have become a group that is a force not only in Zimbabwe but internationally.'

Chanakira was appointed the CEO of the new entity, Kingdom Meikles Africa, which came into being in January 2007. It was, in effect, a four-way merger between Kingdom Financial Holdings and the three businesses under Meikles. It became the biggest merger on the Zimbabwe Stock Exchange and was the largest company by market capitalisation, valued at US$600 million, in mid 2008, on that exchange. The group is also listed on the London Stock Exchange. Chanakira inherited a disparate group of companies under the Kingdom Meikles Africa banner. The group is now split into six subsidiaries: Kingdom Financial Services, Hotels, TM Supermarkets, Retail Stores, the Tanganda Tea Company and Cotton Printers. Kingdom Meikles Africa is the only five-star hotel group in the country and owns the Cape Grace in Cape Town, the famous Meikles Africa Hotel in Harare and the Victoria Falls Hotel. With its two operations in Malawi and Botswana, the financial services subsidiary has ambitions to become a pan-African banking group and plans to expand on its interests in Malawi and Botswana. Kingdom Meikles Africa is the biggest tea grower in Zimbabwe, with a 1% share of the global tea market, and exports on average 6 000 tons of tea annually. Kingdom Meikles Africa also owns the largest supermarket and retail chain in Zimbabwe with about 60 supermarkets and 10 departmental stores trading as TM Supermarkets, Barbours and Meikles. Pick 'n Pay still holds 25% of the supermarket business. Chanakira welcomes the challenge of the new entity he has inherited:

Meikles, Kingdom, Tanganda and Cotton Printers are all well-run, profitable entities in their own right, with loads of potential to become greater African brands. Our intention is not to disrupt these operations unnecessarily. We recognise the fact that a tea estate manager many not make the best corporate banker, neither will a bank operations manager have the wherewithal to be a good food and beverage manager. There was never any intention to confuse the roles.

He has ambitions for the new conglomerate and plans to list on the New York Stock Exchange. He has been conducting roadshows in New York in order to raise US$1 billion in the international capital markets to expand the financial arm and fund further investment opportunities for the group in Africa. Despite the current, challenging operating environment that is Zimbabwe today, Chanakira is very committed to staying on in the country. Where else can one get a 3 000% return on capital in US dollar terms?

> There is no other time in the history of our company where we have recorded the highest growth than now. I come from Zimbabwe. I have managed to succeed in good and bad times. We have made remarkable progress in the face of adversity. What drives us is the desire to raise a success story out of Zimbabwe that will contend us as a global financial services powerhouse.

His ambitions may seem insurmountable given the current situation. Zimbabwe is in its eighth year of recession, is crippled by fuel, water, food, electricity and foreign currency shortages, and holds the unenviable record for the highest yearly inflation in the world. At the country's economic peak, as unbelievable as it may seem today, one Zimbabwean dollar could easily have bought one British pound. Today, given the country's rampant hyperinflation, it would take many more dollars to purchase one pound – and that's assuming you could find any takers. Addressing the 18th World Economic Forum on Africa in June 2008, Chanakira reaffirmed his position on Zimbabwe:

> In the midst of the chaos there are business opportunities. Services are required, basics are needed. The reality of the matter is that countries don't fall off the face of the earth. People live in Zimbabwe, people conduct business and still try and fashion a life out of that.

Although no less of an opponent of the ruling Zanu-PF's economic policies, Chanakira has learnt the hard way about keeping a low profile in a country like Zimbabwe. Although still opinionated, he no longer visibly antagonises the powers that be in the same way that caused him to flee the country in 2002. However, he has clear views on what is wrong with the country:

> Our role as business is to exercise our influence on politicians. Political power without economic power is so discouraging. Africa is too rich to be poor but our politicians don't have the wherewithal to run economies well. New leadership is needed. (Thabo) Mbeki spoke of an African renaissance but my Pastor Tom Deuschle always says that it is more an African reformation that is needed. Africa is full of poor structures, poor institutions and poor strategies.

But he believes and has experienced first-hand that a sustainable successful business can be built in Africa without the need to have politicians in your back pockets. 'Look at Kingdom – no political influence. It was once deemed by some to be an enemy of the state in Zimbabwe,' he laughs. Instead, Chanakira puts his success down to perseverance and a particular attitude towards business: 'I am entrepreneurial. I love risk. I am not afraid; I have faith, my Christianity is a solid foundation for what I do.'

He is also a keen advocate of the life-changing motivational principles he picked up when he attended the Success Motivation International (SMI) course in the US. Holding up a black leather diary filled with small, neat writing, he says: 'Because I am a Christian, people think I hold a Bible but this is my success planner – my diary. I track everything daily, you can go back 10 years; I have one for every year. I am goal-orientated. SMI is unmatched in terms of this.' It is hardly surprising then that his biggest influence is the chairman and founder of SMI, Paul J Meyer. One of the most acclaimed and widely read authors of all time, Paul J Meyer is recognised as an authority on setting goals, personal success, sales and management development. Chanakira visits his mentor every year and continues to be inspired by his achievements.

> Paul invested in 40 different businesses with franchises spanning 70 countries – now that is a conglomerate. He is able to live life to the full; he has impacted the world and has touched me in Africa. I think

that is phenomenal.

Chanakira is also committed to regularly attending academic, professional and business courses to keep himself razor sharp. He refers to himself as 'a learning leader' and finds at least two new courses to attend every year. With that in mind, being 'accessible to many' is also something that Chanakira believes in. As the chairman of SMI in Africa – he purchased the franchise for the continent – he runs regular motivation courses for executives and lectures almost every Saturday.

> I lecture because I'm a product of the product. I was SMI Client of Year in 1996; I got an award in Hawaii. I wanted to become World Client (of the Year) and became that in 2002. I work with people who I encourage to dream to be the best they can for the business and for themselves.

He is also a strong Christian who is actively involved in his church and finds time to speak at numerous church conferences on leadership and motivation. Chanakira is proud of his Christian roots:

> I was inspired to start a bank by my God through a vision of making a lasting contribution to His kingdom. My principle inspiration is drawn from my daily Bible reading, which I attempt to follow diligently. I make no apology to be a believer of Jesus Christ and follower of its statutes and commandments.

As well as a good Christian, Chanakira is a devoted family man, and perhaps the only negative outcome of the high-flying lifestyle he leads is the fact that he has to commute between Zimbabwe and South Africa, where his family and four children still live.

His discipline extends not just to mind and soul, but also to body: 'I jog, I walk, I cycle. I have even played in the Kingdom Football Club which is in the Bankers League in Zimbabwe. I love soccer. I am a Liverpool supporter till I die and love watching (soccer),' he says enthusiastically. For relaxation and pleasure Chanakira reads autobiographies, leadership books and, of course, his Bible every day. 'I read it as a routine. The Bible is my manual; it has everything. I cannot begin to tell you the benefits to my life. "Seek ye the first the kingdom of God and his righteousness and all these things will be added unto you",' he recites.

There is no doubt that Chanakira has had many things added on to his life. His awards – professional and business – cover a page on his profile and include the World Economic Forum Global Leader, Empretec Zimbabwe's Entrepreneur of the Decade and the Zimbabwean Business Personality of the Year award in 2006. The businesses he has touched have also earned him recognition, including Top Performing Company on the Zimbabwe Stock Exchange in 2001, Best Turnaround Company in 2006 and the first share on the Zimbabwe Stock Exchange to post a 100 000% gain within a calendar year in 2007.

And there's more, as well as heading up the largest Zimbabwean conglomerate, with dual listings on the Zimbabwe and London stock exchanges, Chanakira sits on the boards of three companies, including the Christian Community Partnership Trust. Indeed, much has been added to the plate of the wonder boy of banking in Zimbabwe, and there is plenty of food in his house. He once said: 'If you think you can, you can. If you think you can't, you can't.' There is no doubt that Chanakira can – and he has.

Sources:

1. 'Econet Acquires Stake in Kingdom Financial Holdings', 11 January 2005. Online article available at: http://www.econet.co.zw/view_newsflash. aspx?nfid=22.
2. Econet Wireless official website, available at: www.econet.co.zw.
3. 'Chanakira Returns', 27 July 2006. Online article available at: http://www. firstglobalselect.com/scripts/cgiip.wsc/globalone/htm/news_article. r?vcnews-id=344261.
4. www.abetterzim.com.
5. 'In focus: Nigel Muranganwa Kudzayi Chanakira' in *Traders Africa* Issue 18: May – August 2004. Online article available at: http://www. tradersafrica.com/articles.asp?articleid={4617CE2F-2A5D-443E-B1FE-D86B45478BF9}.
6. Chanakira, N. 'Inaugural KMAL CEO Blog', 30 May 2008. Online article available at: http://africanceo.blogspot.com/2008/05/inaugural-kmal-ceo-blog.html.
7. Success Motivation International official website, available at: http://www. success-motivation.com/.

Reginald Mengi – The Philanthropic Entrepreneur

VITAL STATISTICS

Name: Reginald Abraham Mengi
Country: Tanzania
Position/Title: Executive chairman of the IPP Group
Nationality: Tanzanian
Industry: Manufacturing, media, mining, bottling
Highest educational qualification: Chartered Accountancy articles, Coopers and Lybrand, Scotland

I started the business of assembling plastic ballpoint pens in my small bedroom because I did not have any bigger space. I bought the ballpoint pen components from a supplier in Mombasa, Kenya. I was doing this business alongside my employment. I would load my merchandise in the boot of my little car and deliver them to my wholesale customer on my way to the office.

The business became bigger and the bedroom became too small. I moved to the living room and then to the garden. I needed an industrial building when the garden also became too small, but could not afford the rent for this. I asked an owner of an industrial building to rent me part of the outer wall of his building, which he did, although he thought I was crazy. I bought iron sheets, built a sizeable shack against the wall and started operating from there. I diversified into importation of marker pen components. In the first year I made my first million dollars.

It was the first of many millions of dollars this remarkable Tanzanian-born entrepreneur and philanthropist, Reginald Mengi, would make. From his first tentative steps into the world of industry, Mengi is now the best-known and certainly one of the most highly respected businessmen in Tanzania. His privately held business empire, the IPP Group, whose value he declines to divulge, is undoubtedly one of the largest diversified groups in the whole of East Africa. It all started in his bedroom, with the small-scale assembling of plastic ballpoint pens. Now the IPP Group has grown to a substantial conglomerate with interests in manufacturing, media, mining, and managerial and financial consulting. There is no doubt that Mengi has remarkable business acumen and appears to have what can only be described as the 'Midas touch' when it comes to creating and sustaining successful businesses. 'Every one of my businesses was started from scratch,' says the softly spoken Mengi. 'I have never bought a business because it might just be set up in a way that I would not like. Besides, it is boring to go out and buy one. To me, the excitement is in the creation,' he smiles. Mengi is humble about his success; he believes it stems from a simple philosophy and attitude to life that has served him well time and time again. It is the belief that 'he can'.

Once you say you can, your eyes will see opportunities. I have this incredible feeling that I can do anything in this life. I do not see

boundaries around me. I am not afraid of taking risks and I am able
to achieve success by working with the people within my companies
who have good ideas, initiative and commitment to their work. They
are my greatest business asset. I can fly an aeroplane, I can captain a
ship – I can do anything. My ability lies in my capacity to do things
through other people. So long as I can pay one to drive me in a car, it
is as good as me driving that car.

It is Mengi's keen and consistent ability to spot opportunities and
act on them timeously and effectively that has driven his group's
exponential growth within and beyond the borders of Tanzania.
And it all started with a decision to break out of the shackles of
a professional career in accountancy and plunge headlong into a
high-risk, high-return, entrepreneurial environment. His risk-taking
has been rewarded ten fold. Today, Mengi is unquestionably one of
the wealthiest people in Tanzania. Importantly, his success in life is
something he believes strongly in sharing, and Mengi has developed
a reputation for being one of the most active philanthropists in
Tanzania. His biggest dream is to eradicate the poverty of his fellow
countrymen.

> Have you ever seen any businessman in the world who became poor
> as a result of giving to the poor a part of the profits he has earned from
> selling goods or services to the people? The most painful thing in my
> life is seeing poverty afflicting people. Poverty depresses me

This is what drives him to work closely with youth groups, people
with disabilities and disadvantaged women, and to provide
education and start-up capital for those who want to start their own
businesses. Mengi's concern is not just about poverty, it is also about
HIV/Aids and environmental degradation. Until recently, he was
a commissioner of the Tanzania Commission for Aids (TACAIDS)
and was once known as 'the condom king' for his outspoken stance
against certain religious groups and their attitudes towards the use
of condoms. He is a keen environmentalist and held the position
of chairman of the National Environment Council of Tanzania for
four years. He started and funded a tree planting campaign in the
Kilimanjaro region, which resulted in the planting of thousands
of trees. In recognition of his efforts in environmental protection,
Mengi has received several awards, including the East African

Environment Leadership Award. Of his philanthropic side, he says simply: 'It is not about the money, it is about the change that you can bring to communities.' He respects other wealthy philanthropists, such as Warren Buffet, who in their lifetime actively put their wealth to use for good causes.

> Having earned so much, Warren Buffet can sit back and give to charity, to mankind. The end is not about money, money is still a means; the end is to support the poor and the underprivileged. It is not about how much money or wealth you leave behind when you finally depart from this world, it is about what you did with your wealth that will be remembered.

And Mengi certainly knows what it means to be poor. His current lifestyle is a far cry from the one into which he was born, where every day was a constant struggle against overwhelming poverty.

The early days

> I grew up in a little mud hut and you may not believe this, but in that mud hut I was not the only occupant. Next to me there were a couple of cows, goats and some chickens. In such an environment, other creatures like rats and cockroaches come along and share the house with you. These are the things you would normally expect in such an environment and that is where I come from.

Mengi is the last but one of seven siblings and grew up in a small village called Nkuu on the slopes of Mount Kilimanjaro in Tanzania. His parents were peasant farmers who eked out a living from whatever they could grow on the two acres of land on which they lived. It was a tough upbringing for Mengi and his siblings; nothing came easily. He remembers that his parents, especially his mother, sacrificed a lot for him and the family.

> Looking back, I question how I survived because there were times when water and food were very scarce. There were times when we had to do with one meal a day. I remember my mother taking bananas to the marketplace and coming back with meat or a bottle of cooking oil. My brother paid his school fees by money earned from selling six eggs or so, which he boiled in the morning before going to school. He would

eat one for lunch and would sell the rest to his colleagues.

Despite the poverty, Mengi went to school at a much earlier age than his peers and siblings.

> I was very close to my sister who went to school when she was eight years old and I was only five years old then. I cried when I saw my sister going to school in the morning. I thought she was going away to have fun, so I started to go with her.

Given the rural environment in which his family lived, the school was inevitably a long way from home for a five-year-old. Mengi would walk barefoot for two miles every day to get to school. To make matters worse, he had only one set of school uniform.

> I would wash my uniform in the evening and press it in the morning with a charcoal iron. I always went to school looking smart. I think sometimes I was smarter than the kids who had more than one set of uniform.

The long distances and the grooming aside, just making it through the various levels of the Tanzanian education system was another minefield through which Mengi had to walk.

> At every stage, from 'bush school' to district school, one had to sit for an examination and if one failed, one did not go on to a district school. From district school to middle school one had to sit for an examination, and then another to get to secondary school. There were many students who were dropped at each stage. Perhaps only 10% or fewer would pass at each stage.

Mengi consistently fell within that 10%. He attributes his early success in school to a combination of two things:

> I had the drive and school excited me. From an early age, I used to cry because I wanted to go to school. Some children cried because they did not want to go to school. I cannot say I was the most intelligent, but certainly I was one of the top kids in my class. I had the ability, but more importantly, I enjoyed it. I enjoyed reading more than playing.

His rather unique attitude to school continued throughout his time in secondary school right up until his O levels. He was an exemplary student, and was all set to do his A levels and then go on to Makerere University in neighbouring Uganda, as was the pattern for bright students, when he pulled himself off the well-trodden path. For some reason Mengi had set his mind on going overseas, even though the English headmaster of his school, who knew Mengi was bright, had insisted he stay on and complete his A levels. Unfortunately, Mengi did not listen and he lasted just one year in the two-year A level class, at which point he dropped out to pursue a dream. 'I do not know what it was, but something was pushing me. From an early age I was interested in going overseas,' he recalls. Luckily for him, the prospect of going overseas was not completely unattainable.

> There was an advertisement in a local paper which invited O-level leavers to apply to go to Britain to do an accounting course, which meant that I would have become an accounting clerk of some sort. So I applied while I was still at school, without the knowledge of the headmaster. I was awarded a scholarship to go to Britain on a six-month 'accounting clerk' course.

Mengi left for Scotland, ostensibly to embark on the course at the Scottish College of Commerce, but he never actually started it.

> On reporting to the college, I told one of the teachers that I wanted to do something better than an accounting clerk's course. He advised me to attain A levels first. I told him I did not want to continue with the accounts clerk's course any more. I was only there for one day. I did not attend even one class; I never intended to do that course.

He found himself in a tricky situation, entirely of his own making. The Kilimanjaro Native Cooperative Union (KNCU), which funded the accounting clerk's course through its sponsorship programme, refused to finance what now looked like a free holiday in Scotland for a stubborn young man. But Mengi had no intention of returning to Tanzania just yet. He had realised one part of his dream, which was to get overseas, and he was going to do all that was in his power to stay there. He finally took some advice and joined an evening class to complete his A levels. Financially, he was somewhat stuck, and had no choice but to appeal to his elder brother, who was a trader back home in Tanzania, for money to pay for his tuition. His brother came through and Mengi was able to complete his A levels with excellent grades. He was now ready for the next step in his studies.

> I decided to become an accountant after I got my A levels. I had the option of becoming a certified accountant or becoming a chartered accountant – a chartered accountant was superior. So I joined a firm called Cooper Brothers, which later became Coopers and Lybrand, and became an articled clerk.
>
> I was not being advised by anyone. I had a dream; I wanted to get a professional qualification. I was not looking for an easy way out but I was looking for a good way out. Even when it came to the type of accountancy I chose, I took the toughest route.

Five years of hard work and study followed while Mengi pursued his dream to get his professional qualification. He was a personable, smart young man, who easily fell in with the new world in which he was living. He enjoyed his time at Cooper Brothers: 'They made me feel I was wanted, they gave me respect,' says Mengi. He also enjoyed his time in Scotland. Although he stayed in student digs, he became very close to a Scottish family who treated him like one of their own. He remembers his days in Scotland with much fondness.

> Looking back, I sometimes wonder why I was so lucky. I think what you get in life depends on how you are, how you live with other people. You know, in physics there is a law that states: 'for every action there is an equal and opposite reaction', so if you are rude, if you are unpleasant, people will show prejudice against you. I think my humility and my kindness helped me, so perhaps I was getting back the same sort of humility, the same sort of kindness that I had shown to others.

Despite this kindness, Mengi acknowledges that he was treated differently, 'as special', because he was black.

> On the Hogmanay, the Scottish New Year, they believed that if you take a piece of coal and a bottle of whisky to a friend you brought good luck, so I used to get hooked into taking the whisky but no coal because I

was black. I looked at it with a sense of fun; I did not get upset but it shows that they did see me as different.

As much as he enjoyed his time in Scotland, he was determined to return home to Tanzania once he had finished his articles.

> Throughout my life, the idea of living overseas in another country has never crossed my mind. I saw my future in my country. I have seen young people go to Europe or America thinking about how they can make a life there. That never crossed my mind. I was focused on coming back to Tanzania.

After qualifying as a chartered accountant, which he believed was the best professional qualification under his belt that would equip him 'to do anything', Mengi was ready to take on the world. He applied for an internal transfer within the group to return to Tanzania. Unfortunately, his first assignment as a qualified chartered accountant was not destined to be in his home country. Even though Coopers did have an office in Tanzania, Mengi was posted to Nairobi, Kenya. He had no choice but to accept the posting; at least it was closer to home. Within a few weeks, he had packed up the few possessions he owned and left immediately for the warm, sunny skies of Africa.

Mengi arrived in Kenya and reported at the Nairobi office of Cooper Brothers on a Monday morning, signed his employment papers at 9am and by 3pm the same day he had resigned. 'I just did not want to work there,' he says. Mengi left Kenya immediately for Tanzania and tried to get a job with KNCU, the organisation that had initially sponsored his UK clerk's course in accountancy. He was turned down because he was considered overqualified for the position he had applied for. Luckily, an opening cropped up at the Cooper Brothers regional office in Moshi, Tanzania, and he leapt at the opportunity.

Although he was not exactly where he wanted to be, at least he was in Tanzania, and within six months he had managed to organise himself a transfer to the Coopers office in Dar es Salaam. He joined in the position of senior auditor and from there his career took off. 'When I transferred to Dar es Salaam, things changed very quickly. Within two years of qualifying, I was made a partner.'

Mengi rose rapidly through the firm's hierarchy; from partner he rose to senior partner and later to managing partner in charge of 100 staff members and the entire Coopers business in Tanzania. By all accounts, he was doing very well for himself. He was smart, hard working and diligent, and he admits that he became a workaholic who survived on very little sleep.

> At that time, I never dreamt of going into business on my own. I was working hard as a partner. I just loved work; I was working an average of 16 hours a day and surviving on four hours' sleep. Even today, I can manage on four hours' sleep.

All the hard work was paying off for Mengi; life was undoubtedly treating him very well. He was successful both professionally and personally. He was married and had started a family, but it soon became apparent that auditing no longer held any attraction for him.

> At Coopers, auditing became routine and I could not get excited about the work. I started leaning towards the consultancy side of the practice. It appealed to me because it looked more to the future than the past, and that excited me.

What excited Mengi about the consultancy side was the exposure and insights he obtained into the workings of businesses. It whet his appetite and deepened his curiosity to experience business first-hand. But it was his inability to grow real wealth for himself which finally made him take a radical decision.

> At that time I was one of the most highly paid professionals in Tanzania by Tanzanian socialist standards. My conditions of employment were very attractive, but I had this urge to do business but without injustice to Coopers. Even though things were good, my life was hand to mouth because our socialist fiscal policies did 'punish' high salary earners. So I told my partners I would like to cut down my share of profits from 30% to 5%, which I did, because I wanted to cut down my time doing work for the practice and concentrate on an alternative route for myself. I did not want to do it on Coopers' time because it would have been like stealing from my fellow partners. I was very open with them.

In the late 70s and early 80s Tanzania, like the rest of the African continent, was hard hit by the dramatic fall in global commodity prices. It was not the best time for anyone to consider leaving the safe confines of a good job or willingly offer to downgrade their percentage of profits. Tanzania was experiencing an economic meltdown. The country was plunged into debt and the ensuing crisis with its balance of payments was characterised by massive shortages of even the most basic commodities. And in the middle of all this, Mengi spotted an opportunity. 'I went to a shop to buy a ballpoint pen and I could not find one. I thought, how could we be short of ballpoint pens? How?' Rather than ponder the question, which was a very pertinent one, he decided to become a part of the solution. And that single decision was the beginning of a remarkable journey towards the incredible business success that Mengi enjoys today.

Mengi the entrepreneur

Mengi knew his fortune somehow lay in the once ubiquitous plastic ballpoint pen, and he set out to find out how he could capitalise on the shortages in the country by manufacturing the pens.

> At that time one could not import ready-made products, but one could import 'knock-downs'. In other words, you could buy parts or components and assemble them, so I decided to take that route.

Although he had a full-time job, which meant he had an income, Mengi had no disposable capital to invest in any kind of new business venture, but he chose not to let that interfere with his plans. He went ahead and started making enquiries. It did not take him long to discover that there was a ballpoint pen manufacturer in Mombasa, Kenya. Mengi saw no reason to waste time on a business plan or a feasibility study – the opportunity was just too attractive to ignore. 'There was a shortage, the product was required. The time I would have spent on a business plan I could spend getting capital and importing the goods,' he explains firmly. Mengi did not need much convincing.

> I flew to Mombasa to meet with the supplier and asked him if I could buy the components on credit; he said no. I flew back to Dar es Salaam and met an Indian friend who knew the manufacturer in Mombasa.

He told him that I was a reliable person, a man of my word and that I would honour my promises. After a while the supplier agreed to sell the components to me on credit.

Mengi immediately asked for US$4 000 worth of goods for 30-days' credit. He was assured that the goods would arrive from Mombasa within two days, which would give him just about enough time to assemble, market, sell and then get paid for his pens in 28 days. He figured it was worth the risk. But events seemed to conspire against him.

After two days the consignment of components for the pens had not arrived; there was just nothing. Then 20 days went by, then 25 days and still nothing. I started to panic. I found out that the lorry carrying the components had broken down at the border of Tanzania and Kenya in a place called Horohoro.

Aptly named given the horror he was going through. Mengi had to do some quick thinking. He did not have pens to assemble or sell, and he was also in danger of losing his credibility on his first ever entrepreneurial business deal. He had to find a way to rescue the situation. So he did.

I negotiated with a major ballpoint pen distributor in Tanzania to buy my pens in advance. Of course he laughed at me, he thought I was joking. Eventually he trusted me. I sold the pens to him before assembly, even before he had seen them and he paid me in advance two days before payment of the debt to my supplier was due, and I was able to settle my supplier's debt on time!

Mengi had successfully bought himself some much-needed time, but it was only a temporary respite. He now needed to learn very quickly how to put the parts together to assemble the pens so he could fulfil the order he had pre-sold.

I had to ask the supplier in Mombasa how to assemble pens; I had tried myself but failed. The speed of assembling was too slow. They had to teach me the 'technology' of how to assemble with my hands. It may sound stupid now, but it did not seem that way at the time.

As it was, it took him more than a month to get his first order ready for delivery. It came as no surprise that Mengi made his first million dollars that year from a product few would have thought of and a product that gave him a massive profit margin of more than 100%. It seemed that the initial stress, the panic, the near-loss of credibility was all well worth it when he became a US dollar millionaire with his first project.

Becoming a full-time entrepreneur

It is easy to forget that for the first two years of Mengi's start in business he was still the managing partner at Coopers and Lybrand, putting in a full day's work in the office to earn his salary. Although he had reduced his profit share from 30% to 5% to compensate for the time he spent on his business activities, he was still prepared to stay on and reduce his profit share even further to zero.

> I wanted to stay on because I was so committed to Coopers, especially the consultancy practice. I did not want the firm to die and I thought I was a very important player in it. I wanted to make sure that it survived. I told my partners that I would forgo my share of profits and they said no, that I could not work with them if I did not make money with them for myself. So I opted out of the practice.

Coopers survived without Mengi and it is a testament to his leadership skills and ability to delegate and empower those around him that he effectively left behind a firm that worked equally well without him.

> Some people become bosses and they like to think they are indispensable. I delegated everything and then after I left, the firm performed very well. They never sought me out for advice, which meant that the delegation had worked.

With Coopers behind him, Mengi could totally immerse himself in his business. Tanzania was still experiencing shortages in so many other things – pens were just the start. He had been bitten by the manufacturing bug and decided that it was the only way forward. Despite his professional service experience and knowledge of business in general, it turned out that Mengi actually got his kick out of making things. 'Mere business does not excite me. I liked to manufacture things.' So he started doing just that.

> The list of things I have made is incredible! I have manufactured industrial chemicals, toilet soap, bar soap and detergents. I have made furniture, made electrical fittings. I have made shoes, I have made egg trays, I have collected waste paper and turned it into toilet paper and paper napkins. There was a shortage of shoe polish so I made black shoe polish out of charcoal. I made boiler cleaner out of seaweed. I have set up one of the largest plastics companies in the country. I have made brick-making machines, made mattresses, etc. Now I am a Coca-Cola bottler.

And that is how Mengi's empire started; on the back of opportunities many did not see, at a time when many would not have dared take the risk. But the journey was not an easy one. Importing the equipment and the machinery he needed to do the manufacturing was a process fraught with red tape and bureaucracy. According to Tanzania's import laws at the time, the government provided each importer with a foreign exchange 'allocation' to pay for the goods he was allowed to bring in. The process was open to abuse.

> Some people would bribe for allocation of more funds. One thing I am proud of saying is that I never took shortcuts. I always fought for my rights to have my allocations increased if necessary. I wrote letters, I went to see the minister; I just put up a fight. I would rather fight for something that is due to me than lubricate the system to get it, because if I fight for the right, the achievements are much more sustainable.

Looking back, Mengi remembers those early days in business as being characterised by the many fights he took on for things that he believed were his right.

> In Europe, in America, regulations are there and they are followed and are respected, but in our countries people look for ways to bend the regulations so that the 'bending' can be a source of income. There is too much discretion in Africa which allows administrators and the powers that be to bend the laws and regulations. That is where corruption starts. If we give respect to laws and regulations, the instances of corruption would be minimal.

It was during these days of trying to build up his manufacturing business that Mengi developed what would become a lifelong hatred of corruption, a problem he encountered with alarming regularity. It is a scourge that he has actively combated through his media, culminating in a proactive anti-corruption campaign. Corruption aside, the biggest challenge to his manufacturing business was what he believed to be the mindset of his workers and his customers when it came to issues of quality.

> Sometimes employees are not conscious of the need for quality products. Some think that if something is made in Africa for Africans, it does not have to be of high quality. I believe in providing the best quality products.

Despite the occupational hazards of operating in Tanzania, Mengi managed to stay ahead of the game by freeing himself from the day-to-day mundane activities of running a factory. To this end, Mengi's office has and always will be situated away from his operations. And he is open and honest about his failings:

> When it comes to managing business and manufacturing, I am a very bad manager. The only time I was hands-on was when I physically assembled the pens and after that I stayed away. I create something and then I bring in people to manage it.

Given this strategy, it is no surprise that his biggest challenge in growing his businesses has been finding the right people to run them. At times he has had to recruit the best talent from elsewhere in the world rather than rely solely on local inadequate talent, and he admits that this has been a very big challenge to him. Although finding the right people may have been difficult, what Mengi seemed to have found a knack for was spotting new opportunities:

> There are so many opportunities floating around an individual, which the individual can not see. The holy Bible says there are those with eyes but do not see. But if you are blessed, your eyes will see. I believe I am very blessed. I also believe in change and innovation. As time passed, I changed products to meet people's demands and tastes. A business that does not change and innovate is doomed to fail.

From manufacturing to media and mining

Before 1994, private broadcasting was not allowed in Tanzania and the country did not have television, not even a government broadcaster. In addition, the only newspapers that existed then were owned by the government. Then liberalisation of the media was introduced and Mengi decided to diversify his business to include media – IPP Media – after 10 years of manufacturing just about everything he could. Because of his significant media interests, Mengi has been called the 'Ted Turner of Africa'. The IPP Media empire comprises of by far the largest media house in Tanzania and is undeniably the most prolific owner of television, radio and newspaper content in the East African region.

> People in Tanzania do not really know the reality of why I went into media. Many thought and still believe it was a political move that would enable me to run for and win the presidency.

Despite many people's suspicions, Mengi has never been interested in politics. His reason for being engaged in media was much more straightforward: 'I saw an exciting opportunity opening up and went ahead,' he says.

His first media property was a radio station which he called Radio One. It broadcasts in Tanzania in Swahili and is his most successful radio station. It started broadcasting in a limited area and within a year it went national. The station was viable from year one. His other radio stations include East Africa Radio, which broadcasts across the region, and a third station, Capital FM, which broadcasts locally in both English and Swahili.

Mengi was the first person to start television broadcasting in Tanzania. His television station, Independent Television Limited (ITV), was established five years before the government launched its own television station.

> I had no clue of what was involved, but I knew I would be able to run a TV station. There was a very good Englishman managing a TV station in Nairobi. I pinched him and he became the managing director of ITV. I got some people from Australia and America for production and someone from Israel for technology. I gave them all a one-year appointment, within which they had to train Tanzanians to take up

their positions.

ITV started broadcasting on 10 June 1994 at 5pm. Its first major broadcast was the 1994 Fifa World Cup. The fact that it was the first television broadcast in the country and that it was strategically launched during the world's most televised event immediately drew viewers to the station, and ITV has never looked back. Mengi's two other Tanzanian-based television stations, East Africa TV (Channel 5) and Capital TV, are on terrestrial and satellite broadcasts. East Africa TV is a youth-based TV station which broadcasts to Tanzania, Kenya, Uganda, Rwanda and Burundi.

Making money out of media is notoriously difficult, particularly because of the high start-up costs it entails. While his radio station became viable within one year, it took six years for the television station to start providing a return on his investment and Mengi's manufacturing businesses proved to be an invaluable source of revenue. Then he started a newspaper publishing business and at its height, Mengi had 11 newspapers, in both English and Swahili, on the market. His initial strategy was to appeal to niche audiences. For example, he launched a dedicated sports newspaper, which still runs today, but he soon realised that what people wanted more than anything else was good journalism that challenged the status quo. 'I tried to provide more than mere traditional newspapers; I saw people's demand for papers that featured investigative journalism, he explains. So he responded by giving them what they wanted. Mengi admits that, once again, he knew very little about newspaper publication, or even investigative journalism. His belief was, however, that he could do it, so he did.

His obvious success in growing his media business has brought him much criticism. Many people still argue that his media interests are nothing more than a tool to further his ultimate aim of becoming president. This is despite the fact that in the December 2005 presidential elections he threw his full weight behind Jakaya Kikwete, who won in a landslide victory. A rather frustrated Mengi explains that he has no ambition to become president:

This has been one of my biggest frustrations. People think I do things because I want to be president. I have no political ambition. I think they will leave me alone only when I am very, very old and do not have any teeth left.

In the meantime, he has stuck his still good set of teeth into fighting corruption. He believes strongly that the media has a very important role to play in the war against corruption.

> The media has the power to investigate and expose corruption, bring it to the public attention and raise government awareness so that appropriate action can be taken.

Two years ago, IPP Media launched a high-profile campaign through its two investigative titles, *ThisDay* and *Kulikoni*, something no other media owner had dared to do before. 'It made me very unpopular to some people, but the president, and honest, clean, ordinary people appreciate the effort,' says an unrepentant Mengi. Corruption just does not make good business sense to Mengi:

> I have been a fighter all my life and that is why I am not scared of those people who think I am after them. Fighting corruption is everyone's duty; it is my duty. Corruption is an evil which must be eradicated in society. If I bribe a guy today, he may not be there tomorrow to bribe again or the bribe price has increased, which makes the cost of doing business very high. It is not sustainable.

And creating sustainable businesses is what Mengi does best, which is why when he made the decision to engage in mining, especially large-scale prospecting, becoming one of the first local Tanzanians to mine on a large scale, many people sat up and took notice. IPP's mining subsidiary companies own more than 100 mining concessions and are prospecting for gold, diamonds, platinum, uranium, nickel, bauxite, copper, coal and tanzanite. The group has one mine in operation, which is producing tanzanite, the extraordinary blue and purple gemstone named after the only place in the world it is found, Tanzania.

> I did not decide to go into mining for the money only. I think our country has a raw deal in mining, our people have been complaining that they have not benefited from it. But they complain and complain and do nothing. It is not just about lack of money; it is lack of confidence in ourselves as Africans. I want to show that it can be done. We do not have to wait for big international companies to do it for us.

So to prove his point, Mengi started investing in this very lucrative sector.

> In mining you require capital, you require management and technology. All those things can be sourced and you can pay for the capital, management and the technology with just 20% or so of the sales of the mined minerals.

Six years into the mining business, some of the more than 100 mining concessions the IPP Group holds are beginning to bear fruit, and according to projections, Mengi's mining operations will soon take over as the largest generator of revenue for the group.

The Mengi style

Although mining is his current investment focus, Mengi is very diplomatic about which of his businesses he most enjoys.

> Each one is best in its own way. Industry gives me money, media plays its several roles for the benefit of society and mining is a way to show that we can; so I can not say which excites me the most.

What is clear though, is that despite 24 years in business, he is still excited by the prospect of innovating and creating.

> New ideas, new things and new projects keep me motivated. I see a new idea, I chase it, I catch it, I implement it, I seek the right people to manage it. When I get bored, I try the next one.

He is undaunted by the constant challenges he faces; he is the archetypal eternal optimist and prefers to see opportunity where others see challenge. 'I see challenges in problems and opportunities in challenges,' he says candidly. There are a few things in his career he has been unable to navigate around and it is there he believes his weakness in business lies.

> I have lost millions of dollars for trusting other people too quickly and too much, but it is not a weakness that I want to abandon. People may think I am careless, they may think I do not have wisdom, but on the contrary, I trust a person until that person proves that he or she is not

trustworthy. I am not saying that I cannot assess people, but at the end of the assessment I always give someone the benefit of the doubt. It has been very, very expensive.

Indeed it has. He tells the story of one project where his trusting nature cost him a lot of money.

It was a glass project. My supplier in India was supposed to send me 18 40-feet containers carrying the machinery I would need to manufacture a range of glass products. When the containers arrived, they were filled with scrap and rubbish. The supplier was a man I trusted; he even used to send me Bombay mangoes every weekend as a friend!

Mengi's trusting nature goes hand in hand with one of his key business strengths – transparency.

If you are transparent, you are truthful and open, and if you are open, you can get other people's views because they know what you want or want to do. It means I call a spade a spade. I am open.

Mengi is not just open; he is generous with his time and is very willing to share his experiences and business philosophies with the younger generation and the various groups he supports. His efforts have been recognised and rewarded on numerous occasions. In 1994 Mengi was awarded The Order of the United Republic of Tanzania for 'acts and conduct earning praise and distinction for the United Republic of Tanzania'. In 1995 he was awarded The Order of the Arusha Declaration of The First Class for 'earning great distinction for Tanzania economically, politically, socially and in defence of Tanzania diligently and at considerable personal sacrifice'. And despite the accolades he continues to work hard, 'I enjoy working; it is my hobby'. And in between he finds time to continue to keep up with trends: 'I am aware of an English saying that an intelligent person is a person who knows how little he knows. So I keep on learning,' he smiles.

Mengi is still bubbling with ideas and retirement, regardless of his age, is not on his mind.

If you take Warren Buffet for example, he bought his first shares when he was 11 years of age. Then you take Ray Kroc, the founder of

McDonald's who started the business in his seventies. By the time he died at the age of 81 he was a very rich man. Many African people by the age of 50 are looking for places to be buried. They are saying to themselves that they are too old, say, to start a business.

Even now, Mengi still sets himself goals. He has ambitions to list the media side of his empire on the stock exchange and possibly the mining business as well. Both of his two remaining children are involved in his businesses. His daughter Regina is the managing director of East African TV, while his son Abdiel currently works in a consultancy capacity. In October 2005 probably the most significant event in Mengi's life occurred, one that should never happen to any parent. At the age of 31, Mengi's eldest son Rodney died of a heart condition. It changed Mengi's approach to life and his approach to business. 'He was my best friend,' he says of his son. 'His death changed my life in two ways: I no longer fear death; I take it much more casually. And second, I do not crave for material things, money especially. Making money does not give me the excitement it used to.' What is more important to Mengi now is the legacy he wants to leave behind:

> I would like to be remembered possibly in two ways. First, as a person who was able to show that black people can, and not only can, but sometimes do better. And second, as a person who cared for the poor and the underprivileged.

It is safe to say that he has comfortably achieved both already.

Gordon Wavamunno – The Ubiquitous Entrepreneur

VITAL STATISTICS

Name: Gordon Wavamunno
Country: Uganda
Born: 16 December 1943
Position/Title: Owner, majority shareholder Spear Group
Co turnover: Undisclosed
Nationality: Ugandan
Industry: Cars, manufacturing, tourism
Highest education qualification: O levels

It was the middle of 1975, Idi Amin was in power in Uganda and the country would soon be playing host to an Organisation of African Unity summit in the capital, Kampala. Gordon Wavamunno, one of the country's leading businessmen, had just taken a rather lucrative order to supply 60 Mercedes Benz limousines to the government for use during the summit. It was a great opportunity and the deal would net him a lot of money as the newly appointed agent for Mercedes Benz in Uganda. Wavamunno was, without a doubt, a happy man. Along with that order came another one for a Mercedes 280SE from a Lieutenant Colonel Juma Ali, aka Butabika, 'one of the most notorious and dreaded commanders in Amin's government'. Against his better judgement, Wavamunno took the order. It was his first mistake and a decision that would nearly cost him his life.

He duly processed the order and when the car was ready to be picked up, he sent one of his drivers to Mombasa, Kenya, to drive the car back directly from the port to his showroom in Kampala, a distance of 1 240 km. This was to speed up the usual, far longer, process of bringing the car in on a carrier. That was his second mistake. On finding out that his brand new car had been driven 1 240 km, by someone else before him, Lieutenant Colonel Ali lost his temper. He ordered his bodyguards to seal off the showroom and demanded that all the staff kneel before him while two of his guards went off to find Wavamunno. Wavamunno was escorted from his office and forced to join the rest of his staff on their knees. He was to remain this way for more than two hours, with two pistols pointed at him, while the colonel, in a state of hysteria, threatened to have him and his entire staff jailed. When Wavamunno was wondering when, how and if it would all end, a customer wandered in to check on the progress of his car at the service centre. Wavamunno didn't know whether to be happy or more scared, because it was Major Mududu, the officer in charge of one of the most notorious military prisons in Kampala. At that moment, there was a 50/50 chance whose side Mududu would take. As luck would have it, Wavamunno's time was not up yet.

Major Mududu unexpectedly interceded on our behalf and pleaded with the colonel to 'forgive us'. The two men talked a little longer and then, like little children who had just received a new toy, they both started checking and admiring the new special Mercedes Benz.

And that was how Wavamunno got out of the potentially life-threatening situation, with both his life and his business intact. He was lucky.

> It was like walking away from the jaws of death. This sort of incident happened to one Ugandan or another every day of every year. In Amin's Uganda, everybody, including businessmen like myself, had to walk a tightrope not knowing whether today would lead to tomorrow.

Gordon Wavamunno did more than just make it to tomorrow. At 65 he is undoubtedly one of Uganda's best-known and most successful entrepreneurs, with interests in almost every major business sector of the country's economy. Through his wholly owned company, Spear Group, and various other ventures, Wavamunno is into vehicle distribution, manufacturing, tourism, property development, media, commercial transport, insurance, training, medical supplies, flower farming, textiles, furniture manufacturing and retailing, bottled water, publishing and pharmaceuticals – and this list is by no means exhaustive. Over the course of his 45 years in business he has dabbled in everything from mining, film distribution, construction and hotel management to shoe manufacturing, shipping and commercial farming. In his very early years he had a dry-cleaning business, a driving school and started off trading in fresh produce.

His personal worth remains undisclosed, most of his businesses are privately owned, or in some cases he holds a significant shareholding in the company. There is no doubt, however, that his assets could very easily earn him a place on the *Forbes* rich list – in the unlikely event that he is prepared to supply them with the information.

Wavamunno's story takes place against the backdrop of post-independent Uganda – the two are inextricably linked. He has been thrown into jail twice, his businesses have been vandalised and looted almost beyond repair on two separate occasions, he has survived and in fact thrived under six changes of government, including the notorious Idi Amin dictatorship. He has survived one coup, a civil war and extremely hostile business conditions, and has still managed to build one of the largest conglomerates in Africa. An entrepreneur and a philanthropist, Wavamunno is a self-made man who achieved his success without the benefit of tertiary education or business school. He got to where he is today because of his ability to think big.

> I like thinking big, I always have. To me it's very simple. If you are going to be thinking anyway, you might as well think big.

The beginning

Even when he was young Wavamunno always wanted to make a big 'impact on society'. From an early age he was not interested in office work as a messenger or a clerk, as many of his peers would eventually be forced to do. 'My hopes and dreams were to establish a business of my own and rub shoulders with the business giants of those days,' he explains. He did much more than 'rub shoulders with the business giants', he became one.

Born on 16 December 1943 in the rural town of Rugaaga, a remote and underdeveloped area in the south west of Uganda, Wavamunno grew up in a polygamous household with his father's two wives and 17 siblings. Their family home doubled as a retail shop which sold basic commodities, including sugar, cigarettes and sweets. His father was a businessman and trader who taught the young and ambitious Wavamunno everything he knew about business. Wavamunno was fortunate enough to go to school, because unlike the parents of many of the children he grew up with, his father saw the benefits of a good education. More importantly, Wavamunno's father could afford one for his son.

> My favourite subject in school was mathematics, especially those calculations relating to costs, profits, quantities and interest. The businessman in me was already kicking in by the time I left primary school.

During his Christmas holidays, Wavamunno started helping out with his father's various businesses, which included a fleet of buses, a banana coffee plantation, cattle trading and the shop. His primary role and the one which he most enjoyed was the counting of money.

> I was convinced that the sooner I left school and started earning money the better for my future. I wanted to learn the secrets of business under

my father's tutelage so that I would become a successful businessman
in my own right.

So he made the decision not to go to high school and decided to join
the family business. Many of his friends thought he was making a
big mistake, but Wavamunno knew better and subsequent events
were to prove him right. Wavamunno took to his new role as his
father's official number two with great relish. He worked on one
of his father's buses as a conductor, he purchased consumer goods
to restock the retail shop back at home, he supervised the bagging
and storage of coffee and other commodities, and he accompanied
his father on his cattle trading journeys. However, the role he
enjoyed the most was working as his father's accountant; counting
the money, banking it and paying the workers and other expenses.
Wavamunno Senior's decision to bring him into the business paid
off as things improved noticeably with Wavamunno's contributions.
His father drummed into him an appreciation for the way Asians,
who at the time made up a significant percentage of the Ugandan
population, conducted their business.

> My father always admired the Indians' business methods and never
> missed an opportunity to tell me that if Africans wanted to succeed in
> business, they had to behave and emulate their methods and business
> acumen, and I learnt as much as I could from them.

A year after his induction into his father's business, Wavamunno
was sent to a different type of business school. He went to work
for and live with an Asian friend of his father's, Mr Merali, in
the neighbouring town of Mbarara. The Merali family ran a retail
shop and had mining interests, and the young Wavamunno's
role was to be a cashier. While there, he learnt about hard work,
saving money and investing in the business for future growth, but
most important of all, he learnt about credit and working capital.
Wavamunno saw how the Meralis used bank overdrafts to finance
their produce buying and mining activities, and he realised that
the system worked against black Africans. Because they did not
have any security they could not get access to loans, and as a
result they could not get credit from suppliers. 'By the time I left
the Merali family to start my own business, I knew it was crucial
to access credit,' he explains. That wasn't the only thing he left

with; he also left with a very clear idea of what he was going to do next: produce buying.

It was manageable and convenient since it did not require a lot of capital and sophisticated knowledge. With modest savings, it was possible to go into produce buying and gradually expand one's business activities from savings and profits.

Armed with contacts and knowledge from the Meralis, Wavamunno knew exactly where to go to buy agricultural produce. He started trading castor oil seeds, onions, cabbages, beans and ground nuts. He bought from small farmers deep in the interior of Uganda and sold to traders, including the Meralis, his previous employers, all the while sharpening his negotiation skills and building an excellent supplier network. Produce buying was infinitely demanding. Wavamunno travelled extensively and more often than not had to enter into remote and very rural areas, where he was faced with challenging situations brought about largely by the lack of a road network. He travelled by motorbike and if the roads were not good enough, he would enter on bicycle or by foot. He would hire porters to carry his purchases out to the main roads and from there, hire vehicles to get them back to Mbarara to sell. It was a tough but well worth the effort.

Trading in agricultural produce was the launching pad for my business career and during the 60s it remained the core of my business activities, however, I was too restless to be tied down to one sector of the economy. I was conscious of putting all my eggs in one basket.

Wavamunno was to go on to have many, many baskets and divide his numerous eggs equally into them all.

His next move was into transport. He used his initial profits from the produce business to buy a Volkswagen car and started a special hire taxi service, which he ran from one of the local hostels. He personally drove the government officials, police officers and magistrates who were his customers. He described his new business as a 'hard and hazardous occupation'. Not only did he get to know all the prominent people in the town, but he soon became well known around Mbarara and built up a network of 'useful business and social contacts'. A year after he had started his transport business, another car was added; a Peugeot Estate, which he used for the long-distance routes. With two cars, Wavamunno was making what he called 'substantial money', which he ploughed right back into the business, purchasing more cars and eventually moving into buses. He proudly recalls how he bought some of the vehicles in his growing fleet on hire purchase – it was the first time he had used credit. It was a significant moment in his business career, which, for him, clearly demonstrated his 'creditworthiness and reliability as a businessman'.

With his transport business doing well, Wavamunno turned his attention to other opportunities in Mbarara. He opened a dry-cleaning business and added the management of the accommodation, bar and restaurant of a local hostel to his small but growing empire. Given the multiple business interests in which Wavamunno was involved, he began to hire and train people, including his siblings, to work for him. He took on drivers, conductors, dry-cleaners and accounts clerks. He established some very clear guidelines for all his staff, applying the principles he believed had made him successful. 'I made it clear to my workers that I would not tolerate laziness, shoddy work, rudeness to customers and, above all, dishonesty.' Although, he was still only in his very early twenties, Wavammuno was well on his way to becoming a prosperous young businessman. With the profits from his various businesses he built his first home which he looked on proudly as the 'symbol of my graduation from boyhood to manhood'.

The swinging sixties

Like the swinging sixties, the decade in which Wavamunno's fledgling businesses took off, things were upbeat all round in Uganda. Milton Obote, Uganda's first black prime minster, had led the country to independence in 1962, bringing in a new wave of much-welcomed change. Under Obote's socialist rule, Uganda started the partial nationalisation of all foreign banks, sugar plantations and major industries in the country to redress some of the imbalances of the past. Neither Wavamunno nor his businesses were particularly affected by Obote's stranglehold on the country, but Ugandans were beginning to feel the pinch of his ill-thought-out policies and people were becoming discontent. The discontentment spread to the military and paved the way for a coup in January 1971, which overthrew Obote and took the country into its most infamous chapter. Enter Idi Amin, the 'simple' soldier who terrorised Ugandans throughout his eight-year rule and made life difficult for business people like Wavamunno, who sums up this period in Uganda's history very succinctly: 'When Ugandans were busy celebrating the illusion of freedom, the replacement of the rule of law by the rule of the gun was under way.' And that's when his problems started.

The Idi Amin era

Living and working in Amin's Uganda was a daily dangerous gamble. Although I lived in constant fear, not only for my life, but also for those of relatives and friends through Amin's regime, I had made up my mind that under no circumstances would I flee my country.

Wavamunno's stoicism landed him in jail. It was 1971, just after Obote was overthrown by Idi Amin. Wavamunno and his brother were arrested in Mbarara by one of Amin's army generals. The unsubstantiated allegations against the brothers were that they were 'staunch and subversive supporters' of the ousted president Obote. The allegations led to 10 days in jail.

I was severely beaten and tortured. I suffered permanent damage to my left eye from which I still feel pain. We had no drinking water and whatever food we received – if and when we did – was not fit for human consumption.

His experiences proved to be the catalyst that finally caused Wavamunno to leave the small rural town of Mbarara. His success had started to attract too much attention and he made the decision to move to Kampala, Uganda's capital. The move to a big city also saw the rise in his fortunes. Wavamunno quickly joined forces with two local businessmen who ran a taxi service in Kampala. However, the partnership didn't last long as each partner essentially ran separate businesses, with no proper records or demarcation between company and personal funds. Wavamunno soon left, taking with him his six vehicles and the valuable contacts and customers he had established in the brief venture. He set up on his own and called his new business Spear Touring Safari company:

> I chose the name 'Spear' because I was deeply committed to the preservation and promotion of African traditions and our cultural heritage. In every traditional African society, the spear used to be a symbol of protection and success.

Wavamunno was determined to succeed in this city and he was bullish about it. He took a loan to buy a fleet of 10 cars – six Mercedes and four Volkswagen minibuses. He rented office space at the very prestigious newly completed International Conference Centre (ICC) in Kampala; his was the first black-owned business which could boast that address. To Wavamunno, it was a significant moment in his business career that he described as a 'remarkable achievement that I will not forget for the rest of my life'. To give his achievements some context, the business environment in Uganda at the time was dominated by Asians and Europeans. Few indigenous Ugandan businessmen ran high-profile businesses – and certainly none of them had offices at the ICC. But it was just the beginning for Wavamunno; he had bigger dreams.

> Hiring out vehicles was a means to an end for me, I wanted to become one of the most successful tour operators in Uganda in an industry dominated by Asians and Europeans.

He started a tourism agency, establishing contacts with his counterparts in Britain, Germany and Italy. Intent on building a hotel, he bought a piece of strategically located land and began the construction of a hotel in Mbarara, which was on the tourist route between Kampala and the west of the country, where most of the tourist attractions are situated. His timing couldn't have been more unfortunate. It was 1972 and his move into tourism coincided with the period in Uganda's history when Asians and foreigners were expelled, and when Amin banned all foreign tourists from the country. Like the consummate entrepreneur he had become, Wavamunno changed pace and rethought his business.

His fledgling tourism business had crumbled before it had even started. Stuck with a fleet of cars set to service a collapsed tourism industry, Wavamunno knew he had to find ways to generate income and pay off the hire purchase loans he had taken on to buy his vehicles. He immediately started hiring out his vehicles to government officials and private individuals. This proved to be a smart move as the money started rolling in. Despite the harsh economic times that characterised Uganda under Amin's rule in the 70s, Wavamunno's businesses thrived. In fact, in his own words and against all odds, 'business was booming'. It wasn't just business that was doing well; his personal life was also on the up and up. He had just completed his second home, and he had fallen in love.

The two jewels in his crown

They say that behind every great man is an even greater woman and in Wavamunno's case he would be the first to agree that the beautiful half-Scottish, half-Ugandan woman he courted for four years and eventually married was, and still is, an important force in his life and his business. He married Morine in May 1974, and she became not just his wife and a mother, but also a business partner, who is still involved in almost every aspect of Wavamunno's varied business empire. Wavamunno describes his wife as someone who has become his 'principal partner in life and in business – my chief business adviser and a confidante'. It was Morine who took him into the textile and clothing businesses. The company which she started in the early 70s became one of the largest business enterprises in Kampala until it was looted and almost entirely destroyed – first during the 1979 war between Uganda and Tanzania that led to the overthrow of Idi Amin, and then again in the 1985 military coup against Milton Obote who regained power in 1980. Together, the Wavamunnos started a textile importing business that included blankets, bed sheets and bed covers from Italy and Germany.

The year he married Morine was also the same year that Wavamunno achieved his second jewel or what he called 'the most important pillar in my business success story'. That was the year he secured the sole Mercedes Benz franchise in Uganda. It was the most significant business deal in his life at the time and catapulted him into the big league. It started with an informal meeting between the then West German ambassador to Uganda. It was engineered by a friend of Wavamunno's who happened to know that Daimler-Benz was looking for an agent to represent them in Uganda. Daimler-Benz's original agent in Uganda had been one of the unfortunate Asians who had been booted out of the country, their business confiscated and subsequently nationalised. Amin then proceeded, in very quick succession, to 'give' the company to a number of state-run institutions to mismanage. Daimler-Benz objected to the passing around of its business and promptly started looking to appoint its own private distributor. Suitably impressed with Wavamunno, the German ambassador promised to facilitate a meeting for him to meet with Daimler-Benz in Germany. The idea of a Mercedes Benz franchise kindled a flame in Wavamunno's mind. 'There was no doubt that getting a Mercedes Benz franchise was too good to turn down. It was a rare golden opportunity of a lifetime to make money,' he recalls. Wavamunno set about to do all in his power to secure the franchise. He flew to Germany to present his credentials. He felt questions would be raised about his 'experience, technical skills and financial resources', but most of all about his 'ignorance of the German language and limited academic education'. Ironically, despite his fears, the Germans loved him. Wavamunno played on his strengths; he pushed the fact that he had 15 years' experience in transport and tourism, and that he had actually been one of Mercedes Benz's biggest customers in Kampala. Then he played his trump card.

> I knew the local conditions in Uganda very well, I had the right business contacts and, above all, I was creditworthy with a very high reputation in the financial sector.

But it turned out that it wasn't Daimler-Benz he had to convince, it was an adversary much closer to home – Idi Amin's government, in the shape of the Ugandan minister of commerce, who was not too keen on Wavamunno securing the franchise to import, distribute, repair and service Mercedes Benz vehicles in Uganda. It took a meeting with Idi Amin himself, which Wavamunno attended with two of the German company's board members responsible for export. The meeting took place in Amin's home town, Arua, a plane ride from Entebbe airport.

> In those days, Amin had a small African hut in Arua where he used to meet foreign dignitaries whenever he was in a foul mood. As soon as we landed we were taken to the famous hut. For us to enter this traditional hut, we had to go down on all fours and almost prostrate before the big man.

At close quarters, Wavamunno had the chance to form his opinions of Amin and they were not dissimilar to what the world would eventually know him to be. 'He had an inflated ego, and a superhuman conception of his own importance,' says Wavamunno. 'He was very temperamental, impulsive and quick to kill real or imaginary enemies, but he could project the image of simplicity, humility and kindness when it was in his interest to do so.' It was this face that Amin displayed for his meeting with Wavamunno and his prospective German business partners. The meeting lasted one hour. Despite rambling on about Uganda and his plans for the country, Amin never once mentioned anything pertaining to the business at hand and the outcome was less than conclusive. Although he had already registered his company, Spear Motors, to act as the agent for DaimlerChrysler in Uganda, it took Wavamunno one more meeting between the Germans and Amin before the government finally approved his appointment in December 1975.

Not long afterwards, he won the tender to supply hire vehicles to the government during the African Union summit and came face to face with his own mortality and Lieutenant Colonel Juma Ali, the man who brought Wavamunno to his knees because of the late delivery of a Mercedes. The incident made Wavamunno realise just how tenuous his business was in Amin's Uganda. Having said that though, Wavamunno was successful. He controlled the largest market share of any passenger vehicles and trucks sold in the country, and with the support of Daimler-Benz, he established a training centre for mechanics. Today in Uganda, Wavamunno is synonymous with Mercedes Benz and 2008 celebrates 33 years of a highly successful and very lucrative business partnership.

The boom years

It was a partnership Wavamunno leveraged. His relationship with DaimlerChrysler made him an attractive partner for many other European firms looking for partners in Uganda. In 1976, he secured the Bomag franchise for road construction equipment, the Pfaff agency for sewing machines and the Volkswagen Audi vehicles franchise in 1979. The number of companies doing business with him got longer and longer. Through his various agencies and the companies he represented, his business empire expanded into the distribution of vehicle body care products, school materials, the manufacturing of truck bodies, sales of bitumen sprayer trucks, motorcycles, Daewoo cars, firefighting vehicles and equipment, ambulances, agricultural equipment and garbage collection trucks. He also took on the agency for a security printing company which specialised in currency, passports and IDs. Although for many, Amin's Uganda was neither a pleasant place in which to live nor to do business, Wavamunno seemed to have a knack for manoeuvring his way around what was thrown at him.

> I have always believed that politics and business are like fire and water; they do not exist together amicably. A businessman must learn to tame his own political views so that he can serve people of different political persuasions. This belief has always guided and helped me to keep politics at a respectable distance from my business life. I have no doubt that the success of my businesses over the years has been, to a large extent, a result of my doing business with successive governments whether I liked them or not.

But, what goes up must eventually come down and Wavamunno's fortunes were about to take a downturn.

Political turmoil

It was 1978 and Amin was inadvertently preparing for his downfall when he chose to invade neighbouring Tanzania. Foreign exchange, which Wavamunno relied on heavily for his import businesses, was diverted to the war effort and sales were affected as his customers 'saved' their money for essentials. The Tanzanian army retaliated to Amin's invasion and in turn, marched into Uganda. Indiscriminate and widespread looting and destruction became the order of the day. Wavamunno's businesses were severely affected – he lost his entire workshop and stocks of spare parts along with 105 cars and buses across his transport businesses to looting. Office and factory equipment were also 'liberated' – including the shop and dress factory started by his wife. About 600 head of cattle from a commercial farm he owned jointly with his brothers also disappeared. In all, his losses at Spear Motors alone amounted to US$3.3 million. Fearing for his life, Wavamunno fled first to Kenya and then to Germany to wait out the war and the initial chaos but he had no intention of staying away for good.

I am not the sort of man who runs away from problems and challenges. I had built my business career in Uganda and therefore I had too much at stake to think of living anywhere else. Uganda was my home and that was where I intended to stay.

So he returned to assess the damage to his businesses and rebuild his empire. His return was a little premature; things had not yet fully settled down in Uganda and he landed himself in jail for the second time for, he was told, 'his own security and until further notice'. With the benefit of hindsight, his incarceration tuned out to be a blessing in disguise:

> During the four months I was in Luzira Prison, many prominent professional and business people were gunned down by men in uniform and I could have suffered the same fate.

In April 1979, President Julius Nyerere of Tanzania and his Tanzanian army eventually overthrew Amin and in the ensuing euphoria Wavamunno was released. Physically and emotionally exhausted – he had also lost his mother during the period – Wavamunno retreated to Germany to regroup. While there, he took care of business. He negotiated with Daimler-Benz and implored them to relax the terms of payment until he was back on his feet and had time to rebuild Spear Motors. Furthermore, he approached his bank and renegotiated financing agreements. He had no doubt he would be back on his feet soon enough.

After the war, Uganda quickly went through two governments which tried unsuccessfully to unite the country until in December 1980, Milton Obote, whom Amin had overthrown eight years before, controversially returned, aided by Tanzania, to resume power. Obote's return marked the beginning of what Wavamunno called a 'new wave of lawlessness, state-sponsored violence and civil war', and although his businesses continued, they did not 'regain the momentum of the 70s'. By 1985 the country descended into civil war and once again widespread looting of the businesses he had just built up occurred. But this time, it was not limited to his business; his personal effects were also looted and the lives of his wife and children were threatened. Wavamunno was forced to send his wife and their four children away to Europe for their safety. He tells an amusing story that demonstrates the times in which he was living:

There was a family living in a one-room house but they had looted my double bed which could not go through their front door, let alone fit in their house. They kept it under a mango tree and only looked at it day and night. This same family had also looted a fridge, a cooker and a telephone, although they did not have electricity in their home. I had to negotiate with these neighbours and pay them money in order to retrieve my own property.

The irony of the situation was not lost on him, even at the time, but there was little he could do. 'The losses I incurred were devastating to me and they would have broken me if I did not have a passion for success,' he says. Wavamunno set about trying to rebuild his empire for the second time in eight years. But he first had to wait for Tito Okello's government, which took over from Obote's government in July 1985, to give way to Museveni's government in January 1986. At this point, Uganda was a no-go territory with a 'total breakdown of law and order in the country'; even the banks were not lending money. Wavamunno shut down his businesses and patiently bided his time in Germany and London.

In February 1986 he returned, slightly apprehensive about the new man in charge; Museveni, who appeared to have strong socialist leanings. Wavamunno, a capitalist through and through, was naturally very wary. His attitude is unforgiving:

Socialism kills individual enterprise and initiative, it discourages innovation, creativity and investment ... and in any case, in Africa, people only have poverty to share.

Despite his misgivings, he started up his business again. He recalled all of his workers, took a US$3.11 million loan from Daimler-Benz, renegotiated new overdraft facilities with his banks, sold off some of his assets to pay off old loans and inject some new capital, and took advantage of the government's barter trade system selling coffee in exchange for trucks. 'By the end of 1986 my businesses were back on track,' he says proudly.

From the bad old days to now ...

Over the last 22 years of doing business, Wavamunno has consistently built on his successes, looking out for new opportunities and for more ways of making money. As a result of his prominence and his obvious business acumen, he was frequently approached to enter into various ventures, some of which he took up, but in many cases, he opted to start something from scratch. In 1986, it wasn't just his car dealership that was back on track. By then Wavamunno had started diversifying his business and today it is difficult to track his numerous investments. He is either currently involved in, has been involved in or is very likely to soon be involved in, almost any business sector you could care to name. Through his various businesses he directly employs more than 2 000 people.

> While I appreciate the virtues of focus and specialisation in business, I have always believed that in a poor and volatile country like Uganda, it is reckless to put all one's eggs in one basket.

In the early 80s Wavamunno diversified his basket and started a manufacturing company called GM Company, which specialised primarily in building truck and bus bodies, as well as other metal fabrication. Today he is a significant player in the manufacturing sector after purchasing and merging a near-bankrupt government-owned manufacturing plant with his existing business in 1993. The resulting business, GM Tumpeco, has nine separate active production lines, which include fuel and water tanks, steel home and office furniture, hospital equipment, aluminium windows and door frames, wooden furniture, road signs, wheelbarrows and yes, Slumberland mattresses – under licence. The diversity in his businesses shows the extent to which he refuses to be pigeonholed into one particular sector.

Wavamunno owns a fleet of trucks that transports goods to the port in Mombasa, Kenya. He has a printing company that prints everything from T-shirts, caps and vehicle graphics to vehicle licence plates. He has a retail operation which retails imported furniture – mainly Italian. He started a tourism initiative in the shape of a lodge for backpackers at Kayabwe on the equator. He is the majority shareholder in an insurance company called United Assurance Company Unlimited, which specialises in short- and long-term insurance products. In 2000 he sold some of his shares to UAP Kenya, a leading insurance company in East Africa, and the company was later renamed. He plans to list on the Ugandan Stock Exchange in order to raise money and to get more people to participate in the economy.

In 1998 he added media to his ever-growing portfolio and purchased a radio station which made its name broadcasting the soccer World Cup contests live. He later added a television station and today Wavamunno Broadcasting Services (WBS) is the leading indigenous station in the country. The company resides at Spear House, a five-storey steel prefabricated building, shipped in block by block from Germany by Wavamunno and put up in less than 12 months. He is also the majority shareholder in one of the first five flower exporting businesses in Uganda – Victoria Flowers. The eight-hectare farm supplies roses to the European market – exporting mainly to the flower market in Holland. It's a business he describes as both 'interesting and frustrating', due to the nature of the sector, which is highly specialised and very competitive. In 2000, he started a small publishing company which publishes, among other things, educational books and books for authors who wish to self-publish.

Along with a Japanese and Singaporean partner, Wavamunno was involved in a large-scale clothing and textile manufacturing operation, which, under the African Growth Opportunity Act, exports organic cotton garments to the US and manufactures clothing for the local market. In 2008 he put up his shares in the company for sale. In 2003, he started Wavah Water, a rather lucrative mineral water bottling manufacturing plant, built to international standards. Wavah Water now supplies Uganda, Sudan and other neighbouring countries with still and sparkling mineral water. He is currently in the process of expanding his plant to double its output in order to satisfy local and international demand.

But not all his businesses have been successful. In 1995 he embarked on 'by far my most ambitious but abortive venture' by starting a commuter bus service to replace the state-run bus transport service which had collapsed. A year later he bowed out and folded his company, City Link Buses, when it was no longer financially viable. Three years later, Wavamunno decided to enter the banking sector. He secured a banking licence and incorporated a bank called Nile along with 17 shareholders. He was the first chairman and chief financier of the project. For a number of years the bank did well, but the central bank stepped in over allegations of mismanagement. After an investigation, the bank was eventually returned to its shareholders to continue to run, but much damage had been done. It was eventually sold to Barclays Bank in 2007 after the giant made an offer which could not be matched by anyone else.

This is by no means a comprehensive list of Wavamunno's assets and interests. The single common denominator across the myriad of businesses is Wavamunno himself and it is hardly surprising that he has won the title of Ugandan Businessman of the Year for seven years running. His current projects, which are still in the making, are a commercial business park development in Kampala and a pharmaceutical company, which among other things, will use indigenous herbs as a base for creams and other beauty products.

Like his business interests, the Wavamunno name is ubiquitous in Uganda. To give you an idea, there are a number of roads named after him in the country and at least two schools. And when you thought he couldn't possibly have time to do anything else, Wavamunno adds that he is also the honorary consul of the Republic of Hungary in Uganda, responsible for the issuing of visas and the promotion of trade opportunities between the two countries.

Somehow, in the middle of building his empire, Wavamunno found time to build his dream home; what he calls his 'most precious asset'. It is Cape Villa, Wavamunno's seven-storey home, complete with an elevator, on the shores of Lake Victoria in Kampala, which took seven years to build. The entire area taken up by the house is six and a half acres of terraced splendour, built on the slope of a small hill which looks out on to a spectacular view of Lake Victoria. It is built on the original land which Idi Amin occupied after deporting its occupants, and in which he married Sarah Kyolaba in 1975. Wavamunno proudly refers to Cape Villa as 'one of the most beautiful and creative works of art and one of the most majestic buildings I have seen and admired'. It is a monument to his success, built on sheer hard work.

Although Wavamunno admits that his earlier years were about satisfying an insatiable desire to 'do business' and 'make money', he admits that the making of money was merely a means to an end and not the end in itself. It was his way of escaping from poverty and initially educating his siblings, and then his own children. However, the more money he has amassed the more he realises that 'making money carries certain social responsibilities'. As a result, over the years, he has been involved with various philanthropic initiatives in Uganda, focusing particularly on education. Apart from various schools he has built for communities, Wavamunno's bursary scheme has sent thousands of Ugandans to school.

At 65, after a lifetime of building, Wavamunno finally has a little more time to relax – although he is clear that he is not ready for retirement. He reads fiction and business books and is currently writing part two of his autobiography. As part of the diplomatic community representing Hungary, he entertains frequently at his palatial 67-roomed home. He spends time on his boat, time with his children and grandchildren who are dotted across the world. But most importantly, Wavamunno strategises about his next money-making venture, forever looking for new baskets for his many eggs.

Sources:

1. Wavamunno, G. *The Story of an African Entrepreneur*, Uganda: Wavah Books, 2000.

Ndaba Ntsele — The Suntanned Entrepreneur

VITAL STATISTICS

Name: Ndaba Ntsele
Country: South Africa
Born: 6 October 1952
Position/Title: CEO Pamodzi Holdings
Co turnover:/Assets: R2 billion
Nationality: South African
Industry: Investment holding company
Highest education qualification: Executive business management diploma

On 5 August 2007, the South African Sunday newspapers broke with a financial story that would have caused some consternation among the various players in the local financial sector. That morning and the following week, headlines on all the major business papers across the country told of the launch of South Africa's largest private equity fund. The fund raised US$1.3 billion, easily dwarfing the two largest funds in the country by R3 billion. Even more remarkably, all the money was raised offshore, with the backing of US investment companies First Reserve and American Metals, and Coal International, one of the world's largest coal companies. The launch caused one financial weekly to applaud the fundraiser's 'knack of persuading international investors to part with their money'. Other newspaper headlines talked of a 'new investment giant' and sang the praises of the company that had created the fund. The company behind the headlines was Pamodzi Investment Holdings, one of South Africa's first black-owned and -run investment companies.

'It means I have convinced America and Americans that I can grow their money, pay them back and retain a lot of money,' says Ndaba Ntsele. 'It's the first time in this country, on this continent, that so much money – money that is not a grant – has been raised. It's money that I have to pay back,' laughed the key figure behind the fundraising and the man who, along with his partner Solly Sithole, started Pamodzi Investment Holdings in 1996. 'It doesn't happen every day that suntanned people like ourselves are given authority for such a lot of money!' he jokes.

Ndaba Ntsele is the 'suntanned' entrepreneur and millionaire who made his mark in South Africa way before Nelson Mandela's very long walk to freedom in 1990. Ntsele was one of the very few black success stories that came out of South Africa during the struggle years. He, along with his two partners, Solly Sithole and Ncedi Manyoni, had a knack for making money, even back then under apartheid's restrictive and punitive laws, which saw them become millionaires before their 30th birthdays. These days, Ntsele is operating in the much more empowering business environment that is South Africa in the 21st century. The chief executive of Pamodzi Investment Holdings, Ntsele runs the privately owned company that he launched in 1996 at a time when he says 'empowerment was fashionable'. When he talks about empowerment, he is referring to black economic empowerment

(BEE), the government policy instigated by the South African government to fast-track the participation of blacks in the economy. When Pamodzi Investment Holdings was launched, just two years after the first democratic elections were held in South Africa, many white-owned companies were rushing to implement their BEE strategies, selling stakes in their businesses to black consortiums to abide by the new regulations. It was a lucrative time for black businessmen in South Africa and Ntsele's company was one of the first at the starting block, waiting to capitalise.

Ntsele describes Pamodzi as a multibillion-rand investment company with a few private shareholders, including Ntsele himself and his long-time business partner, Sithole. Detailed figures about their investments are not easily disclosed; Ntsele is unsurprisingly reluctant to give away too much. 'We're running a big company,' he says. 'If you look at our underlying assets it should be at about 20 000 people. In terms of the value of the company maybe it's somewhere close to R2 billion.' The company has 13 investments in six strategic sectors: finance, food, leisure, vehicle retail, technology and resources. Since it started operating in 1996, Pamodzi has raised R16 billion, of which R12 billion has come from offshore fundraising activities – an art which Ntsele seems to have perfected. Pamodzi's investment strategy is to go for controlling interest in any business it targets and to add real strategic value. Ntsele explains:

> What differentiates Pamodzi from a lot of (other companies) is that from day one, we said we're not going to buy 2% or 3%. We said when we get into companies we want to take control in terms of controlling the board, so we could hire and fire management.

Ntsele laughs as he talks about the company's unique way of dealing with the boardroom politics of South Africa. Typically good-humouredly, he says, 'We don't put one person on one board because these boards are full of white people and if you've got one black person among 12 white guys, give him six months and he'll be thinking exactly like them. We put in two or three.'

Business under apartheid

The light-hearted reference to racial politics in South Africa gives an idea of the dynamics of doing business in the country today. Although Ntsele can joke about it now, back then, when he was starting off, it was no laughing matter. For a black person in apartheid South Africa, doing business was fraught with all manner of difficulties. Ntsele and his partners struggled to raise money to finance their building projects in the sector in which he built his fortune, and they never seemed to be able to get to the decision makers to make their case.

> You must understand it was during apartheid, we were very, very oppressed. When they heard my accent it was difficult to get to get to the top ... not even just the banks, all the institutions.

In the early days, even when they tried to cut themselves in on a deal to become part of a consortium – which included the major white-owned construction companies that were bidding to develop land in black townships – Ntsele and his partners weren't taken seriously. The project they were bidding on was part of the apartheid government's initiative to create better, but separate, living areas for the country's black population. It was done through an organisation called the Urban Foundation, run by Justice Stein.

> We went to the Urban Foundation we said: 'We don't want to be contractors, we want to be developers.' The difference being that a developer makes a lot more profit from developing the serviced land. We were in the game and we understood the game and we wanted to have that cream. We had to take Justice Stein to my house in Pimville (Soweto), sit with him until 4am to convince him that we must be part and parcel of this thing. The big white companies also didn't take kindly to it, that we were now playing at their level because they were the ones that had the privileges of doing these things ... it was tough.

Even finding a suitable place from which to run a business was tough if you were a black company. The law was very specific about where black people could set up offices, and it wasn't where their customers were.

> Our clients were working in the central business district (CBD) and by law, as blacks we weren't allowed to have offices in the CBD. So we had offices in the townships, but it was difficult for us to operate because during the day our clients worked in the CBD, so you woke up in the

morning and you could not talk to anybody unless you drove to their offices in Johannesburg.

Their solution to the problem was to get one of their suppliers, a white furniture manufacturer who did a lot of business with Ntsele, to front for them and make the application in his name to secure office space at the very prestigious Carlton Centre in the CBD. The upshot was that Ntsele and his team became 'the first black guys to have offices at the Carlton Centre'. At the height of their business, Ntsele and his team at Pamodzi were employing in the region of 600 people and a sizeable number of them, interestingly, were white, an unusual arrangement for a black company. 'The irony was that we were supposed to call them "boss" but they ended up calling us "boss",' laughs Ntsele.

The early years

Since then Ntsele has been breaking the mould in various other ways throughout his life. As a young boy growing up in Soweto, he seemed destined for a life that was different to that of most black people in South Africa. When most little boys were playing in the streets, Ntsele was off selling peanuts, apples and bananas with his aunt, who ran an informal stall. Some of the five-year-old's earliest memories are of the times he spent with his aunt. He enjoyed interacting with people, counting the money and providing customers with the correct change. Looking back, he was developing skills that would one day help him achieve his ambitions. Ntsele was a smart child who was in the top 10 at school; maths and science were his favourite subjects. He always knew that selling was an important skill to have, and between the ages of 15 and 18, he started trading apples. He soon graduated to selling newspapers in downtown Johannesburg over the weekends. Even then, Ntsele realised the power of teamwork and would put together a team of newspaper boys on all the street corners and share the profits at the end of the day. As well as an understanding of teamwork, he developed a passion for money and was smart enough to devise legitimate ways in which to get it. He made his first 'fortune' in peaches, buying from wholesalers and selling on to fruit shops and directly to consumers on the streets. It was going to be the first of many fortunes he would make in his lifetime.

One of eight siblings, Ntsele was born on 6 October 1952, in Soweto, Johannesburg. He grew up in Orlando West, an elite area where the black middle classes, lawyers like Nelson Mandela and Walter Sisulu, lived. He went to Orlando High, finished his matric in 1971 and went out into the world to make his mark. His first job was working for the Johannesburg City Council as a clerk, which earned him the princely sum of R110 per month. From there he progressed to the traffic department and spent some time as a traffic officer. It was the 70s and South Africa was under the grip of apartheid. Things were heating up in the townships; black people were burning the ID documents which they were forced to carry around and things were to culminate in the historic 16 June uprisings, which put Soweto on the world map.

Ntsele was a part of that significant period in South Africa's history but he realised early on that political activism was not for him. He decided that it was easier to create change through capitalism. He believed firmly in wealth creation and that 'commercial warfare is greater than political warfare'. And although there were not that many opportunities available for a young black man, aged 19, from Soweto, Ntsele's ambitions remained intact.

> To be number one is something that I loved – I mean from childhood. I wanted to distinguish myself from the rest. Even at high school I saw myself as a millionaire.

Ntsele looked at the multimillionaires in the country at the time; the Ackermans who ran a retail chain, the Oppenheimers who were into mining. He realised that they all had one thing in common: they all ran their own businesses. Right there and then he made up his mind never to work for anyone. In addition, Ntsele came from a family of entrepreneurs; his aunt, whom he says was the biggest influence in his life, and his various uncles never worked for anyone. They had realised that the traditional path for black entrepreneurs was down the retail route as small-time business owners. But this did not interest Ntsele. Although he may have had little idea of how he would make his millions, he did know what he wasn't going to do. 'I was not going to run a shop and I didn't want to be a sole proprietor,' he says firmly. But as a means of supplementing his meagre income from the council, he continued his independent selling. This time though, he sold clothing. He already had a car at 18, a Morris Minor, given to him by his father, which he used to drive across the border to Swaziland to buy stock from the factories there.

Ntsele strongly believed in team work; he had already experienced the power of pooling effort and profits when he sold newspapers on street corners in the Johannesburg CBD. So in 1979 he joined forces with two friends, Solly Sithole, who is currently the executive director of Pamodzi, and Ncedi Manyoni. Together they started Pamodzi Property Construction. The name itself, a Swahili word meaning 'oneness', reflects Ntsele's business philosophy that 'unity is power'. The three set out to make some real money.

The building business

Even back then the young partners had a clear vision that they were building a business that would be around for years to come. The three friends made a vow of total trust, not even family would come between them. And although Manyoni left after the business took a downturn some years later, after 27 years, the partnership between Sithole and Ntsele is still very much intact and stronger than ever. The partners had been introduced to each other because of their mutual love for money and their vision of becoming millionaires. Ntsele's uncle had introduced them after realising that they had much in common.

> From day one we decided that when you start a corporation there must be a leader – irrespective. So we decided to have a secret ballot, the three of us. My name came out as managing director of the company. Both of them put my name down, so I became the managing director. Solly became the sales director and Ncedi became the financial director because he had a BCom degree and knew the sums. We each had 33.3% of the company, but the fact that we agreed that one must be the leader, that showed a level of maturity at that time and it worked.

They decided to enter into the construction business. Back then, in South Africa, black people were only allowed to live in remote, rural, undeveloped and non-commercial areas. These 'townships' as they were called, were developed by the government to house black migrant workers and their families. All families, regardless of size, were housed in tiny 54m^2, four-room structures called 'matchboxes', which were built on 240m^2 of land. They were usually flimsy, poorly constructed and built on land with no drainage, no sewerage system or road infrastructure. Ntsele and his partners took their first risk. They gambled with their future security using the only money they had access to – their endowment policies. The young men cashed in the policies to create working capital and used that to start their construction company. Ntsele's uncle, a builder himself, referred to the trio as 'the three blind mice', a reflection of their level of knowledge of the industry in which they were about to enter. The idea they wanted to experiment with was to create more living space and maximise the use of the 240m^2 each family was given. They planned to build simple structures, standalone extensions set behind the main houses, consisting of two rooms and a garage – and they did.

> What excited us about building were the numbers – they're big numbers. When we started building the garages, we would sell one for R6 000, so if you build 10 houses, it's R60 000, so it's a lot of money. Psychologically, for all of us, the big numbers were exciting and also the freedom of doing business.
>
> How did we start when none of us were builders? It's what we're actually doing right now at Pamodzi – it's management. You must get the expertise from people that can build. So when we started, I went on building sites, constructions sites and we were talking to their foremen, we wanted to know who was who. We hired one guy who was a foreman who understood building. We offered that guy more than what he was earning and we bought him a brand new van, a Toyota. He was so happy with that car and the wife was so happy, it was unbelievable.

But their business wasn't just about building houses. In order to sell the houses they had to help their clients find and raise the money. At that time, banks were not giving home loans to black people. However, Ntsele and his partners eventually found a building society that agreed to offer loans to people in Soweto. They would fill out the applications for their clients, submit the forms, make their money, and then move on to the next building.

From building the two-room garages, the trio graduated to building three-bedroom homes with a kitchen, a dining room, a lounge and two bathrooms, on serviced land which they purchased from the Urban Foundation. The margins were good and they knew exactly how to juggle the financing to make sure they were never caught short. Pamodzi Property Construction would put down a 10% deposit on the land and they had a six-month window in which to come up with the balance. They would build the house and when they were paid through their client's mortgage, they would pay the Urban Foundation the 90% balance and pocket the rest as profit, all within six months. The new homes were selling for a lot more than the two-roomed garages – R50 000. But soon the banks changed their tune about giving loans. This was largely because the houses that Ntsele and his partners were selling came with a 99-year leasehold. The challenge was to re-educate their clients about the way they spent money.

> There were a whole lot of black people who were only spending money on clothing and cars and nothing else, because we couldn't have ownership of anything. Now to move people from that to a 20-year bond was quite a tall order. There was a whole new generation of teachers, doctors, lawyers, that could now afford to have a house for R50 000.

Ntsele was determined to encourage those teachers, doctors and lawyers to buy his houses and he was obviously successful in changing spending patterns because business was booming.

> We were in our twenties when we started and before we reached the age of 30 we had made so much money that we bought three 380 Mercedes Benz, the top of the range that time. I mean those cars were driven by people that really have status in the community and they're big and we were young and we bought them! I mean we bought three of them!

Ntsele and his partners were so busy living large and making money that they actually forgot to calculate their real earnings.

> When we started, we got so involved in building houses, selling houses, collecting money and making good profits that we didn't actually do the numbers. We went for maybe 24 months without checking how much were making because there was cash flow. We just kept on buying stands; more and more, and building until after about two years Ncedi

called us and said: 'How much profit did we make?'

It was clearly a surprise for them to discover that Pamodzi Property Construction was not just making money – it was making a lot of money.

> When we started with the Urban Foundation our turnover was about R4 million (a year), which was a lot of money at that time. In year two, it went up to about R7 million. Ncedi had done the calculations and called us into a meeting. At that time, I must be honest, I was thinking of hundreds of thousands of rands, I didn't even think of millions.

Spurred on by the ready cash flow and the big profits, Pamodzi Property Construction wanted to join the consortium of white companies that was to work on the Urban Foundation's property development project in Soweto. So they approached Urban Foundation with a novel concept for a black construction company.

Joining the big league

Pamodzi Property Construction asked to join the Urban Foundation's consortium, which was comprised of the major white-owned construction companies. The consortium was tasked with putting in the sewerage lines, roads and the other infrastructure that would create serviced land for 2 400 houses in Soweto. It was novel for a black company to seriously consider that it had a chance at this, and the three were duly discouraged from joining the consortium.

> The Urban Foundation said it would cost us too much money. We said fine, we'll find the money. That was a real test for us. In order for us to participate we were supposed to have R6.5 million to do the roadworks, and for a year or two you would not be able to draw anything because that's infrastructure. Nobody believed that we could pull that amount of money, but at that time I had super confidence because we had always had good dealings with our bank, Standard Bank. Our cash flow was good.

Their cash flow may have been good, nevertheless, their own bank turned them down.

I needed them to lend me R6.5 million and the bank manager said that I must be going cuckoo because his limit was about R150 000 as a local bank manager. My track record was not going to work so I went to Barclays Bank and we met Chris Paul and he gave us the entire amount. All he said was that we must just give him back his money.

Although they had lots of cash floating around their business, Pamodzi Property Construction's actual net worth in assets combined was only about R300 000 – the value of their three homes, which they had bought for cash. So it was all the more significant that the three managed to secure the loan. Ntsele explains:

The loan was based on our cash flow projections, but then there was a holiday for the first 18 months so we were not supposed to make repayments, because during the first 18 months you're putting in infrastructure. But after 18 months you've got to start selling.

Literally two weeks after they secured the loan, the boys from Pamodzi won another tender to build a school for Anglo American. Already owing Barclays bank R6.5 million, Ntsele went back to Standard Bank to raise the working capital needed for the new project. He clearly impressed them too, because he walked away with R2 million for the new project. It was money he felt he deserved.

The biggest thing is that without marbles you cannot play the game – we must be given access to capital. It was a double whammy getting both R6.5 million and R2 million – that positioned us. Because the numbers were huge, the profit was huge too. That was the height of our careers.

Even back then Ntsele seemed to have perfected a skill for getting institutions to give him money and it was one skill that he would hone to perfection in later years. In the meantime, the three friends had many homes and a school to build. They were the biggest black developers in the country and had achieved their dreams of becoming millionaires. On average, the margins they were making on each home they built were about 15% or 20% after tax. And the team had various sales tricks up their sleeves when it came to selling houses.

There's one that I built for R11 000 in Pretoria but I sold it for R71 000. I would borrow furniture and put the furniture in the house. Even today, all over the world, people pay more for a house that is furnished even if that furniture is not going to remain there.

Pamodzi was doing well, but they were also putting something back into their community. They started a programme that provided education to young black men and women who were interested in construction. Once they had completed the programme, the trainees were invited to work at Pamodzi.

That far back, we had started to empower our own people. You come on board, you must work on projects, you'll get bonuses and you'll buy shares in the company.

Things were good, but as they say, what goes up, must come down, and things were about to come down very rapidly for the boys from Soweto.

The housing boom was really big; we were building big schools, we were building filling stations, we were building halls, and everything went well until the late 80s when the political instability was very high.

The lean years

In the 1980s the South African National Civic Organisation (Sanco) advocated for the boycotting of the payment of rates and taxes. The banks panicked, anticipating that people would also soon stop paying their bonds. They withdrew their money from all the urban black areas. It was a blow to Ntsele's business. 'We were not aware that we were so dependent on the banks. That's a lesson in itself. Without the banks we could not play,' he says ruefully. Ntsele and his team had not just been building homes to order, they had accumulated stock – lots of it – and they were about to pay the price for their optimism.

We were stuck with houses because we had also been doing some speculative jobs. People couldn't get loans – even people with good track records. The banks didn't do it openly ... you put in an application and they come back and said: 'We regret ...' We found out from our black friends who were working for the banks that our time was up.

The experience taught Ntsele another hard business lesson about cash flow.

> That's when you actually understand the theory of saying somebody is so rich yet poor. In terms of our assets we were very, very rich, but in terms of cash flow, paying the staff, we were very, very poor. We were retrenching people because there were no jobs. Things were getting bad; we couldn't sell our property, we were virtually penniless. Money was not coming in as before.

Then Pamodzi was dealt another blow. The building trade suppliers refused to deliver building supplies to the township, believing it to be too dangerous. The result was that Pamodzi was severely affected by the embargo and had to downscale its building activities. One unfortunate outcome of the massive slump they faced was that Ncedi Manyoni, their long-time partner, parted ways with Ntsele and Sithole. The stakes were a little too high for him.

> We owed the banks a lot of money, we had a lot of pressure, and at times, we couldn't pay people on time. Some banks were issuing summonses for the money we owed them. We had ceded our homes and everything, so if anybody had pressed a button I would have had to tell my kids that they didn't have a home any more. Things were tough. We were at risk at one time and that is why we lost our partner.

Despite all the pressure, Ntsele identified an opportunity – a stopgap that tided Pamodzi over until their next big money-spinner. Pamodzi moved out of residential and into commercial construction. They started building filling stations for emerging black entrepreneurs and it just managed to keep their heads above water.

> Filling stations delivered good profit margins. The petrol companies were fighting each other to build filling stations in the same spots. The numbers were big.

But the bubble was about to burst on commercial building too as the contracts tailed off and, as Ntsele put it; 'we went south'. Pamodzi put its construction work on hold while they looked around for a quick financial fix. The quick fix turned out to be something they had been dabbling in all along. And it was not the most obvious move for two ex-construction men.

> When we were in construction, our part-time thing was to sell jewellery. We sold jewellery because we loved jewellery. In fact, Ncedi was called Mr T (from the A-Team) because he always wore three or four chains.

They sourced their jewellery stock directly from a contact in Hong Kong, cutting out the local middleman who had initially introduced them. 'We had discovered that gold is never second-hand. Once you polish it, it's new. The jewellery was going very, very fast,' explains Ntsele. From jewellery, it was a small step into trading gold krugerrands; South African gold coins that contain exactly one ounce of gold, first minted in 1967 to help market South African gold. They were introduced to the business by a Jewish trader who approached them in a mall because they were 'dressed well' – back then Ntsele and Solly spent much time and effort on clothes. As well as selling them the krugerrands, the trader became their main buyer. At first, they had no clue about how the gold trading business worked, but they caught on fast.

They were juggling the jewellery and the krugerrands business to keep afloat. Their jewellery contact in Hong Kong was impressed by the volumes they could shift and introduced them to another business opportunity which turned out to be very lucrative indeed. He sent them a shipment of half a million dollars worth of electronic goods, branded radios and speakers.

> Immediately I told my housing sales team that they must go and sell these samples to all the shops that were selling radios. I don't know what the supplier did in Hong Kong, he was buying very cheap and our prices were very low. Business started flying.

Their cheap prices didn't only undercut the market, it also upset the competition. The established distributors with agency agreements to sell the same electronic products tried to stop Ntsele and Sithole bringing in their goods by trying to get them arrested at the port.

> I had enough knowledge to know that what we were doing was not

illegal. I went with an attorney to clear my goods, so the suppliers then talked to me nicely. They said: 'Please don't bring any more goods in; we'll buy what you have at a premium.'

Not one to turn down a golden opportunity like that, Ntsele handed over his products and tried to focus on building up his construction business again.

Back on the up and up

It was the early 90s and South Africa was about to enter into an economic boom. Mandela was out of jail and the first democratic elections in the country were around the corner. Although Ntsele had 'a lot of balls in the air', he made one last-ditch attempt to resuscitate his main business – construction. Pamodzi went into partnership with one of the country's largest construction companies, Murray & Roberts, to put up the biggest building materials supply store in Soweto. Sadly, this was to be their last major construction project, but there were other big fish to fry. In 1992 Ntsele went on a trip to America with one of his engineers, ostensibly to look at US engineering and construction methodologies. But he was really on the lookout for other business opportunities. His real mission was to find some franchise opportunity to bring back to the new South Africa. 'We were positioning ourselves so that when apartheid was over, we would have the first bite of the cherry,' Ntsele explains.

Ntsele and Sithole flirted with a number of US companies, including the underwear company, Victoria's Secret, and McDonald's and Nike. But it was Nike that came through in the end and the most exciting days of Ntsele's career were about to start. Although it has been well over 10 years since Nike stormed triumphantly into South Africa, Ntsele's excitement is still palpable as he tells the story of how they won the Nike franchise for South Africa.

> There were 236 companies that applied, some were moving very, very fast. There was the Edgars group, Total Sports and some other big names. Nonetheless, we interviewed and we beat everybody.

Ntsele put it down to a single factor: 'It's a will to win. We had developed a culture of not failing.' Of course it helped that he and

Sithole were a well-established partnership that had been going for more than 10 years and had survived various ups and downs. Nike seemed attracted to their entrepreneurial spirit – and the fact that they were black. The boys were back in business.

The Nike years

Getting the licence was just the first part; Nike laid down strict terms of engagement for Ntsele and his partners.

> Nike gave us some tough conditions: 'Don't cede the licence to any bank, don't cede your shares. We're a big company and we sell all over the world. We're number one in the world. Everybody buys Nike so the bank must give you money based on your cash flow.' Coming from a situation of apartheid, black people were not being given a lot of money in terms of millions. Now I had to get this amount of money to run Nike.

The sort of numbers Nike was throwing around were high and the three-year cash flow projections would have put off the faint-hearted – but not Ntsele.

> The turnover the first year was going to be R23 million, the second year R25 million, the third year R27 million. These are the numbers that we had to give to Nike.

Getting people to part with money was Ntsele's special skill, one that he had honed over the years. 'The banks wanted to have equity but the rules were that we must not sign anything. Nonetheless, there was one sympathetic banker who gave us the money,' he explains proudly. Not only did Ntsele raise the money to start the business, he met the cash flow projections, and went on to exceed them by more than 100 %!

> The first year we made R49 million – now that was nice – and the second year I think we made R62 million. It was huge growth.

The guys in Portland, Oregon, must have been patting themselves on the back for choosing Ntsele and his team. They had clearly made the right decision. Ntsele and his partners achieved their phenomenal growth by adopting the same strategy they had employed when they started out in construction. They brought in the expertise and paid top dollar for it – while still ensuring that they put black people in key positions.

> I went to all the guys that were running sports marketing businesses: we got the guy who was distributing Reebok during apartheid (and) we made him our first MD. And then he went and stole all the guys that were selling for the competitors, some of the guys we found were selling Nike before their disinvestment (in South Africa). So we had a solid team and that's why we hit the ground running.

Nike people were well-paid people, Ntsele says: 'We gave our sales guys and management a lot of money so they were sharing a lot of profit with us as shareholders at that time.' But growing at that exponential rate meant that Ntsele and Sithole had more and more funding requirements.

> When you grow like that you also need money and we were now desperate. This one merchant bank became a shareholder. When they bought the shares they said they were going to give us money but then Nike International felt they must protect us, so they took a 25% stake and the bank took 20%, which meant the company remained 55% black-owned.

Even though they had a bank as a shareholder, they still couldn't feed the cash cow quickly enough.

> The guy (from the bank) that was sitting on our board blamed the credit committee. We needed about R50 million to R60 million capital for growth, so I had to take that bank, and I won't mention their name, to Portland so they could see how big Nike was.

The female bank executive that came out to see the Nike operation was quite literally given the red-carpet treatment. 'When she came down from the plane, she thought there was a movie star there because we had laid out a red carpet and limousine for her,' laughs Ntsele.

> She looked and she looked and she still refused so Nike told her: 'Bye-

bye, lady, thank you.' The lady would not be moved. With all that treatment she said 'no' and she was a shareholder!

But all was not lost; Nike International had a back-up plan for their South African team. It was clear that they believed in Ntsele.

> Nike brought the president of Citibank from America and he talked to me, (asking) where I want to take this business to, and I told him all my dreams. You can see from my stories I love these big dreams. He said: 'Fine, you go back to South Africa and we're going to call you.'

And with that, the money was raised and the business continued to grow. When Ntsele and Sithole sold Nike in 1997, their turnover was in the region of R400 million a year. Looking back fondly, the best part of the Nike experience for Ntsele was the dynamic way they did business. He still admires their winning spirit:

> Nike is a marketing company through and through, and it's just full of energy and big hearts. The way Nike started from humble beginnings but went on to become number one in the world and they sustained that number-one position. Everybody that's linked with Nike has to be part of that culture.

Under Ntsele's leadership, Nike South Africa went ahead and did its own thing. It capitalised on all the major sporting events that came South Africa's way, including the 1995 rugby World Cup, which was held in, and won by, South Africa. Nike always seemed to pick the winners.

> We sponsored the Springboks the year they won the rugby World Cup. In all the airports, every single store was full of Nike jerseys. Now that was brilliant marketing.

There were many other brilliant marketing strategies that set Nike SA apart from its competitors. They brought out several top athletes to South Africa. Alberto Salazar, the marathon runner, came out to run the Comrades Marathon, which he subsequently won wearing Nike shoes. Andre Agassi came to South Africa on a promotional tour. The Brazilian soccer team came to play South Africa's national soccer team, Bafana Bafana. Nike hosted high-profile events, including the under-14 soccer tournament, which brought young people from all over the world to South Africa.

> But the greatest lesson that I got from Nike personally was that Nike takes everything seriously. When they prepare for Wimbledon, it's serious. When they negotiate for sponsorship, it's serious. Before bringing the Brazilian football team here I had to go to Miami; they showed us how they prepare for a big tournament. For the under-14 tournament I had to go to Germany to see how they prepared.

There was no doubt that it was exciting times for Ntsele, but all good things must surely come to an end and Ntsele and his partners decided to sell Nike South Africa back to Nike International for a very tidy sum. They were at the very top of their game at the time: 'We were in the big league, we were turning over R200 million, R300 million. We sold when we were at a level of about R400 million,' he remembers. When they sold, Ntsele was already planning the next big thing.

Pamodzi Investment Holdings

Once again, Ntsele had read the signs and realised that there were new ways to make money in South Africa. It was 1996, two years after the country's first democratic elections and it seemed everyone was bending over backwards to implement the government's black economic empowerment policy.

> The concept of this thing excited us very, very much because it puts you in a position to buy into these white companies, and you can be diversified, which is something that I believe in.

While still at Nike, he had started putting the team together. 'I wanted to do business with people who were thinking like me, the same ideology, and hard workers who are professionals,' he explains. It took Ntsele one year to put his dream team together. Ntsele joined forces with Peter Vundla, who became the chairperson of Pamodzi, Felicia Mabuza-Suttle, Sifiso Msibi, Solly Sithole, Kobus du Plooy, Jan Roesch and Andrew Wheeler.

> I didn't want them to work part time, I wanted everybody to resign from

work and put money in. We started the company with eight people. All eight of us put in money and everybody resigned (from their other jobs) except two people. At that time I was in the middle of selling Nike so I couldn't go. I was an absent CEO, but I believe if you're a good leader you must also be led, so I said they must they must manage themselves for three months until I come back. Pamodzi opened its doors in 1997. In late 1997 I sold Nike and then the great story began: Pamodzi Investment Holdings.

The 'great story' of Pamodzi Investment Holdings is actually a simple story of a very successful black-owned company that is taking full advantage of the opportunities in the BEE arena and providing excellent returns for its shareholders.

Our internal rate of return has been very, very high – I think about 40%. People got their money back, we sold some assets, we made profit. There's only one business where we got involved and we didn't make money in all our underlying assets.

The first deal Pamodzi completed in 1997 was the R45 million purchase of a hospital – Auckland Health. That was soon followed by a sports marketing company and then a 45% stake in Sodexho, an industrial catering company with significant government contracts. The buying spree didn't stop there; Pamodzi bought into a telecoms company, InfraCom, then Technicare – both of which have since been sold. Their current assets cover the financial sector – where they own stakes in Wesbank Auto, a fleet management finance operation, and Pamodzi Brokers, which specialises in short-term insurance. Their IT portfolio includes a 25.1% share in the Johannesburg Stock Exchange-listed IT company Digicore. They also own a 28% stake in NamITech, a high-end security technology company that produces chip cards for the telecoms and financial sectors. Pamodzi has a 49% share of a BMW dealership which is one of the top-five performers in South Africa. In addition, they own 30% of Kulungile Metals and Pamodzi Gold, their joint venture with Canadian-based resources, and Superior Mining, which is also listed on the Johannesburg Stock Exchange. In 2006 Pamodzi became the top black-controlled junior mining company on the exchange.

But perhaps the most exciting deal Ntsele has been involved

in as part of Pamodzi Investment Holdings was when they added FoodCorp Holdings – a food manufacturing, marketing and distribution company that handles some of the country's best-known food brands – to the company's asset list. At the time, Pamodzi executed the largest management buyout in the country when it delisted FoodCorp. The 1998 deal was worth R1.9 billion, with the Dutch bank ABN Amro contributing R450 million in equity.

> We were competing with all the banks in the country with that opportunity and we won and that took FoodCorp from a R3 billion turnover company to about R4.5 billion. We also empowered 3 200 people in that deal.

Six years later, in 2004, they completed the largest secondary buyout of the same company when Pamodzi raised the first high-yield Eurobond by a South African company. The deal was underwritten by Citibank and secured R175 million from more than 100 European institutions. When they merged FoodCorp with First Lifestyle, Pamodzi went back to the markets to raise another Eurobond worth €135 million. Everyone gets to share the upside at Pamodzi, says Ntsele.

> We gave the staff members here, including the tea lady and the PAs, share options. I think our tea lady's options are close to R1 million now. I said to her: 'You can go and be a manager anywhere' but she said: 'No, I'm a professional tea lady.'

It's a reflection of Ntsele's leadership style and his personality that his team have remained loyal. He is an affable, team player who has a ready smile and an innate confidence in his ability to achieve whatever he sets out to do.

> My leadership style is very, very simple. I motivate people and I tell them that once a person doesn't have fear, once a person doesn't have a complex, he works better. A complex from the colour of one's skin, one's educational background; that's one of the killers for our people. Particularly coming out of the apartheid situation where we were told that our minds and our education were inferior.

Although he was educated largely under the 'inferior' education system, Ntsele has not once let that get in his way.

> I was super-confident as a leader, but then I educated myself. I read a lot of books. I'm not ignorant, you cannot catch me. I've developed myself with my team. I learn from people; I'm a good listener.

His ability to listen and learn has kept him in the boardroom discussing high finance with some of the most sophisticated investment bankers in the world. 'I listen to the guys who are doing the financial model and get the logic,' he says simply. Ntsele is also a decision maker who acts.

> There's not a single day where I don't make a decision. I don't want to postpone things – that's my style. We'll sort it out when it's wrong after we've made it, but I hate to sit on the fence.

He is still very much enjoying what he is doing and, at 56, Ntsele still has a big vision to fulfil. His dream is to list Pamodzi on the New York Stock Exchange to prove to black business people across the world that it can be done. He believes that bigger is better and wants to see Pamodzi 'bulk up' even more. 'Your Bill Gates are dominant in this world; your Anglo Americans are dominant because they're big,' he argues. Ntsele's vision to go big is to create what he calls a 'sustainable business' based on his philosophy that unity is power.

> If you look at the whole continent, we're working as individuals, not forming corporations that are sustainable. With Pamodzi, the difference is that it must be a sustainable business run by suntanned people like me.

When he is not thinking up ways of making more money and growing his investment group, he is playing games with one of his three daughters, sometimes gaining insight into himself:

> When we're playing games they get cross when they're losing. With my second daughter, she wants to go to sleep having won the game ... she would like to win four games and then she wants me to go and sleep. I discovered that I'm also like that, when I've lost too much, I want a comeback.

Ntsele has had a few comebacks in his career and that makes him that much more of an entrepreneur. In November 2007 he was the South African winner of the annual Ernst & Young World Entrepreneur Award. At the time he was quoted as saying: 'The greatest honour which can come to an entrepreneur is to be recognised by your own peers in your lifetime.' In May 2008, along with the 40 country winners of the previous year's competition, Ntsele was inducted into the World Entrepreneur of the Year Academy. Now, that's some achievement for a boy from Soweto.

Sources:

1. Anderson, B (2007). 'Groundbreaker' in *FinWeek*, 6 August. Article available online at: http://www.fin24.com/articles/default/display_article. aspx?Nav=ns&ArticleID=1518-2125-2126_2159652.
2. Bain, J (2007). 'Pamodzi unearths resources fund', *Business Times*, 5 August. Available online at: http://www.thetimes.co.za/business/businesstimes/ Default.aspx?id=375861.
3. *Financial Mail* (2007). *The Little Black Book 2006/07*. Johannesburg: BDFM Publishers.
4. 'World Entrepreneur Awards 2007 South Africa', 15 November 2007. Online article available at: http://www.ey.com/GLOBAL/content.nsf/ International/Strategic_Growth_Markets_-_Entrepreneur_Of_The_Year_- _National_Winner_-_South_Africa.

Keith Kunene – The Family Entrepreneur

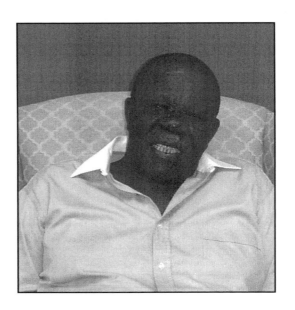

VITAL STATISTICS

Name: Keith Kunene
Country: South Africa
Born: 23 February 1942
Position/Title: CEO Kunene Brothers Holdings
Nationality: South African
Industry: Coca-Cola bottling and diversified investment holdings
Highest education qualification: BProc, University of Zululand

I think, back then, one just accepted apartheid. In hindsight, certain things that were happening made me very angry; very angry. To give you an example, we lived on a street that bordered what they used to call 'single quarters'. These units were built to accommodate four families in one room with four doors. People tried to make the best of it. There were three rows of these quarters and then there was an opening and another three rows. In the middle were the communal toilets and taps. So if you wanted to go to the toilet and you were a male, you had to walk down all that way, and when you got inside the toilets it was one long cement block with seats carved into the cement – nothing for privacy. It could have been my father, my uncle; there was no privacy.

One went on happily with life and school. It is only now that one sits and thinks and I get very angry. It was very inhuman but we never saw anything wrong with it; this was how the black man was supposed to live.

Keith Kunene never set out to live how 'the black man was supposed to live' in South Africa. If he had, he would never have gone to university; he would never have qualified as an attorney of the supreme court of South Africa. He would certainly never have set up what would become the longest existing black law partnership in South Africa, he would never have started a business that grew into the largest Coca-Cola distributor in South Africa, and finally, he would never have created – along with his four brothers – a multimillion-rand investment company with interests in bottling, distribution, financial services, telecoms, business consulting and the motor industry.

Dudu, Zanosi, Zoli and Menzi are the brothers without whom Keith Kunene's story could not be told. From very early on in their lives, the five brothers worked closely together as a team, and eventually built what is today a highly successful diversified investment holding company – in which they are all equal partners. Keith Kunene modestly describes the family-run group as a 'small business', which each brother contributes equally to running. 'There is a great amount of trust between the brothers; we never have to look over our shoulders,' he says. But it isn't just the trust factor that has led to the success of the brothers' business. There was a natural pecking order and respect in the relationship between them which also contributed greatly to the sustainability of the business that exists today. Kunene explains: 'I was the natural leader and if I was to drop dead, the next eldest brother would naturally take over.' Although he is nowhere close to dropping dead just yet, Kunene, now 66, is officially retired from the business and Dudu, the second eldest, is at the helm of the family investment group, Kunene Brothers Holdings (KBH). Clearly their way of running a business is working because KBH has been described by a leading financial magazine as a 'substantial business empire' and the brothers have been credited with being 'pioneers of black empowerment' in South Africa.

KBH is seen as 'different' from many of the other black-owned investment groups that proliferate in the country. According to BusinessMap, an empowerment research and consulting firm, what adds more credibility to the KBH story is the fact that the brothers 'have been in business a long time and have managed to build up their own capital, unlike some newcomers to the empowerment scene'. But Kunene puts his success down to the brothers' business skills. And categorically dismisses any suggestion that KBH is just another black-owned company that sprung up overnight following the introduction of the South African government's black economic empowerment (BEE) policies. 'We haven't grown on the back of BEE,' he says emphatically. 'We are business people who happen to be black, but first and foremost we are business people.' In fact, KBH is an atypical BEE company – it is largely low key and remains behind the scenes quietly, growing its business and bringing real value to its deals.

> We have avoided making business dependant on politics and we have seen when the guard changes your business changes. You don't depend on the politicians. Whoever is in government we will support but you know, we never go to business and say, 'I have got a line to President Mbeki.' No, we have never done that.

Kunene Brothers Holdings resides in offices in the upmarket business suburb of Sandton in Johannesburg. The holding company comprises 20 people who, between them, oversee the group's strategic investments in bottling, distribution, financial services, telecoms, business consulting and the motor industry. As a family-owned and -operated business, Kunene is understandably reluctant to put a value to the entire group. Since 1994 and the inception of KBH, which houses all of the five brothers' investments, the group has conducted more than 26 financial transactions, acquiring interests in a number of businesses, two of which are listed entities on the Johannesburg Stock Exchange. The brother who started it all and the visionary behind the brothers' success is Keith Kunene. An entrepreneur and a businessman through and through, he continues to participate in KBH's investment activities despite his so-called official 'semi-retirement'. 'I remain involved in the issues of strategy, which is what I enjoy. I influence the decision of which businesses to get involved in,' he explains. Kunene is also an intellectual at heart who studied law and even understands Latin. Over a 20-year period, he simultaneously created and ran two businesses full time: a Coca-Cola wholesale and distribution company, which started off the KBH empire, and a three-partner legal practice called Kunene Inc.

Kunene the young entrepreneur

From an early age, Kunene displayed one of the typical characteristics of a true entrepreneur – a healthy interest in money.

> When I stayed with my grandfather we had chickens and cattle. My grandfather sold eggs and I would walk with him and deliver them to white families and collect the money – that excited me.

It was but a small step to his own moneymaking venture at the age of 12:

> We lived next to a mine operation with a dump, and somebody used to dump offcuts of rubber strips with which they had made doormats. I would pick them up and take them home and I would make my own doormats. Visitors who came to our home would see them and say, 'make me one', and they would give me R2 or R3 and so on.

Once he had started making money, his grandfather taught him perhaps one of the most important lessons Kunene would learn about money.

> There was a little savings box in which I had to put the money – my grandfather taught me that. I never went to a shop when I was young

to buy sweets, never ever. Even if someone gave me money I was supposed to take the money to my grandfather and show him, and he would order me to put it in the savings box. I was told that you can't just get two or five cents and run to the shop to buy sweets.

Being the first son and the first grandchild in a Zulu family, it was tradition that Kunene be brought up by his grandparents, who lived in Boksburg, east of Johannesburg, where he admits he was 'pampered and spoiled'.

I grew up in a family were we could afford a pair of shoes and meals every day. One would never say we struggled, because we weren't rich but we weren't poor. We lived comfortably in the circumstances.

He remembers his childhood as a happy time, one where his grandparents and parents, particularly his father, Fortune Kunene, provided a stable and nurturing environment for him and his four brothers.

My father taught me one thing: if any one of his children fought, he would never make a judgement in the presence of both of them. For example, he would call the younger one and say: 'He is your elder brother, you must respect him. Don't do that.' Then he would call the other one and say: 'He is your younger brother. If you behave like that he won't respect you.' I found that it worked.

His parents, who were both teachers, understood the importance of education and Kunene was sent to a tough Catholic boarding school in Vryheid in KwaZulu-Natal, which soon beat him into shape, literally.

It was very harsh conditions. For example, there was no warm water. Typical Catholics, they made us go to church three, four, five times a week! You had to wake up at 5:30am, go to church at 6am and then go to breakfast at a certain time. In the month of October we went to church every afternoon. After supper we had half an hour then we had to go to study. But it was fine and I came out well. I must say that I think it instilled discipline in me.

Kunene was very bright and like most bright children he thrived in an academic environment that encouraged excellence: 'I really enjoyed school. I enjoyed being with my equals,' he says. Although he excelled at most subjects, numbers were just not his game, and he failed miserably at maths and science, which was a great pity because his father wanted him to be a doctor. He certainly was not adverse to the idea, but he rebelled against the only way into the profession for a young black man in South Africa.

> I sort of resented going to the so-called 'bush colleges': Fort Hare, University of Zululand. They were apartheid creations. Zulus had to go to Zululand and Xhosa people to Fort Hare and so on. So I went and looked for a job and I worked as a clerk.

Kunene put any ideas of further education on the backburner for a while and joined the work force. But he was totally uninspired by his first job, which was in a hospital, dealing with admissions. He had little good to say about his experiences there.

> There were no challenges; you were sitting there taking people's details all the time. What's your name? Where do you stay? Where do you work? How much do you earn? Okay. Right. Finish. Next one. I spent the whole day doing that – I learnt nothing absolutely nothing.

The unchallenging environment in which he found himself gave Kunene time to plot and manoeuvre his way into the life of a young, rather attractive nurse who worked at the same hospital. It turned out to be the only good thing that came of the six years he spent there, because he eventually ended up marrying her and living, as the fairy-tale ending goes, 'happily ever after'. Unfortunately the same couldn't be said for his position as an admissions clerk, and soon that came to an end. 'The idea of being a doctor had been so ingrained in me that I didn't think of anything other than being a doctor.'

He eventually got his act together and applied to study medicine at the very same 'bush college' he had initially refused to attend, the University of Zululand, in what is now known as KwaZulu-Natal. His poor maths results meant that he did not secure a place in the medical school, so he compromised and applied for the next best thing.

> In my first week or two I registered for a Bachelor of Science with

zoology and biology. That's when I came into contact with people who were studying law. I wrote a letter to my dad and I said, 'Look, I don't think this is thing is going to work. I want to be an attorney.' He said, 'Go ahead.'

So he did.

I knew about being a lawyer and what it was, and of course, those days, what one thought lawyers did was to go and represent people who had become involved with the law. One never grasped that there were contracts to be drawn up and a whole lot of other things other than being a criminal lawyer.

It was one of the best decisions he ever made, because it turned out that he loved the law and was actually rather good at being a lawyer. 'It was the best thing that happened to me. I did very well, and I ended up running a very successful law practice,' he explains. It wasn't just the law he loved, he also loved the language of the law – Latin – it appealed to the intellectual in him. And while there may not be too many people with whom he can converse, he still sees the benefits of having slogged through the classes.

There were only two of us that sat for the final exams of that year. Latin helped my English; it boosts your English grammar, so I found English easy. I could analyse a sentence. You ask a lot of people about verbs and adverbs, they don't know.

While at university studying for a full-time law degree, Kunene married his hospital sweetheart and she had the first of their three children while he looked for somewhere to do his articles in apartheid South Africa.

There were only five or six black firms back then. To get one's articles was very difficult and I was just lucky that somebody recommended me to this white firm and they took me on.

And that could have been the beginning of the story of the successful lawyer who ended up starting and running the longest existing black law partnership in South Africa – but there's more to the story. Although it was clear that he had a good solid profession as a lawyer ahead of him, it was not enough for Kunene – he desperately wanted to be a businessman. During the second year of his articles, he spotted an opportunity and made his move.

The Coca-Cola business

I always wanted to run a business. I wanted to run a business outside of the law because I wanted a good living.

The opportunity to make a good living came in the shape of a dairy retail outlet near where he lived which sold mainly fresh milk to locals in the area.

It was by coincidence. Somebody who knew me and knew I was in a law firm had a sister who I was told had a little problem. I said I would sort it out for her. The sister was a widow and her husband had died not too long before. She had no children and they had this milk depot. I had been watching it change hands for some time – almost every two months. So I said to her, 'Next time you have a vacancy, just offer it to me.' And it was hardly a week when she called me and said, 'Here are the keys, you go and run the place.' That was, to me, a big exciting challenge.

It was also the start of the Kunenes' family business. The fact that the milk depot was a small business made it even more appealing to Kunene; he saw an opportunity to build something up from the very beginning.

I knew I would love to grow it and it was also the only one in the area that sold milk and its other dairy products – there was no competition.

Kunene was shrewd enough to see the opportunity that lay in this dairy retailing business, an opportunity that various managers before him had failed to realise. It didn't take long for him to put in an offer.

I leased the business. I paid her a monthly amount. I would receive the stock and I had to sell it by the evening because it was dairy produce. Initially it was a big struggle, because there was no profit. In fact, there was actually almost no profit other than the products that we consumed at home. At the end of the month there would be R500 or R300 left over and I would use that to increase my stock.

Kunene's father, Fortune, was the first in the family to join the business. The retired school teacher ran the milk depot while Kunene continued with his articles at the law firm in Johannesburg. Apart from the fact that the income from the milk depot was not enough to sustain him, it simply never crossed his mind to leave his law articles behind. That was not part of the plan. Kunene was determined to be a lawyer and a successful businessman. Over the next 17 years he topped and tailed his legal day first with the dairy business and then with the KBH investment business.

> I went to the dairy in the evenings to cash up and close, and I would wake up in the morning, go there and open up, give them change, receive the stock and go to the office.

The rest of the day would be spent in the legal world doing battle with the unjust apartheid legal system. Kunene had big plans for that world too. In the meantime, however, he had a business to oversee. The dairy business was tough, but Kunene and his father persisted and their hard work and foresight eventually paid off. Things started to turn around when Kunene introduced a popular brown, sweet liquid to their product range. 'I managed to sneak in Coca-Cola,' explains Kunene. And with that, the business suddenly took off.

The next thing he did was change his client base – he stopped retailing and started wholesaling to other retailers. His silver bullet was a big old refrigerated storage facility, which gave him the space to store large quantities of cold Coke. Kunene knew he had a monopoly because he had identified the real operational issues that the small shops had with other wholesalers, and he cleverly managed to address them both by doing two very simple things. He opened up his wholesaling operation for more hours and for more days than his competition. The effect had a direct impact on the working capital of the retailers he served, and thus on the amount of business that came his way.

> The spaza shops had two problems: one, there was no storage, and secondly, the owner had no capital. I had established that the Coke

bottles cost a lot and they could not afford to have their capital tied up for too long. So I operated seven days a week. A spaza shop owner would come in on Friday and buy three or five cases. By midday on Saturday they'd be gone, so he comes back and buys more with the revenue he has made, and by sunset on Saturday that is also gone and so on. So over a weekend I would sell 15 cases to this person who could never afford to buy 15 cases upfront. He pays me cash, I am happy.

Almost by default, Kunene became the preferred wholesaler.

I started getting spaza shops saying: 'I need to buy from you in bulk so you give me a discount.' So by giving him a little discount, he could make a bigger profit. I relied on bulk sales, so we both won. I had a big turnover.

The move from dairy retailing to Coca-Cola wholesaling was the catalyst that caused the business to take off.

The law business

Despite the growing success of the Coke wholesaling business, Kunene did not miss a beat with his professional career as a lawyer. He had continued with his articles and in 1976 he was admitted as an attorney to the South African Bar. Rather than try to secure employment in a predictably white-owned legal practice, he decided to add his proven entrepreneurial flair to his profession and started his own law firm.

The first partnership I started was in 1976 and ended in 1980. It was very short because there were a lot of hitches, not from me, but from the law. For example: the owner of the building didn't want me to use the toilet – I had to go down to the second floor. I had not been party to the lease and when they went to the bank to ask for an overdraft, they had to put me in the cupboard – not literally, but I could not be a party to the overdraft.

Frustrated, he left that particular partnership and soon after started another one with two new partners. Kunene Inc opened its doors for business in 1981.

The partnership was unique in South Africa, especially in those times, in that it consisted of an Afrikaans gentleman, a Jewish gentleman and me. I practised in this partnership for 17 years and it became the longest existing black law partnership in South Africa.

For the next 17 years Kunene continued to go to work every day as a lawyer, while he ran a growing business on the side with the help of his father and his brothers.

The start of Kunene Brothers

It wasn't just Coca-Cola the Kunene brothers were selling. They had come across an opportunity to take over a liquor retail outlet that was previously owned by the government. They submitted their tender, won it, and became alcohol retailers. One of the brothers stepped in and started running this arm of the business. They decided to buy more liquor stores; with the aim to have his three younger brothers, Zanosi, Zoli and Menzi, managing a store each. But they needed to raise money, so they approached the bank. Unsurprisingly, Kunene faced what most black entrepreneurs in South Africa faced at the time: an unhelpful bank that demanded assets from people whom they knew were not allowed, by law, to own any.

We said we wanted R150 000. The bank manager looked at us as though we were a bunch of clowns. It was not easy. I remember I got angry with him because he said: 'What collateral have you got?' I said: 'Do you want me to bring my children and my wife into the bank?' In the end we got some money, because ironically, they (the same bank) then opened up a branch in Soweto led by a black guy who actually gave it to us.

With the overdraft, Kunene and his brothers, who had all joined the business full time in 1981, purchased their second bottle store. Soon after, they bought a third bottle store, which they were able to purchase for cash from the profits of the business. Shortly after that, they bought a fourth bottle store, again for cash.

By now we were running a big business. We had four separate bottle stores and we had just opened the second Coca-Cola wholesale – so one brother was running each store.

Their first Coca-Cola wholesale operation, which had started life as a milk depot, had now spawned a second outlet, and then a third. The brothers owned four liquor shops and three Coke wholesale operations, which were all doing rather well. Between 1983 and 1987 the Kunene brothers were the largest independent wholesale distributors of Coca-Cola in South Africa. By 1991, as a result of consistently high sales volumes, they were appointed official distributors of Coke products in the East Rand region of Gauteng and in their first year, they sold well over half a million cases of Coca-Cola. It was at this time that the brothers started thinking about becoming more than just distributors; they wanted to be bottlers. The main source of their revenue was coming from their Coca-Cola wholesale business and they wanted a bigger slice of the very sweet cake.

Coca-Cola was one of the many multinational companies that officially pulled out of South Africa in support of the anti-apartheid movement in 1986. It was to return in 1994, when Mandela's new democratic government officially marked the end of apartheid. In the meantime, Coca-Cola was looking to 'dispose of' its assets in the country. The Coca-Cola empire, one of the oldest and most successful corporations in the world, was built on a global network of more than 300 bottlers worldwide. Bottling franchises, like the one Kunene was after, are given out by region and each bottler is responsible for the entire chain – the manufacturing plant, the distribution and the sales – all with Coca-Cola's full marketing support. The brothers had big plans to involve themselves higher up the food chain in the Coca-Cola empire. In order to pursue their vision to become official distributors and bottlers, Kunene and his brothers went to London to negotiate with Coca-Cola. They were offering to buy a 51% stake, valued at R25 million, of an existing bottling operation that Coca-Cola owned in the province of Mpumalanga.

The negotiations went very well and to this day Kunene will describe it as the high point of his career. The bulk of the R25 million needed for the deal came from Coca-Cola itself and with various bank loans the brothers secured. Their track record in wholesaling Coke products over the years, coupled with Coke's desire to partner with black-owned businesses post apartheid, made the Kunene brothers' bid an attractive package to both the banks and to Coca-Cola. They were now in the bottling business

– where the real money was.

Throughout the negotiations with Coke, Kunene, surprisingly, still maintained his law practice and continued to work there full time. Although he loved the law and the intellectual stimulation it provided, the business of running a law practice was proving difficult to sustain. His Coca-Cola business was doing well, however, he was heavily invested in it along with his brothers and had no spare cash for the law practice. Kunene and his two partners had hit a brick wall.

> The three of us worked very hard and it grew, but at a certain point I knew it needed a cash injection. We had a lot of restraints and the business got stuck, and other than insurance policies, I didn't have any collateral to offer the bank. The situation was lopsided because my partners relied solely on the practice but I had a business on the side.

And this business on the side accounted for more than 60% of his personal income! For some time, Kunene had been splitting his time between the practice, his business and a fair number of other interests.

> I was involved in a whole lot of things. I was chairman of the Black Lawyers' Association, I was holding a couple of board positions and it was very hectic.

Kunene had become the chairman of the Black Lawyers' Association (BLA) in 1985. The lobby group was formed in 1977, not to 'effect change in the South African political community', but to 'ensure the dignity of all lawyers, irrespective of race or colour'. It was an important, high-profile role. When Kunene took over, of the 6 000 attorneys in South Africa, only 600 of them were black. Kunene, as head of the BLA, was tasked with increasing numbers and improving the conditions for black lawyers. One of his key responsibilities was to take the regional operation into a national one and he travelled extensively in this capacity. His business acumen was increasingly being recognised, and he accumulated a number of non-executive board directorships. Throughout his career, his directorships have included Aveng, Southern Bank of Africa, National Employment Trust and the National Exhibition

Centre. But it was the Coke business that proved to be the making of Kunene and his brothers.

The Coca-Cola deal was the first of many acquisitions the brothers would make. It was 1994 and the new South Africa was the place to be for black businessmen. There was certainly money floating around and the brothers realised that the way to get to it was by creating an investment holding company that could capitalise on the many empowerment opportunities in South Africa. Along with their partner, Graham Royston, the brothers registered the company Kunene Brothers Holdings (KBH) in August 1994. Although he was still running his law practice full time, Keith Kunene, as the eldest, became CEO of KBH. The new entity consolidated the various businesses the brothers had been operating independently, into one, along with the jewel in their crown, the 51% shareholding in the Coca-Cola bottling company. The bullish business climate in South Africa at the time meant there were plenty of empowerment deals to be made and the Kunenes, given their track record as successful businessmen, where well poised to capitalise on them.

Their first investment outside of the Coke deal in August 1995 was driven by Zoli Kunene and was the purchase of an initial 10% stake in Grintek Electronics, one of South Africa's leading electronics companies. It was here that the brothers established their 'active ownership' philosophy, which saw them actively participating in the operations and strategic development of the businesses they bought into. With Grintek Electronics, Kunene and Zoli provided management and other services, as well as being appointed to its board. Three years later, as a testament to the value the brothers were adding to the business, Zoli was appointed chairman of the company.

In 1997, the brothers created a private equity firm called Kunene Finance Company (KFC), which was set up to raise short- and medium-term money to fund their investment activities. In acknowledgement of the brothers' business acumen, four major South African institutional investors, including Old Mutual and Sanlam, took a stake in the company. Their investment strategy, driven by Kunene, was to 'spread risk' and take the focus away from their Coca-Cola assets.

> The idea was to secure our business as things can and do go wrong. For example, we know that when the weather is cold, Coke sales will drop, but when it's hot, you wake up and clap your hands.

So from Coke and electronics the brothers diversified into the motor business by purchasing a 30% interest in McCarthy Motor Holdings, a successful Mercedes dealership in Mpumalanga. By 1998, a year after Kunene was voted one of South Africa's 50 most influential black people by *Ebony* magazine, he was totally immersed in the Kunene brothers' financial dealings and finally, sadly, gave up on his 17-year-old law practice. The legal practice had stagnated because it needed money and it needed fresh new blood. Kunene, at one stage, had hoped his daughter who had studied law and practised for three years elsewhere, would ultimately take it over, but she was not interested

> I stopped the law practice because I got too involved in business. Things had changed. It was a difficult time in my career because I had no money to put into the practice. I couldn't survive as a law firm so I sold it. Today you can't survive by being a small firm, you have to join larger firms. Since I qualified as an attorney I had never worked for anybody, so it would have been difficult for me to work for a large firm and be told when I must come to work.

The closing of his firm meant Kunene could, for the first time, focus his time entirely on KBH. And in 1998, he finally joined the company he started, as a full-time director. In the meantime, KBH had been extremely active and was churning out all manner of financial deals. They were involved in more acquisitions in different sectors, some listings and delistings, four rounds of capital fundraising activities, a share buyback and yet more purchases of Coca-Cola assets. In 2000, the brothers moved into the financial services arena, acquiring a 10% interest in the financial services group Glenrand MIB. Three years later, they added another motor dealership to their existing McCarthy Mercedes investment, Ford and Mazda. Their most recent acquisitions are a 25% stake in a telecoms company, Connecting Africa, the largest satellite installation company in South Africa and a stake in a business consulting firm called Ovation Technologies.

But Coca-Cola continued to be a major focus for the business. KBH had acquired a small stake in a listed bottling company, Kilimanjaro, which ran the East London bottling franchise. They were now involved in bottling operations in two regions and Kunene's aim was to become the largest black bottler of Coca-Cola on the continent. The brothers increased their share in CCBM (Coca-Cola Bottling Mpumalanga), they bought even further into Kilimanjaro, on whose board sat Richard Maponya, another black entrepreneur, and they eventually took over its management. KBH merged with another Coke bottler, Coca-Cola Sabco, to create Coca-Cola Fortune, which became the second-largest Coca-Cola bottler in South Africa. Today KBH controls 75% of the soft drink giant's geographic bottling area in South Africa. No mean feat for five brothers who started off selling Cokes from a milk retail outlet in their township. Kunene credits and acknowledges his brothers for their role in the birth and growth of what became KBH. It is clear that without their involvement, the group would not exist today.

> As I look back, I know that it was the hard work and entrepreneurial spirit of the Kunene family that led to the success of the enterprise. My brothers worked very hard. I was not very operational; I was involved in strategy and I loved my law practice. I also know, however, that our partnership with the Coca-Cola Company has been a critical factor in our success.

Today, all the brothers hold directorships and chairmanships across their various investments. The next in line to Kunene, Dudu, at 60, is the executive director of Glenrand MIB and chairman of KBH. His younger brother, 57-year-old Zanosi, is the executive chairman of Coca-Cola Fortune. Zoli, at 55, is the CEO of KBH and the chairman of Grintek. And the youngest of the five, Menzi, is responsible for the group's motor interests and is the executive chairman of Action Ford.

Winding down

Kunene, now claiming semi-retirement, is focusing on spending even more time with his family and improving his current golf handicap of 22. But his retirement doesn't look like it's going to happen any time soon.

> I love business and any other situations where I initiate something on my own and see it become a success. I am starting a new business; trying to build a consultancy, just for the kick of it. I want to sit and tell people what to do.

With one eye on the future of the business, his three children who are all 'very well educated professionals' are being groomed to carry on the legacy started by Keith and his father, Fortune.

> They are all graduates and they are all doing well. I have no fears. In their own right they will survive over and above their inheritance. I have given them the tools of life.

The five brothers between them have 19 children, 14 of whom are at university or have graduated. While Kunene is clear that he is not offering sheltered employment to the next generation of Kunenes, he is clearly expecting them to take up their positions within the group.

> The idea is that they must know that when they come here, they will add value. They must not think they can go and work in the family business. They must know what it is like to get up in the morning and work for someone because then they are responsible.

Like every entrepreneur before him, his biggest challenge in business has been about money.

> We didn't sit back and cry and say we have no money – we just kept on trying. To me that is the challenge. You have to take risks. I remember I had given up each and every insurance policy I owned as security. If I had dropped dead, then my wife would have had nothing. Not reckless, but take risks, that is business. There is the possibility of failure and that you must guard against.

Kunene considers himself a natural leader who has always been 'very assertive in life'. He honed his leadership skills over the years with a collection of chairmanships, which include the National Soccer League, Mpumalanga Gaming Board, the Central Energy Fund (from which he controversially resigned), and the Council of the University of Zululand. Through them he has evolved a collective approach to decision making.

In his downtime, he finds time to read books about the successes of other individuals. He is particularly inspired by Warren Buffet and the South Africa mining family, the Oppenheimers. But his most favourite pastime is foreign travel. It's a hobby that feeds his inquisitive mind:

I would like to visit all corners of the world. I like knowing places. I was in Red Square and it gave me goose bumps. In 1980 I went to the US for the first time. I met Red Indians. I've met Aborigines.

But perhaps what excites Kunene most of all is the sense of his own achievement:

When I sit and look back, I think all what my parents left me was a piece of paper – a certificate – and all I have is my own effort, and that excites me.

Sources:

1. Kunene Brothers Holdings official website, available at www.kunene. com.
2. 'The Economic Impact of Coca-Cola on South Africa', University of South Carolina: Moore School of Business. Article available online at: http://www. uscdmc.sc.edu/moore/research/presentstudy/Coca-Cola/SoAfrica/chapt5. html#top.

Geoffrey Mwamba – The Material Entrepreneur

VITAL STATISTICS

Name: Geoffrey Mwamba
Country: Zambia
Born: 15 March 1959
Position/Title: Executive chairman of GBM Group
Total Assets: Undisclosed
Nationality: Zambian
Industry: Food and transport
Highest education qualification: O levels

Business is about money and I enjoy making money but it's never enough. The moment you think you have enough is the moment you are gone. Let me tell you what money is for: money is about generating more money – every single day. Then when you have the money, it is about financial discipline. There was an Asian friend of mine who told me that most Asians are successful, not because they are clever or they were born with a talent, simply because they have financial discipline. I have noticed that most of my friends, when they get excited, they want to buy things that they have dreamed about without realising that tomorrow if they do not generate more money, they will not be able to buy these things. Whatever I make today, it ends here – it is for today. Tomorrow I must generate more money and if I don't, I'll be mad with myself. That's what keeps me going, that is my strength.

These are the words of Zambian millionaire, money man and entrepreneur Geoffrey Mwamba, talking about his favourite pastime – making money. GBM, as he is more popularly known, is a larger-than-life character whom everyone in Zambia seems to know. In his 25 years in business, Mwamba has been in and out of several sectors in the pursuit of money. He currently owns and runs Zambia's second-largest maize mill, a transport company which has a fleet of 28 luxury buses, a brewery that specialises in traditional beer, and a trading company that supplies basic foodstuffs. In between all of that, Mwamba dabbles in the money markets business, occasionally trading foreign exchange while looking for the next opportunity. 'Where we can make money, we go for it,' he explains. He chose the milling business for exactly that reason. 'Milling is lucrative in the sense that it is the staple food in this country; we all eat pap.' He's in the transport business because 'it's a cash business. People travel every day. People come to you so you don't have to follow them around.' And he trades foreign exchange simply because he 'can take advantage of the situation, when the dollar falls, you buy the dollar in abundance'. Taking advantage of situations for profit is something that Mwamba has been doing successfully, ever since he launched himself into the world of business at the age of 22, with start-up capital of US$1 000, which he got from his mother.

Mwamba began trading foodstuffs: rice, beans and Kapenta – a type of sardine – mainly to the government, which was buying food to feed prisoners and police officers. The government was the only sector that could afford to buy so they became his only customers.

It was the early 80s, during the time of Kenneth Kaunda, Zambia's first president, who had been in power since the country broke away from Rhodesia in 1964. Zambia was going through tough times and the country was being crippled by shortages, but like many post-independence failure stories, there was always a good reason.

In the 70s, the price of copper and other commodities worldwide dropped dramatically. The Zambian economy, which was almost solely dependent on copper, started to decline as a result. Initially Kaunda turned to international lenders for relief, but as copper prices continued their downward spiral, it became increasingly difficult to service its growing debt. Kaunda decided to withdraw Zambia from the International Monetary Fund and World Bank programmes with the intention that the country could effectively stand on its own feet without donor support. The result was that Zambia experienced crippling shortages across the board – from fuel to soft drinks. But in scarcity there is opportunity and as the old saying goes, 'A chicken doesn't stop scratching just because worms are scarce'. Mwamba took full advantage of the situation in Zambia and slowly built up a business that thrived because of rather than in spite of the situation in Zambia. He had different things to worry about.

> My biggest challenge was to get paid by the government. Once I got the money I knew that selling or securing an order would not be a problem. At the time we had so many shortages, so whatever one had, it would sell. What was important at that time was to secure the order and secure the goods. I had both.

It didn't take long for Mwamba to understand the system and make sure he got his money out on time. And in the process he got himself noticed.

> I became so popular within the circles of the paying officers and it became automatic that each time there was an allocation of funds to be paid to suppliers, my name was always included.

He soon became one of the country's largest suppliers of foodstuffs to the government.

> At that time the margins were very high; I was making about 60% profit. It took about three months for me to be paid my money but as

soon as I was paid, I reinvested the entire amount into buying the same commodities, secured myself another order and supplied again.

For a young businessman with no formal education, Mwamba was not doing badly at all. He had figured out the most important thing about business at a very early stage: 'My late father taught me to differentiate between profit and working capital,' he explains. Once he had learnt that, the rest was a piece of cake.

The learning years

Mwamba had picked up his business know-how when he was a young boy working for his father in the family-owned bakery. As the only bakery in the area, it was a very lucrative business. His father, a strict disciplinarian, took the young Mwamba under his wing.

> I started working from the age of 12. Each day I came back from school my father always wanted me to be close to him in the running of the family business. He didn't allow me to see a lot of friends. He allowed me to go to church on Sunday to see friends then. But from Monday to Saturday, I joined him in the business; my father wanted me to be part and parcel of everything.

His father was undoubtedly a major influence on the young man and Mwamba never once questioned his father's authority. In fact, he was proud of his father's achievements:

> The day I was born, 15 March 1959, was the day that my late father became the first African minister of agriculture. It was just before we got independence. That's the time when the colonialists were integrating those Africans who would be influential (into the government).

His father was one of them but his influence extended beyond the government; he was also a member of the royal family. When Mwamba turned 19, his father was made a chief and could no longer oversee the day-to-day functions of the family bakery. He left his son in charge. Mwamba was the seventh of 10 siblings and seemed to be the only one of his brothers who was interested in the business.

Most of my elder brothers tried to work with my dad but unfortunately they didn't enjoy it and they didn't stay long. They decided to go and get employment somewhere else. My father saw potential in me, and I think being involved so young made me enjoy the business.

He started at the very bottom and worked his way up to manager:

I started as a sweeper. In the bakery industry if you become a professional baker you have to start sweeping because you have to be clean in whatever you are doing. So I started sweeping. I moved on to being a moulder, then from a moulder to mixer, from a mixer until I rose to the rank of manager.

Mwamba's family lived in the northern part of Zambia, in an area called Kasama. They moved to Lusaka, Zambia's capital, when his father started working for the government. When his father retired, the family moved back to Kasama when Mwamba was just eight years old. Two years later, his parents divorced. Mwamba stayed behind in Kasama with his father.

My father coming from a royal background wanted to marry a second wife, which my mother thought was slightly odd because she was not used to that kind of life, so she decided to divorce my dad.

Despite this, Mwamba remembers a happy childhood, 'I have never had a hard life,' he says. 'It was fun.' He enjoyed school tremendously:

I was very good at maths; I was always above average in my class, and that is something which has helped me be where I am today. I very rarely use a calculator.

Despite this success, Mwamba stayed on at school only until he had to and jumped at his first chance to leave.

I did my O levels and that was all. My interest was in business and I honestly thought that I would do better in that than going on to further my studies.

His father supported him in his decision to leave school but wanted

Mwamba to explore his options solely within the family business. Although he wanted to explore other types of businesses outside the bakery, his father wouldn't allow it. But Mwamba was patient and level-headed and made a decision to learn as much as he could from his father. But this placid attitude didn't last long. Managing the business on his own when his father left made the ambitious Mwamba realise that he was, unwittingly, being held back by his father.

> I had brilliant ideas but he (my father) didn't take them on board. Elderly people, when they have a business, they are very particular about what they do and how they run it. They don't want to start taking on new ideas because that would mean fresh problems. My father, at his age, was quite content with what he had, but I wasn't.

Mwamba took matters into his own hands: 'I finally decided to leave the business because there were so many family members who wanted to join at that stage.' Fed up with battling with his family, Mwamba decided to try his luck elsewhere. It was a decision that started him on his path to success and money.

The making of an entrepreneur

> I had a dream and I had a vision to become a successful businessman. So after I left the family business, I decided to run my own business in Lusaka; I had free will to do what I wanted.

Mwamba may not have been sure of what he wanted to do initially, but he did know that he did not want to work for anybody else. In fact, the thought never crossed his mind.

> I wasn't interested in being an employee, that I can tell you, because I knew I would do better in business. I saw the potential in myself. I thought it was a waste of time to work for someone else. Apart from my father, I had never worked for anyone and I had no intention of doing so.

Before he left Kasama, Mwamba married his sweetheart, Chama, who was 21. He was planning to leave Kasama for Lusaka to pursue his dreams. With no money and nowhere to live, he had no choice but to leave his young wife behind. 'I was running a family business and nobody would allow me to take any money out of that business. I didn't have any money,' he explains. He quietly moved in with his mother who ran a small shop in Lusaka, and after about a month, she eventually asked him about his plans.

> She asked me why I was there. I explained to her that I couldn't continue to run the family business because there was too much interference from the family members. She wanted to know what I was going to do next. I asked her if she had any spare money so that I could start a small business. She told me that I should give her some time and she would think about it and come back to me the following week. So the following week, one evening she called me in and told me that she had some spare money – about US$1 000 in her account – it was her life savings. She said I could have it as long as I put it to good use. She blessed me and the following day she gave me the money. That is how I started running a small business.

With a 'no strings attached' gift from his mother, Mwamba went straight off to buy 50 bags of rice from National Milling. He had found out about the food trading business through some friends, and he realised that there was money – lots of it – to be made.

> I chose rice because it was profitable. During the few months I had been in Lusaka, I had contacted a few friends in government who actually showed interest in buying rice from me, so I started supplying government departments.

Six months into his business, Mwamba's wife, Chama, came to join him in Lusaka and from day one she was hands-on in the business.

> There are situations when we started our business when it was very tough. We would buy things like Kapenta, maybe three or four bags, to sell at the market. We look at what has happened to us today and we laugh at that. We know where we come from.

Over the next 10 years Mwamba continued to trade and eventually built himself a reputation and a pile of money. He began to diversify into other businesses in pursuit of more money. In 1990 he registered a company called GBM Trucking, which started distributing Mosi beer – the country's most popular locally brewed beer – along with sugar, maize and assorted groceries to major market outlets. He was still trading foodstuffs with the government, but was beginning to get tired of the increasingly long periods between the delivery of the goods and the payment from the government. 'I decided to go into a cash business where I could control my own cash flow, where I didn't have to wait for a cheque from anyone,' he explains. He chose the transport business. The primary form of public transportation in Zambia was then, and still is, minibuses, which the vast majority of commuters use to travel to and from work. Mwamba saw an opportunity to make money in the largely self-regulated sector. He bought himself 10 minibuses and in 1991 started a small public transport business which ploughed Lusaka's streets carrying passengers around the city. Unfortunately it didn't last long and he eventually left the business for good reasons: 'There was too much killing of the drivers. I decided to do away with it as it had become unprofitable.' But it wasn't clear which of the two reasons provided the more compelling urge to leave!

Mwamba then got involved in several other businesses, including a car hire company and a traditional beer brewing operation. In 1995, he registered a company called GBM Wholesale & Distributors, through which he imported various goods into Zambia. Although he seemed to change businesses fairly frequently, and he was undoubtedly making lots of money, it took the advice of a friend for Mwamba to move things up to the next level.

> A good friend of ours, an Asian bank manager, who looked at our performance and read between the lines, told me that I should think about diversifying into manufacturing. So Chama and I considered going into any manufacturing company, but fortunately that is when we came across the milling company.

At the time, Zambia was under the rule of President Chiluba, who had taken over from Kenneth Kaunda in 1991. The country was going through a major privatisation programme, where many government assets, including the mills, were being sold off to local businessmen through tenders. This was during the so-called 'second recovery' period of Zambia's history in the mid 90s. One mill that became available was Kasama Mill and was sold on a competitive tender basis to Mwamba. 'I knew that mealiemeal was the staple food of this country. There were eight or 10 other bidders and ours was the highest.'

Mwamba paid in excess of US$1 million for the mill without having to borrow a cent of it: 'We had the money in the bank already. It wasn't a problem,' he explains proudly. He duly took over the business and proceeded to build it up. Part of the conditions of the sale was that Mwamba had to take over the entire staff complement of 133 largely inefficient workers. Despite that, through hard work and the support of his wife, he managed to build up the business to the point where it is currently the second-largest mill in the country and employs more than 200 people. He is making plans to expand into neighbouring Democratic Republic of Congo (DRC), and is in the process of building a factory in one of the Congolese towns close to the Zambian border.

> Compared to the way we found it, the business has done very well. When you start a new business you have to attract your customers. One way is to reduce the price of your commodity, and that's what we did.

Currently the factory has a capacity of about 10 tons per hour, and produces four types of corn-based porridges, including a branded breakfast mealiemeal called Family Choice. With its eight trucks, the company supplies retailers and markets throughout Lusaka, and recently stopped supplying the government due to non-payment. While Mwamba is reluctant to provide details of his turnover, he will admit that he is operating at a current profit margin of 25%.

He continued his trading business concurrently with the mill and eventually stopped in 2004, two years after the Mwanawasa government came into power. He wasn't prepared to give too much away, but it was clear he was no fan of that particular regime.

> It became very political. Each man has got his own rules so probably I didn't agree with the rules so I decided to withdraw. I made it a point that I stopped dealing with the government.

With one source of revenue gone, Mwamba started looking around for another. He was specifically looking for another cash business because, 'we didn't want to continue to work for our money'. He decided to go back into transport. Having learnt hard lessons from the minibus business, this time he went for luxury coaches. He explains why:

> Zambia is a land-locked country. People need to travel from one point to another and the only reliable source of transport they can use is the bus.

He and Chama currently own 28 60-seater luxury buses under a company called Gemini, which travel the country carrying holidaymakers and small traders. It turns out, that of all his business interests, past and present, the luxury bus business is the one that he most enjoys:

> The transport business keeps me on my toes 18 hours a day. You have to talk to drivers, you have to talk to mechanics, and you have to talk to passengers.

But Gemini is also the business that provides him with the biggest challenges.

> There are lots of ups and downs. The rainy season is the worst time for anyone running a passenger-based business. Any minute from now it could start raining and then you hear that a bus has been involved in an accident – those are my lowest moments. First and foremost my concern is for the passengers – are they hurt? Up till today no lives have been lost in my buses, but we have had several accidents.

Mwamba is very hands-on in all his businesses, particularly Gemini. In order to minimise internal fraud, drivers have to phone in with the number of passengers and the amount of money collected before they can start their journey – and Mwamba's phone is never far away.

> Previously we relied on the passengers going through the operations manager but unfortunately certain complaints did not reach our ears, which is quite dangerous for this business.

The Mwamba dynamic

Gemini, and in fact all of Mwamba's other businesses, is split evenly between his wife, Chama, and himself. Mwamba is the executive chairman and Chama is the managing director and the general operations manager. Mwamba speaks proudly of his business relationship with Chama:

> She is my assistant. She has been my right-hand person since the word go. We were married at a young age and she comes from a family of business people. At one point, her grandfather was one of the richest men in Zambia. She has contributed quite a lot to the growth of the business. And I have no doubt that if something were to happen to me she would take over the business without any problems. My wife is a businesswoman; she understands business. She is just as good as I am.

Chama's unique talent, according to Mwamba, is her ability to sniff out potential issues of theft within the business – a perpetual problem with many small businesses in Africa.

> Basically my wife is very good in terms of reconciling figures. We have employed accountants and often they may not detect any problems but my wife can.

Chama has another role in the business, which by all accounts is a very vital one. Mwamba is well known in Zambia for having a bit of a temper and the consequences have led him at least once into the pages of the national newspapers. He concedes that his temper is a problem.

> I am a very friendly person as long as you don't step on my toes. If you do that, I can be a very difficult person. I have noticed that some people keep repeating the same mistakes. Sometimes I discover faults by my senior staff. I caution them, write to them and say these things should not happen. You find that they repeat it again. Then I get so mad. Once a mistake is made and is corrected I don't expect that mistake to be made again.

His temper outbursts have seen him arrested and in court on charges of assault on at least one occasion. One story that ran in the *Times of Zambia* newspaper on 12 December 2007, details his arrest:

> Police yesterday arrested Lusaka businessman, Geoffrey Mwamba for

allegedly assaulting his former chief security officer. Mr Mwamba was released on police bond and would appear in court soon.

Mr Mwamba reported himself to Lusaka Central Police Station around midday and was detained for most of the day before being released on bond. He was released on his own recognisance following the arrest after he reported himself, a police source said.

Mr Mwamba said at the weekend that he was innocent and accused his former employee of fabricating the allegations against him.

Mwamba is not just in the papers for his dalliances with the law; he generates a fair amount of publicity purely because he is a very wealthy and generous individual in Zambia. He has also attracted attention when he chose to run for a seat in Zambia's parliament for the country's ruling Movement for Multiparty Democracy (MDD) party. He subsequently lost, and although he is reluctant to confirm anything, he has not completely set aside his political ambitions.

> I did have political ambitions but I would not like to comment on that simply because you never know what could happen. I don't want to say never, if I must do, then I will serve. If the people of Zambia say, 'come and be part of us', then why not?

Mwamba is extremely patriotic about Zambia: 'This is my home. I love Zambia. I love the people and the people know me,' he says. More importantly, the Zambian economy, according to Mwamba, is conducive to making money.

> If the economy was not doing well I wouldn't be what I am today. The foreign exchange rates have stabilised, which makes it easier for any businessman to plan. For the last couple of years I have been able to plan and focus my business. I can do projections. Before I never used to know because every morning you wake up and find the Kwacha (currency) has been depreciated. For now, Zambia has one of the best economies in the world. We have no restrictions in terms of foreign exchange; basically it is a free market. Those who work hard will make it in Zambia.

The Mwamba legacy

Mwamba has certainly worked hard and has made it to the top, and he is now in the comfortable position of looking forward to leaving behind a legacy. He is determined that his children will become business people and hopefully continue what he has started. The elder two of his five children who are living in Zambia are both working full time in the family business. Like his father before him, Mwamba is directing them towards a career in the family business, although with perhaps less zeal.

> Yes, it is important they work in the business, this is what my dad did to me. I am trying to groom my kids into good business people. I have three girls and two boys; the firstborn son is a miller by profession. We sent him to school in Switzerland. Sibongile, my daughter, helps in operations in both the milling and the bus companies. My last born is still doing A levels. We've agreed with him to go abroad to study finance and banking, hopefully he'll open up his own bank.

He is, however, reluctantly realistic that despite his children's genetic predisposition to becoming great business people, they may not all end up that way. He has a plan for that eventuality too; he is building up his property investments, which include assets across most of Zambia and in the UK so that his not-so-business savvy children can inherit them.

> They might not all have the same business acumen that I have, but when it comes to property, it will be difficult for them to squander that. So we are also into property development; when we have a bit of money we buy properties. With properties you never go wrong.

Mwamba is still on the lookout for new opportunities to make more money, but what is certain is that he has earned his money fair and square through hard work. He consistently puts in 18-hour days and works six days a week.

> I think the most important thing that has made me what I am is hard work. I have very little time for leisure; most of my time is spent on planning for my businesses. As we are seated here I am thinking how business will be in two years.

He allows himself Sundays off and admits that the quality of his family life may be compromised as result of his stringent attitude to business and work.

We devote most of our time to business rather than the family. It's not good, but at the same time, in order for the family to be happy, we need to be in business. I am happy my family has understood our position and that is why we have Sundays, which we devote to our family and friends. Sundays are special to us.

He has few outside interests – 'I don't even have time to read the paper. My wife reads the paper and usually narrates the key stories to me, and I don't play golf,' he says firmly. Mwamba is almost entirely focused on business – his businesses. He admires Bill Gates, mainly for his work ethic, which is similar to his own.

He comes from a humble education but he is one of the richest individuals in the whole world. The reason behind it is that he is creative and hard working. Look at him now – he is regarded as one the richest men in the world but he still goes to work.

Despite his success in life and his obvious wealth, Mwamba remains a humble and content man.

I started with almost nothing (and look) where I am today, so I respect every human being in society. I am a very happy person, very, very happy, very proud of myself. I don't suffer from high blood pressure because I am happy, very happy.

Mwamba was once famously quoted as saying that he had enough money 'to move the Queen from Buckingham Palace to Lusaka'. Now, if that is the case, he has every reason to be happy, very happy.

Sources:

1. Zambia Privatization Agency. 'Privatisation Transaction Summary Sheets 1992 – 2005', June 2005. Available online at: http://www.zpa.org.zm/trsum.pdf.
2. Zambia Travel Guide, available online at http://www.zambia-travel-guide.com/bradt_guide.asp?bradt=170.
3. Ndola (2007). 'GBM Arrested', *The Times of Zambia*, 12 December. Available online at: http://allafrica.com/stories/200712120372.html.

Richard Maponya – The Defiant Entrepreneur

VITAL STATISTICS

Name: Richard Maponya
Country: South Africa
Born: 24 December 1926
Position/Title: Executive Chairman and MD of the
Maponya Group
Co turnover: Undisclosed
Nationality: South African
Industry: Retail
Highest education qualification: Kagiso Teachers' Training
College

Then there was a hit squad that used to raid families and shoot people dead. I was on the list and they paid me a visit, but by the grace of the Lord I escaped. It was a miracle because they were waiting for me at my house. They knew what time I closed my business and what time I got home. I had a big dog which was very well trained. This one day, my dog started barking when I got home. Three white boys in balaclavas came running out and the dog was on them. One of them jumped the fence, the other two ran past me and when I got out of the car to see what was happening, they got in their cars and disappeared. I was lucky that time.

At one stage they wanted to burn my supermarket down. My next-door neighbour phoned me one night. He said: 'Come quickly, there are people burning your store.' I woke up my boys and we took our guns. When we arrived we could see policemen standing around. These guys have a substance that they pour; it burns bricks and I found it had burned the area around the doors. But we had strong sprinklers and the fire was contained. The man in charge came to me and asked if I was the owner of this business. I said yes. He turned to his colleagues and said; 'Kom, kom, ons gaan loop' (Come, come we are going); they got into their cars and drove away.

These were just some of the occupational hazards of doing business in South Africa during the apartheid era if you were black and influential – like Richard Maponya. He was, and still is, one of South Africa's best-known and best-loved entrepreneurs.

The reason I succeeded during the apartheid era was because I never took 'no' for an answer; because if you say 'no' to me, there must be a very good reason. If there wasn't reason I would keep on knocking at your door demanding to know the reason why.

Maponya made his name during the 80s when the apartheid government kept on saying 'no' to him. But they did not reckon on the obstinate entrepreneur, who describes himself as an 'economic activist'. Like many highly politicised black South Africans, Maponya chose to make his difference by challenging the frustrating apartheid laws and bureaucratic systems which governed the business sector.

I wanted to prove to the white man that a black person, given a chance, could also make the grade. And I proved it beyond doubt because here I

am today, despite all the things that were legislated against us. As black
people we were not allowed to get into business, we were not allowed
to form companies, but I was driven by something which said to me:
'If a young white boy can become a businessman and be successful,
why can't I?' I fought a battle that I actually won.

Maponya may not be fighting the same sort of battles as he did back
then, but at age 82, he is still very much in the game. Today he is
more likely to be found battling with the banks to raise the money
for future projects – and there are quite a few in the pipeline. On
27 September 2007 Maponya's dream was realised when Nelson
Mandela officially cut the ribbon that declared open Maponya
Mall, his R650 million upmarket shopping complex development
in Soweto.

> I didn't want anything less than Sandton City. I wanted to bring a
> product that could be better than Sandton City to the people of Soweto.
> They deserve the best.

It was a simple but moving ribbon-cutting ceremony, and one that
must have played out in Maponya's head many times over the years
in which he had strived to make it a reality. In his speech to the
huge crowd that gathered to witness the event, Maponya shared
with them, in a single sentence, the secret of his success: 'I never
gave up when the door was slammed in my face,' he said simply
and firmly. And over the course of his 60 or so years in business,
the door has been slammed in his face many times. But equally,
many doors in business were kicked down and opened as a result of
his battles. Not just for him, but for the many black South Africans
who came after him.

And although many would argue that at 82 he is a little past the
traditional retirement age, Maponya doesn't seem to want to stop.
In fact, the completion of the shopping mall has launched him
into a whole new career and his sights are set equally high. 'I am a
property developer,' he says with a certain amount of pride.

> At the present moment I am embarking on another mall. I am being
> asked by one of our neighbours to put up a similar mall, even if it is
> a little smaller but a similar product. We are developing office parks
> throughout the country.

How it all started

Richard Maponya describes himself as a 'self-made man':

> I am what they called 'vuka usenseli' – wake up and do it yourself.
> I wasn't pandered to by anybody. To me, this means I am a born
> businessman. I never got the training to get into business, I just woke
> up and said: 'I have a dream and my dream is to produce a certain
> thing.' And then you pursue that and you make it happen.

Since he was about 17 years old, Maponya had already started
making the seemingly impossible happen – much to his father's
concern.

> Back home (in Limpopo) there was a river flowing just down past our
> fields. I looked at these fields and I thought I could grow vegetables
> there. I saw what the white people across in the other fields were doing
> and I thought, 'Why can't we do the same?' So I diverted the water from
> the river and made a little dam. I started irrigating an area and then I
> started planting cabbages, tomatoes, onions – all kinds of vegetables.
> All of a sudden I had produced enough for us to eat at home and I
> started selling the surplus to the neighbours. My father said that I was
> a very naughty young man as I was doing things a big man couldn't do.
> My father asked how I had thought to do it (and) I said I just felt this
> could be done because I had seen it done on our neighbour's farm.

Maponya grew up on a farm in Limpopo. His parents were farm
workers who could rarely afford to put three meals on the table.
Nevertheless, the smart young Maponya went to school and
developed a reputation, not as the best or brightest student, but as
the 'cleanest student' in the class. He recalls how his teacher would
stand him on the desk and say: 'Look at his feet. Look at his clothing
– look how he is dressed. Look at his hair – how neat he is. When
I am talking about cleanliness this is what my pupils should look
like.' To this day Maponya takes his appearance very seriously:

> I used to love clothing and I grew up like that even when I came into
> Johannesburg. At one stage I was voted as one of the best-dressed men
> in Johannesburg.

Sadly, the vote of confidence in Maponya's dress sense did not do much to influence his career path. Like many educated black people with ambition, he planned to become a teacher, one of the few careers open to him in South Africa.

> During those days, teacher training was a prestigious thing and if you were a teacher you were highly respected and the community looked up to you. You were really a special person. I wanted to become a teacher, so I came to Johannesburg.

Luckily for him, it was not meant to be, and what the teaching profession lost, the retail industry gained. A relative of Maponya's told him about a job opportunity at a clothing manufacturer for 'an educated black person' and he went along for an interview and got the job. His boss was a Mr Bolton, who would later become his mentor. Maponya's job at the clothing manufacturer involved the sorting and packing of the newly manufactured clothing for distribution. He was smart and learnt quickly; he took to his new job with enthusiasm and excelled at it. Within six months, much to the chagrin of the older employees, he was made an *induna*, the 'boss boy' of the department. In the three and a half years he spent at the factory, Maponya became a clothing expert:

> I would just touch a piece of cloth and I would be able to tell you this was 10, 11 or 12 ounces and also tell you that it was made in London, Italy or America.

Early on he got himself involved in selecting the styles and ranges the factory supplied to the rural black stores, and his department, under the benign figure of Mr Bolton, thrived. But this was apartheid South Africa and no matter how good the young Maponya was, he was going nowhere fast. When Mr Bolton was promoted out of the department, Maponya realised that the prophetic glass ceiling was built a lot lower than he expected.

> Mr Bolton told me: 'There's nothing I can do for you because you are a black person – you cannot oversee white people. You can just be a boss boy and that is it.'

Maponya appraised his situation and knew it was hopeless:

I knew I couldn't go further because the laws of the country were such that a black person was not recognised as anything. I couldn't even resign and go and join a company that could give me a more responsible job.

Maponya the informal entrepreneur

That was one of the first doors that was slammed in his face, but another door, organised by Bolton, would soon open. Bolton tried to compensate for the situation in which Maponya found himself by offering him the opportunity to buy the factory's soiled clothing and samples at a discounted price, which he could then sell for extra money. 'That,' said Bolton, 'is the only thing I can do for you in recognition of your achievements.' Maponya couldn't have been happier with the opportunity.

> I started selling. I created what we call 'pay while you wear'. I come to you as a lady and I show you the garments I am selling, and you say: 'I love this one and that one but I haven't got money.' So I ask, 'When will you have money?' You say: 'Maybe at the end of the month.' And I say, 'Ok, take it and pay me at the end of the month.' During those days people were good human beings, very trustworthy – what we call *ubuntu*.

Maponya continued to work as a boss boy at the same company, but over the weekends when he was off work he would travel far and wide to the black urban areas, hawking his clothing and pushing his unique credit offering to an eager clientele.

> That's how I raised my working capital. No bank would give me an overdraft. It was unheard of for a black man to even have a chequebook.

Chequebook or not, Maponya was making good money on the side, but unfortunately it didn't last. Bolton retired and his successor felt that Maponya, as an employee of the factory, should not have had this extra source of income and took it away. Maponya promptly resigned. He had his eyes set on bigger things anyway.

> I hated being employed and having to keep saying 'Boss' to boys who were my equal. I decided I was not going to do that any more. I was

going to be self-employed and I was going to create jobs for other people. I was driven by something which said to me that if a young white boy can become a businessman and be successful what is wrong with me doing exactly the same?

Maponya's plan was to remain in clothing and retailing, but the apartheid government had other ideas.

When I resigned I was going to start up my first clothing store because that's what I was trained in and I understood it very well. I wanted to put up clothing stores in Soweto. I applied for a licence and the powers that be said: 'You must be dreaming! You are here to work for industry not to get into business.' Then they told me I would never be given the right to sell clothing or put up a clothing business because it was a white man's job.

Challenging the status quo

It was South Africa in the 50s and black people were only permitted by law to start businesses in what were called the homelands. These homelands were independent states to which Africans were assigned by the government according to their record of origin, which was often inaccurate. All political rights, including voting, held by an African, were restricted to the designated homeland. Four of these homelands were created, including Bophuthatswana, Venda, Ciskei and Transkei. Soweto was not a designated homeland, despite the fact it was populated by black people, and Maponya's application to run clothing stores in Soweto was subsequently turned down.

I looked at Soweto and I said: 'Yes, but here in Soweto there are black people.' Soweto was created by apartheid, you know. They removed people there from Sophiatown and from Braamfontein; they moved us and threw us out there. It was actually created as a dormitory for people to sleep there, wake up and catch trains to go to work. I wanted to service these people.

Not ready to take no for an answer, and certainly not scared to challenge the mighty apartheid system, Maponya took his argument to the courts. Interestingly, it was the legal firm of Mandela Tambo, Nelson Mandela and Oliver Tambo's legendary law practice, that took on the case. Maponya recalls how the partners operated:

> Nelson would never be in the office but Oliver was always there and he was the one who opened my file and took my case. They made a representation for me – it was a big fight, they actually shook them up.

The 'them' Maponya was referring to were the lawmakers of the apartheid system. Tambo and Maponya threw the ridiculous apartheid laws back at their creators, using the powerful weapons of logic and reason.

> Our argument was: In terms of your own laws you say we must trade amongst our own people. In Soweto there are only black people, there are no white people there and I want to do business amongst my people, therefore I should be given the right to do so.

Maponya sustained himself by continuing to buy and sell clothing informally to his existing clientele while he waited. His patience was rewarded, and eventually, a door, not the door he wanted, but a door nevertheless, was opened. Maponya was granted a licence to sell what was vaguely referred to as 'daily necessities' in Soweto, by the apartheid government.

> I thought, well, 'daily necessities' means you can get into the grocery business or any business that sells food and I had a background of milk from the farm I grew up on. I figured the one thing I could handle best was milk.

So milk it was. But although running a milk retailing business was a far cry from the clothing emporium he had envisioned in Soweto, it still proved to be a very lucrative launch pad for Maponya into the world of business.

> I was the only one selling milk in Soweto. I employed five guys; we were buying milk in 25-litre cans and then we would decant them into smaller bottles to deliver. As Soweto grew we were running up and down selling milk. It was hard work because I would wake up at 4.30am to wash the bottles, fill them with milk and then load the bicycles so that at 5am when my guys arrived, the bicycles were loaded and they

could hit the road and deliver.

The dairy business was a raging success. At its peak, Maponya had more than 100 men on bicycles delivering milk every day around Soweto. Success like that doesn't go unnoticed and it didn't take long for the bigger, more established, white-owned dairy players wanted a piece of the Soweto pie. They say the sign of a good businessman is one who knows when to leave the game, and Maponya knew his monopoly days in the dairy business were over.

> I thought these guys would crush me; they have got the power, they have the money, and if they were coming to Soweto, I knew I had to look for something else.

Maponya decided on the grocery business and duly applied for and secured the necessary licence. He was allocated a site and was told he could put up whatever building he wanted.

> I had to build it myself. I started with a butchery and then I put up a grocery. On the other side I sold fruit and vegetables, and in the middle I had a very big room which I turned into a restaurant.

The conditions of the licence were almost ridiculous in their detailed requirements, as was the behaviour of the law enforcement agents:

> They itemised the items I could sell and if I was found selling asparagus or tuna fish, which were classed as luxuries, I would have lost my licence. They used to raid us as if we were selling drugs and when they came into your shop they jumped the counters as if you had killed a person and had hidden him behind the counter. That's how rough they used to treat us. The laws were terrible.

But that wasn't all, for an arbitrary reason that only the apartheid government understood, the grocery licence went as far as to stipulate on which days of the week he could sell meat:

> At that time, there wasn't any electricity and we were not allowed to sell meat on weekends. So you can imagine: people have knocked off from work, they are spending their weekend in Soweto, they want meat

but they can't find a place to buy meat in the whole township.

The absurdity of the situation irked Maponya and he was itching to do something about it and the other ridiculous rules and laws that black people in business had to comply with. He had come up against the brick wall of apartheid enough times to know that with enough pressure, it could come down.

By the 70s a trickle of black-owned businesses popped up around the country. Maponya started lobbying, initially in Soweto, for black businessmen to come together and fight for their rights.

> I realised that if you spoke to these officials on your own they would always turn you down and they would always shut their doors in your face. I decided that I should organise black businessmen so that we form a chamber of commerce and speak to these people with one voice.

That was the beginning of the Johannesburg Chamber of Commerce. It grew into a powerful lobby group which made frequent representations to the government on business issues. Maponya became the commerce's chief crusader; he took to the road, travelling across the country, encouraging black businesses to come together and form similar chambers.

> I wanted to make a point that a black person is not what the white man believes us to be – merely labourers. We can run businesses and be as successful as they are if things are equal. It was deliberate that black people were run down and made to be nothing.

Maponya the greengrocer

In between his activism, Maponya's business was growing into a very lucrative operation. His initial grocery-cum-butchery-cum-restaurant grew into a chain of eight Soweto-based discount supermarkets, each grossing in the region of about R2.5 million to R3 million a month at their peak. He was the single largest employer in Soweto, with up to 170 employees working in shifts during the busiest periods.

> Maponya's Discount Supermarkets were very successful. We had queues from sunrise till 11pm. All the leaders of my country – the

Tutus of this world, Sisulus, Mandelas – they were buying there.

The stores were popular because Maponya was a good businessman. He sold his stock cheaper than the established competition, opened his shops for longer hours and treated his customers with respect. It was about more than just the money:

> I remember Dr Molane walked into my store he wanted a can of baked beans and a can of fish. He found me selling my baked beans and fish much lower than OK Bazaars. He actually made a scene about it – he could not believe he could get cheaper food in his own township store than he could buy in the supermarkets in the white urban areas. People were surprised; they asked me how I survived. I said: 'Listen, I survive because I am serving the community.' I survived on turnover. You can make money on selling more with a smaller mark-up margin than selling little with a huge mark-up, and that is exactly what I used to do.

The political situation in South Africa at the time helped somewhat. By the 80s South Africa was a hotbed of political activity, the African National Congress (ANC) leadership had gone underground, it was a dangerous time and of course, Maponya was right in the thick of things.

> The boys would come to me and say: 'We are going to boycott town – stock up, stock up as much as you can.' Then I would get goods for about R5 million and take them up to the roof, and believe you me, in a week's time everything would be sold. The boys used to say to me: 'Don't exploit us but stock up.'

Apart from providing the goods which fed the anti-apartheid movement in Soweto, Maponya was an extremely outspoken member of the banned ANC. It was a time when prominent and not so prominent black people were simply disappearing.

> They had guys who were pinpointing all influential blacks, because if you were an outspoken, influential black, you were called a communist. So we were communists – all of us – even though we were capitalists.

If a death list existed, then Maponya was almost definitely on it.

There was at least one attempt made on his life and one of his supermarkets narrowly escaped being burnt down.

> I was very outspoken but I continued to put my point across as I felt it was correct. I would not compromise on anything and the powers that be most unfortunately tried at one time to keep me quiet, but if the Lord sends you a sign you always escape these things.

Maponya was certainly above the radar – at one stage, according to Maponya, a newspaper claimed he was the 10th most influential man in South Africa. His position wasn't helped by the very high-profile and expensive hobby in which he indulged. Maponya came to the attention of many white South Africans in the 80s when he became the first black person in South Africa to enter the exclusive world of owning and racing horses. He went on to own more than 70 horses during his reign, each valued at between R150 000 and R500 000 per horse in winnings. But that wasn't the point. To Maponya, the very fact that no black people owned horses, despite most of the punters who bet on horses being black, was an anomaly.

> These guys were shouting at horses but none of these horses were black-owned. Why? Black punters must have the opportunity to back a black-owned horse and must cheer a black horse winning at the post.

So he took it upon himself to correct the situation. It took five years of doors slamming in his face before he was granted the colours which allowed him to buy and race his horses. 'They thought I was a joke because this was a white man's club and here I was, a little black boy, wanting to join,' he explains. The club members threw everything at him and he patiently threw it right back.

> They said: 'Show us your balance sheet.' I took out the balance sheet and showed them. It took six months before they came back to me. They said: 'Yes, we saw your balance sheet but it's not quite satisfactory. Can you give us an audited balance sheet?' So I produced one. It would take another six months before they came back to me and I had written so many reminders. They then said: 'Yes, we saw your audited balance sheet, can you please show us a receipt from the receiver of revenue in

order to establish that you are paying tax?' And it would take another six months.

When he finally secured the licence, they refused to let him use the colours he had cleverly selected for his jockeys.

> I selected ANC colours (green, yellow and black) and I did it on purpose. I knew I was flying the ANC flag and the ANC was banned then. They refused; they said: 'These are ANC colours we can't give them to you.' Then Eric Gallo, one of my sponsors, said: 'Colours are just colours. If you want to politicise colours then you can politicise anything. Give the man the colours, he wants them, they are his colours!' Then they granted me the colours. The first horse I bought I named 'Another Colour'.

The diversification of the empire

The cut-throat world of horseracing, arson attempts and near-assassination, all these were nothing compared to Maponya's attempts to keep his discount stores operating profitably and within the accepted levels of shrinkage.

> The only stores that were making money were the ones run by my wife and I personally – the others, they would just break even, sometimes lose money. I realised that to expand was a not a very good thing until such time that you have developed a good managerial team that can help you control things.

Maponya's eight children were still all young and in no place to help run the retail empire he was building. But he was driven to continue to expand his businesses – for the sake of his children.

> The Lord was kind to me; he gave me eight children. I created all these businesses so that when they grew up I could give each child a business and say: 'Now it is yours. This is your beginning. Build it up and be on your own and if you let it fall down it will be of your own irresponsibility.'

From supermarkets, Maponya diversified into retailing fuel. He opened up a filling station in Soweto. It seemed a logical move:

The car population was growing and I could see there was a niche, something was needed. So I made provision by putting up a filling station so these guys could have a place to buy petrol and to service their cars.

Then there was the General Motors dealership which he secured and called Mountain Motors, which sold Chevrolet cars. His reasons for entering into that particular business were much the same as his reasons for starting the filling stations:

I thought: this is a growing little town, why can't we have a place where the people of Soweto can buy motorcars? So I applied for a dealership and I negotiated with General Motors and was granted the opportunity.

Although Maponya was doing very well and selling his quota of cars, he eventually closed the dealership when General Motors disinvested from South Africa. He turned to BMW, where he encountered operational problems which proved what he had always believed: there was a huge amount of disposable income in the black township – even for luxury items. His problem was that he couldn't keep up with the demand.

I would be given a small allocation of cars to sell and I would easily sell that allocation within a week. When I asked for more cars, there would be no cars and then I would eat up my next allocation by borrowing from other dealers. For the next two weeks, I would have nothing to sell. And here I was; I had staff to pay and people asking me to give them cars which I didn't have. It was a frustrating situation and there was nothing you could do about it. So you wait, thinking that next year they will increase your allocation.

In the meantime, Maponya, along with his business partners, took advantage of Coca-Cola's decision to disinvest from South Africa in 1986 as a result of apartheid. Coca-Cola was on the verge of selling its South African assets to a white-owned company. Maponya saw it happening and was enraged by the injustice of the situation. Here was a company supposedly sympathetic enough to the black cause to pull out of the country, yet insensitive enough to sell its assets to a white company, ignoring the very people it claimed to want to help. It was like a red flag to a bull and he decided to challenge Coca-Cola.

> I went to Atlanta with a friend, Gibson Thula. We made a very strong case and they listened to us very attentively. Within two weeks they cleared a meeting in South Africa and a decision was taken that we must be given a bottling plant. We were given one in East London.

Maponya was now an independent bottler and distributor of Coca-Cola products. He had joined forces with some other business partners to form a company called Kilimanjaro, which listed on the Johannesburg Stock Exchange, and operated a lucrative bottling plant in East London. The company was eventually taken over by the Kunene brothers, leaving Maponya free to to focus on his other businesses. His BMW dealership was still struggling along. He never seemed to be able to supply enough cars to meet the demand and he was getting frustrated with the situation and blamed the system.

> The people at the head of BMW were white. Their idea was that I must be played down as much as possible; I shouldn't be allowed to grow to become a very big dealer and it was very frustrating. I lost money, so I gave up the BMW dealership as well.

But before he gave up on the dealership, he transported a very special passenger on a very special day, which became one of the most significant moments in modern South African history. It was the day Nelson Mandela was released from prison in 1990. Maponya recounts the story of how his BMWs came to the rescue. 'When I am released you must pick me up in your car as I hear you are running a BMW dealership.' This was the requestmade to Maponya by his friend and relative, Nelson Mandela, on a visit just days before Mandela's official release on 11 February 1990.

> I promised him I would do it and on the day he was released I organised for eight BMW cars to be waiting for him – all chauffeur-driven. I was one of the chauffeurs and I drove him myself. We took him into hiding and this was the most frightening experience because when he was released, every single black person in the county was so excited to hear that Mandela was out. When we picked him up we were chased by motorcars, by motorcycles, by helicopters. So we disappeared.

The following day, I was supposed to drive him to the FNB stadium (in Johannesburg). I had never ever seen so many people in one place – there must have been more than 100 000 people in the stadium and more than 200 000 outside. People were arriving by bicycle or whatever form of transport they had – just to meet Mr Mandela. We realised that people could kill him without realising it, just because they wanted to touch him.

Maponya's wife was a cousin of Mandela's, and the two men had been friends for a long time. However, it took 18 years, for Mandela to return the favour for the day he hitched a ride to freedom in Maponya's BMW. In a very rare official outing in 2007, Mandela agreed to be the guest of honour at the launch of Maponya's dream mall in Soweto.

From retail to property

Of all the businesses in which Maponya dabbled, it was his super-markets in which he spent most of his time and for which the Maponya name is best known.

> I was very lucky that I married a lady who, when she comes across a customer, she never forgets the customer's name. You come today, she welcomes you in and she says: 'Hello Ms Makura how are you?' When you come the following day: 'Welcome Ms Makura, what can I do for you?'

Maponya expands on his particular breed of old-school customer service, which he believes was a major factor in sustaining his business.

> A mother would wake me up at night and say: 'I forgot to buy food for my child.' I would wake up and go to the store, take a packet or tin of baby food and give it to her and say: 'You will pay me tomorrow when we are trading.' That is how we help people out and because of that, today the Maponya name is a brand, a strong brand amongst our people. And believe you me, if you ask about Maponya they will tell you the type of people we are.

Sadly, the Maponya Discount Stores no longer exist. Over the years, Maponya has let them go. The final three sites were leased to his biggest competitors, Shoprite Checkers, in 2001. Maponya bowed out of the grocery business because he had a big vision that needed his attention. Back in 1994, when the law changed and finally allowed black people to own land, Maponya bought a piece of land in Soweto on which he planned to put up a shopping complex, which 13 years later, became the R650 million Maponya Mall. It took him seven of those 13 years to put a professional team in place and get the project to the stage where the banks would even look at him. It was the biggest deal of his life and Maponya was not about to let that door slam in his face.

> Some banks were sympathetic but other banks were diplomatic. They would engage you in a discussion, but in a discussion that went nowhere. They keep talking nicely to you as if they planned to write a cheque tomorrow, but that cheque never arrived.

Eventually one bank came up with a solution that would help make Maponya's dream mall a more attractive proposition. The main problem was that Maponya did not have the collateral to qualify for a R500 million bank loan he needed. So the bank suggested he get himself a partner. Enter Zenprop Property Holdings, a privately held property investment, development and management company which proved to be just what Maponya needed.

> Zenprop was exactly like me, in tha, they intended to hold the property and not resell. They too wanted to grow their portfolio. We created a 50-50 partnership. We went to the bank and the bank gave us money. To date they have given us R665 million.

After the dream

With the paintwork barely dry on the Maponya Mall, Maponya's eye is already on the next deal:

> My other dream is to put up a Maponya motor town in Soweto. I would like the people of Soweto, if they want to buy motorcars, to be able to wake up and walk to the centre of town where they can buy a car instead of travelling into the cities and going to look for a car there.

Clearly, Maponya is not about to slow down any time soon – well, not if he has his own way. Under the watchful eye of his daughter Chichi, who helps him run the family business, Maponya is being forced to cut back. His days of weightlifting and boxing are long over; the 82-year-old grandfather now relaxes by watching rugby and soccer, and listening to music. His favourite artists include Michael Jackson and Aretha Franklin. Since his wife passed away, he has done far less travelling. His eyesight is not what it used to be, so he does far less reading of the business books he read so avidly to broaden his knowledge when he was younger.

In business, Maponya admires Raymond Ackerman, the founder of one of the largest fast-moving consumer goods (FMCG) retail groups in South Africa, Pick 'n Pay. Maponya admires his spirit most of all:

> He resigned from the company that employed him because they did not agree on certain things. When he resigned, he woke up a bank manger and asked for money to buy a certain business so that he could be in competition with his previous employers. He was granted that money and he started very humbly, and today he owns one of the biggest chain stores in South Africa.

Throughout his life, Maponya's success has been built on the premise of a simple philosophy and a single location: that as a black man, he was no less capable than a white man. And that the people of Soweto had the right to spend their money in Soweto. With the former, he has proved himself time and time again, and with the latter, the Maponya Mall stands as testament to his belief that 'Sowetans deserve the best'. Maponya sums it up in his own words: 'I fought a battle that I actually won,' he says proudly.

Daniel David – The Emerging Entrepreneur

VITAL STATISTICS

Name: Daniel David
Country: Mozambique
Born: 15 February 1966
Position/Title: CEO Soico Group
Co Turnover: US$10 million
Nationality: Mozambican
Industry: Media
Highest education qualification: Business management degree from Instituto Superior Politécnico e Universitário (ISPU), Mozambique, management diploma from the University of South Africa (Unisa)

When you go underground, you realise that you are at risk – it is do or die. If something happens down there, you have no chance of surviving it. Every day I used to think that I don't want to die, that I want to go back to my country. I was thinking of my family, thinking of my girlfriend – every single day. The only thing that kept me going was that I would make money to help me start my life back in Mozambique.

Eighteen months later I finally arrived back at home with all my goods. At the border I had rented a truck into which I put all my things. I remember it was raining the day I arrived at home and all my family came out to meet me. It was very emotional; my brothers and sisters were hugging me, they had not seen me in months. No one remembered to take my stuff out of the truck and the driver drove off with it. All the things that I had collected over the last 18 months were gone. My mother started to cry, but I felt nothing.

It was going to take more that the loss of everything he owned to make Daniel David cry. At 19, he had just survived 18 months of hardship working in a South African mine. His entire life before that point was also typified by hardship and poverty in a country that had been at war with itself for nearly two decades. By the time he returned from the mines to Mozambique, the country had suffered virtual economic collapse, leaving much of its population either dead or in distress. Millions of Mozambicans were displaced internally or had fled the country, living as refugees in neighbouring states. The year David returned, 1986, was the year in which the country's president since independence, Samora Machel, was shot down on a flight from Zambia, along with members of his government. His successor, Joaquim Chissano, continued the peace reforms that his predecessor had started, but peace did not come to the embattled Mozambique until 1992, and economic stability was still a very long way away.

But at that moment when his possessions were liberated by an opportunistic truck driver, David was not so concerned with the political or economic situation of his country. He was more concerned about what he would tell his girlfriend about the missing gifts he'd bought her and how he would now survive.

Daniel David subsequently survived. In fact, David did much more than simply survive. On the contrary, he has thrived. At 40, he is that very rare breed of Mozambican – an entrepreneur with a fast-growing, privately owned conglomerate entirely of his own creation. David is the CEO of Soico Group Ltd, a diversified, predominantly multimedia organisation, with interests in television, radio, print and production. The group employs more than 200 people and has a turnover of US$10 million a year. David's media group, Soico, owns and operates one television station, Soico TV (STV), which is the country's most popular channel and has been in operation since 2002. In 2004 David launched Soico FM (SFM), a Maputo-based radio station that is slowly growing its footprint. In 2007 David launched his first weekly newspaper, *O Pais*, which is gaining a reputation for delivering hard-hitting news. The group also owns a television production company, S Live, which makes content for his TV and radio stations, as well as advertisements and films for external clients. One of his claims to fame is that S Live was involved in the production of the Hollywood movie *Blood Diamond* which was partly filmed in Mozambique.

And those are just his media interests. David's first business, which he launched in 1990, was a marketing communications consultancy which created and sold strategies to corporates. It still exists today and falls under DHD, the holding company he established to house Soico and his ever-expanding non-media interests. Since 2006 David has focused on expanding his interests outside media. He recently started Graphic, a web-printing business; LPT, a procurement company based in neighbouring South Africa; Vuka Mobile, an airtime reseller; Interactive, a consumer mobile technology provider; and Massala, a below-the-line advertising agency. David explains his strategic decision to incorporate non-media assets in to the group:

> I discovered that media is not something that makes you rich. It positions you in terms of credibility but I must find a cash cow that can help me consolidate, because when you work with media in Africa, things change. It's like in Zimbabwe, they can close you down.

But David's passion remains media, and because of the very real threat of operating in Africa, he understands the need to mitigate his risk.

> There is no political censorship on my stations, which means that I am at risk if people in the government don't like the way I am using (content). I have found it is better to create and consolidate other

businesses so if something happens, I can still achieve what I want for my family and for myself.

What David wants for his family and for himself is a life very different to the one in which he grew up.

I don't want my wife, my kids or future generations of my family to experience what I went through. We were a poor family; my life was tough and hard. It was painful.

The early years

David is the eldest of nine children who grew up in the area of Mozambique called Ressano Garcia, close to the border with South Africa. His father was a payroll clerk who worked for a company that recruited workers for the big mining companies in South Africa. His mother looked after the family's smallholding, which grew just about enough lettuce, tomatoes, potatoes and maize to sustain the family, with a little left over to sell in the market. David remembers his youth as a time of sheer, physical, hard work:

We used to wake up very early to help my mother in the field and then we would go and sell the lettuce and potatoes on the roadside. Sometimes I would have to brew up batches of the local beer, which we made from mealies, to sell to the miners on their way back from South Africa. Then I would wash and go to school. When we came home, we would clean the house, help with the cooking – whatever was necessary. It was very tough.

His mother was a disciplinarian and she pushed him very hard:

My mum used to say: 'You must cultivate from here today, when you are finished you can go.' We would work quickly and then when we were done, my mum would say it was too early and that we must go to another place.

But farming and selling fresh produce were not the only responsibilities David had. As the eldest of the siblings in a large African family, much was expected of him. For example, when his father started building a house in a middle-class suburb in the city of

Matola, David, aged 10, was put in charge of the building project. Once a week his father would give him cash and David would travel the 90 km to Maputo to pay the builders and sort out any issues on the site. When the house was completed, David and his entire family except his father left the border town and moved into the home his father had built. His father remained behind to continue with his job, after sending his family away in order to give them a better life. David fondly recalls a ritual his father started in order to keep in touch and remain a part of the day-to-day life of his children.

> I used to have to keep a diary for my father because when he came to see us, he wanted to be able to read about what we had been doing all week. So if I woke up at 6am, I had to write: 'I woke up at 6 o'clock, I brushed my teeth, I went to help Mum,' etc.

The exercise must have helped to improve his writing skills and sharpen his memory for detail, because despite the physical hard work and apparent focus on housework rather than homework, David did very well at school.

> I think my family was proud of me because at school I was really quite the student. I was good at school and good at science subjects and maths – anything that had numbers.

Given this, it was hardly surprising that David left school with good grades after performing well in the Mozambican equivalent of his O level exams. Career advice was an unnecessary inconvenience, which the schools didn't provide, because the socialist government at the time made all the decisions.

> You were not allowed to choose what you wanted to do or where you wanted to go. The government did that for you when you finished grade nine.

Despite his good academic performance in school, the career that had been selected for David by the government was as a sports teacher. The decision was final and incontestable, and he was sent to the Institute for Physical Education to learn his new profession. David was frustrated by the decision because he knew that his talents could have been put to much better use.

I was very upset at the time. Mozambique is a poor country and I was seeing a future where I would have to tell my children that I was working in sport! But I had no choice; I learned to teach basketball, athletics and I was so good that in my second year – a year before I was supposed to finish – they gave me a job teaching at the same school where I had studied.

The Matola Secondary School was David's first and only job as a sports teacher. He instructed the second and third grade but he was not very happy about it. Quite simply, this was not the life that he had imagined for himself.

During my childhood we worked hard, hoeing in the fields, until our fingers turned red with blood. I wanted things to be different when I grew up. I wanted to be the type of person who had a car and had a radio; someone who had a different type of life to the one I had. I didn't think that I would get these things as a sports teacher.

So he told his father that he wanted to go to neighbouring South Africa to try his luck there.

South Africa was the place where young people dreamt of going to, because when you came back, you would bring T-shirts, hair products, Colgate, food or whatever, and the girls would think, 'oh this guy is great – he has Colgate!' People would look at you differently because Mozambique had nothing.

If owning just a tube of branded toothpaste could make a young man more popular with the girls, it was no wonder David was keen to go. But the easiest way he could get there was by joining the thousands of Mozambicans who regularly crossed the border to work on the South African mines. Even though he was only 18 at the time, it was easy for him to jump the queue because his father still worked at the mining recruitment company.

I was not looking forward to working on the mines but in Mozambique there was no alternative. At that time we were starving. There was no water, there was no food; there was nothing. If you wanted to buy meat you would have to queue for maybe two days. You could only buy 1 kg of rice at a time, we used to eat only one type of fish, called Carapau (a type of mackerel), and there were no clothes – we used to get second-hand clothes from overseas. We were suffering; Mozambique was not an easy place to live.

The problems were compounded by the fact that Mozambique's neighbour, South Africa, in an attempt to stop the military arm of the ANC utilising the country as a base to fight apartheid, started financing a destabilisation war in Mozambique. David and many other Mozambicans were forced to leave and try to make a life for themselves outside its borders. So it was fortunate that he managed to get himself a job with one of the large mining houses in Bloemfontein in the Free State province in South Africa, as 'a 'white guy's assistant'. It basically meant that he worked for the mine surveyor, who was white, and helped him carry his bag everywhere. Luckily it was not a manual job, but it still required his presence down the mine every day at 4am.

> The only thing that kept me going was that I would make money to help me start my life back in Mozambique. I told my father and my girlfriend that it wasn't what I had expected – it was not my life. I knew more than some of the white people working with me but they got paid a lot more than I did. I wasn't happy but I tolerated it. I kept thinking that at least if I worked, I would make some money and be able to get married to my girlfriend.

His objective, apart from marriage, was to save up as much as he could by spending as little as possible of his meagre salary so that he could buy the things he needed back home. His saving plan included economising on clothing:

> I went to the mine with just two pairs of jeans. During my 18 months there I never wore anything else; I would wash one pair and wear the other. I was saving all my money to buy blankets and dinner sets, preparing for my return to Mozambique.

It was the longest 18 months of his life, he was doing a job that brought him face to face with his mortality every day, but more importantly, David was doing a job that he felt was way beneath his capabilities. He was worth more than a simple bag carrier. He just wanted to go home. Halfway through his contract, with 18 months still to go at the mine, David packed up all his belongings, hired a truck and left South Africa for Mozambique. His dreams of a new beginning with the little capital and few goods he had amassed to help ease the hardship of Mozambique were dashed when the truck driver drove off with everything he had saved up for in the previous 18 months. He had come back in no better position than when he had left. His father, although initially reluctant to see David work on the mines at such a young age, was even more reluctant to have him back in war-ravaged Mozambique. He insisted that David return to South Africa. But David chose to stay; his plan was to try to fight in the civil war. He was only 20, but his future was looking decidedly bleak.

One thing that kept him going, however, was a very strong belief in God. Before he left for South Africa, David had joined the Anglican Church and was a regular churchgoer. He had become a catechist, a layperson who instructed people in the basic principles of Christianity, and spent much of his time preparing other young people for baptism and confirmation rituals. To this day, David's faith is still a very large part of his life and value system. Although the church provided him with some spiritual reward, unfortunately it did not provide him with the sort of financial reward he needed to live day to day, so he started looking around for something that would ensure him a salary. He stumbled on to an opportunity in entertainment. David knew of two local bands that played well and he offered to become their agent. He decided to organise a show where the bands would perform and he would make money out of the ticket sales. The bands bought into his vision and agreed to perform at his concert. All he had to do was promote the show and sell tickets. And that couldn't be too hard, could it? He started well. Without many resources to help him in his new quest to become a music promoter, David learnt to be resourceful. He carefully drew up a poster announcing the bands' performance at the local school hall, photocopied it on his friend's father's photocopier machine and then stuck posters up all over the school. On the day, he employed two people to collect money at the entrance and got the bands started. Unfortunately, his lax security arrangements let him down.

> There were a lot of people there but many of them got in without paying so we didn't make as much money as I would have hoped. I was bankrupt but the bands just said: 'Ok, you can pay us back after the next show', because they knew there was nothing to do in Mozambique.

The second show went much the same way and David soon retired from his fledgling career as a music promoter. Instead, he took to performing arts with a similar moneymaking scheme.

> A friend of mine was in an acting group and I decided to join them and put on a production. We decided we were going to write the story ourselves and perform it ourselves. So we went around to various companies trying to get sponsorship money to pay for the theatre and the actors – we planned to stage it at one of the best-known theatres in Maputo.

David managed to secure some sponsorship money, but that only paid for the production and advertising costs. He just about broke even on the project and soon realised that after two unsuccessful forays into business, getting an established job might be a more productive way of earning a living. He didn't have to look too far.

> The first door I knocked on was at the Mozambican national broadcaster, TVM (Mozambique Television). They had only been operating for one year and everyone was talking about them. I went there looking to become a journalist but I was told that there were no vacancies for that. I was told to go to the admin department.

Within weeks, David was hired as an admin assistant. At that stage, TVM only broadcast twice a week; on Saturdays and Sundays, broadcasting a regular news bulletin. Given the economic climate in Mozambique, the station was understandably poorly funded. David remembers the early days when he first started the job and would have to stand all day because there weren't enough chairs to go around. Things improved as the station grew in popularity, and soon enough, he secured his own desk and chair. TVM grew from broadcasting solely on Saturdays and Sundays to the rest of the week and David ended up spending 13 years with the broadcaster, learning everything he knows today about the business of television. He was a quick learner and very adaptable, so he moved rapidly through the organisation.

> I started at TVM as an admin assistant for the department that cleared the broadcast equipment purchased from overseas. Eventually I became the head of that department. From there I was promoted to director of International Affairs and my job was to visit other state broadcasters to secure operational and staff training assistance – I travelled all over the world. After that I was promoted to programme director, then training director, then marketing and commercial director.

According to David, his upwardly mobile trajectory through the broadcaster was due to the fact that he was not only good at his job, but that he had integrity. 'They trusted me,' he says simply. 'I learnt that I could achieve anything I wanted if I stayed dedicated and did my job properly.' He did both, and was eventually rewarded by a nomination to the station's board in 1996. The year he was elected to the board was the same year that he realised his ambitions for himself would not be met while someone else was responsible for his income. David had already married his childhood sweetheart and they had started building a home and planning their family.

> My experience was that people working for state companies in Mozambique at that time never became rich. They retired and they were still poor. I didn't want that for my future.

He made a decision to take the responsibility for his future into his own hands, and quietly started a company called Visao Ltd, which specialised in drafting marketing communication strategies for businesses. According to David, the Mozambican government frowned on multitasking state workers who dabbled in their own businesses, so David had no choice but to register the company in his cousin's name, and keep his involvement quiet for the next two years while he grew the business.

> Back then there were party controls – you could not work for government and have your own business. I was scared of the government's control over everything. I feared that one day they would come and say: 'You cannot do that!' and fire me from my job.

Nevertheless, he went ahead and rented a small 2m² office which housed one computer, one photocopier machine and three members of staff. One of them was David's cousin who ostensibly ran the business. But David was not your typical silent partner, stealthy yes, but not silent, because every evening after work he would go straight to the office to give them instructions for the following day. The money he was making from Visao just about paid the salaries of the three staff – there was no extra cash for him. David soon realised that he needed to move up a gear if he was ever going to make some real money. So, in 1999, after 12 years at TVM, he finally resigned to focus on creating personal wealth. He was determined to fight the spectre of poverty that had dogged him all his life.

> I used to have friends who came from quite well-off families and I always felt that I couldn't invite them to my place because we were not as wealthy. I had friends who had four meals a day. When I went to study with them they used to have lunch at 4 o'clock, which I didn't have in my house. I used to go to the plot to work, they didn't do that. I used to have red hands because I worked in the fields. I never told them that I had to get up at 4am to work with my mum. I was proud of my family because my father kept fighting for us to get more and more, but we were not rich.

And David wanted to be rich. He started up a second business, one that would make him some real money and one in which he was personally involved.

> When I started working at TVM, I did a training course with International Trade and Commerce. They organised one-month courses on international trade, which taught me how to import, how to export and how to do procurement. So I started doing it for other companies. I would help them open a line of credit at the bank and help clear their goods through customs. I enjoyed it because I was making cash.

News of his import-export business spread via word of mouth and through the various contacts he had established during his years at TVM. He imported mainly industrial-type equipment into Mozambique and brought the products in through South Africa. David enjoyed the business and he certainly knew how to play the game. He laughs as he recalls the lengths to which he went to impress suppliers at meetings in Johannesburg:

> There used to be a big five-star hotel downtown called the Johannesburg Sun, and next door to it was the Grand Hotel which wasn't so upmarket. I would book into the Grand Hotel and sleep there, but when I had my meetings, I would have them at the Johannesburg Sun.

On the work front David had taken up new responsibilities and he had been appointed as the vice president of the Union of National Radio and Television Organisations of Africa (URTNA). He was still a director at TVM and David went all over the world procuring equipment, buying content and setting up exchange programmes for training staff. But in between that and the deals that took place in Johannesburg hotels, his day job was becoming untenable. A new board had been elected at the national broadcaster and David did not see eye to eye with them on a number of key issues. In 2000, after 13 years, he finally resigned from TVM and was free to pursue business. He immediately started yet another business. Visao, his communications agency, was still going strong, but he put the import-export business on hold to focus on this new venture.

> I started a company which organised conferences. I would coordinate the entire project; I secured a keynote speaker and the sponsorship, and charged the delegates a fee to attend.

David started organising two- to three-day economic and business conferences in Maputo. It turned out to be quite a lucrative venture and after a few months he spotted yet another business opportunity.

> After organising a two-day conference talking about Southern African integration, I realised that there was a lot of content that came out of these sessions that could be utilised. People had prepared speeches, there were interviews, there were handouts, and after the conference, what do you do with all that?

What you do if your name is Daniel David, is plan to start a weekly economic newspaper using all the free content collected during the conference and make it pay for itself through sponsorship and advertising revenue. He carried out a feasibility study for the project and was ready to launch the business when a chance meeting in a Johannesburg hotel with a former industry colleague changed everything. It put in place a series of events that started David down a much more exciting path, which would set him on the way towards his media empire.

> When I worked at TVM I met a guy who worked for the state broadcaster in South Africa. I met him again in Johannesburg in 2002 on a business trip and he asked me what I was doing. I told him that I wanted to start an economic newspaper and he told me that there was a company in South Africa that wanted to start a pan-African TV network called TV Africa, and they were looking for partners. He offered to introduce me to them and helped me set up a meeting with them.

TV Africa was essentially a television content provider that delivered free content to African broadcasters in return for a share of the airtime sold around their content. They were operating all over Africa and David was about to become their Mozambican partner – even though he was not a broadcaster, at least not yet. David was very excited by the prospect of starting his own television station; his 13 years of service to the national broadcaster was about to pay off. Although he didn't have a broadcasting licence, any broadcast equipment, or even premises for that matter, he was determined to make it happen. Having worked for the state broadcaster for 13 years, David was concerned that the government would turn down his application for a broadcasting licence if he planned to compete against his previous employers. The solution, which was similar to the one he had found for the communications agency, was to keep his involvement under wraps. So he applied for a TV licence under his wife's name.

One problem solved. He then needed to solve the next problem which was his lack of broadcasting equipment. He tapped into his communications agency business, Visao, which was doing very well at the time. But he needed more than it could spare, in fact he had calculated that he would need US$700 000 more to buy equipment. He approached a bank for a loan, and it was only after a friend stepped in as a guarantor that the bank finally agreed to lend him US$80 000 to purchase equipment for his new TV station, but it was not enough.

> I knew a guy called Hennie who sold TV equipment and he was prepared to help me. He said: 'Daniel, let's make a plan. I give you

second-hand equipment; you pay me in two years.' I bought some new equipment and a second-hand Apple Mac computer to do the editing.

His so-called 'broadcast centre' was actually a residential flat situated on the top floor of an apartment block that he rented. The sitting room was the studio, one bedroom was the control room and the other bedroom housed the Apple Mac and mixers. On 25 October 2002, along with his seven members of staff, David started STV – Soico TV – and started broadcasting free content from TV Africa in the Maputo area. It didn't take long for him to realise that the TV Africa partnership was not the best direction for his station. TV Africa provided him with foreign content – usually American – which he realised his viewers didn't really want to watch.

> After three months I saw that TV Africa was not a good business model. They thought global and I thought local. I decided to invest in local content and started bringing in my own programming; signing agreements with other organisations, including producers in Brazil. It did not take long for me to become self-sufficient and I got to the stage where I eventually took only sports content from TV Africa.

As well as acquiring content, David soon began to produce his own local content. He began with a five-minute local news flash and progressed into hosting live studio debates and music shows. The success of his new channel proved what he had believed all along; that advertisers and viewers wanted local content. The proof was there as his viewership numbers grew and advertising poured in.

In 2008 the station broadcast 24 hours a day across the main provinces in Mozambique, including Maputo, Gaza, Inhambane and Sofala. It is Mozambique's most popular television station and competes with the state broadcaster, his previous employers, and the Brazilian-owned Miramar. It was recently voted the best television station by a local magazine.

STV is well known for its political, economic and social debates, and has developed a reputation for being a frequent critic of the government. Apart from potentially controversial content, it also consistently broadcasts some of the most prestigious international events, such as the soccer World Cup. It has secured licences to show popular international soap operas and series, including some of the best-loved Brazilian telenovellas.

> My biggest challenge is that many people don't believe the TV station
> is mine. A lot of people thought, 'oh this young guy, how can he run a
> TV station?' They thought it would become bankrupt within months
> and instead they saw it was growing.

David's next move was to launch a radio station, Soico FM (SFM)
in 2004. It was run from the same premises and used much of the
same infrastructure as the TV station. In fact, the TV and radio
stations often shared content. In a unique move, shows like the
news and some of the live debates were broadcast simultaneously
on TV and radio. With clever economies of scale like that, SFM
quickly became a profitable concern for David.

David continued to reinvest in his business. The year after he
started the radio station he bought a newspaper; *O Pais*, which, like
his TV station, is also growing in popularity and will soon become
a daily paper. 'I want *O Pais* to become the largest and best-known
newspaper in Mozambique,' he says firmly.

David is undoubtedly ambitious and his drive has paid off.
He is in the enviable position of having to turn down potential
investors who are lining up to buy up, or at least buy into, his TV
station – but he's not selling. The creation of his conglomerate is
in full swing.

> When I open a business I go in fighting, and some of my colleagues
> say: 'Daniel, let's slow down, please!' But if there is something that
> excites me, I go for it.

David realises that he has been going for a few too many things now
and that perhaps his business has grown a little too quickly. Since
2002, he has started at least nine companies. His current focus is to
consolidate the business and put some proper structures in place.
He laughs as he explains his dilemma:

> I don't know how to slow down. I am trying to do that now. I am
> consolidating what I have got because I know it will make my
> businesses stronger and more effective. I want to be number one in
> whichever sector I am involved.

David believes the route to his success has been hard work and vision, and he looks to entrepreneurs like Richard Branson and Donald Trump for inspiration. 'I admire both for their approaches to business and how they have grown their businesses. And like Trump, I also want to enter into property investment.' Although he is not saying much, plans are certainly under way in that direction. Aside from his ability to visualise and turn his dreams into reality, David's strength in business is in strategy. Surprisingly, he couldn't care less about the numbers.

> My feasibility study is easy, I don't do calculations. I just think to myself: I want to open this business, if I fail what will happen? If my answer is that I will still be eating bread and drinking wine as usual, then I have done my feasibility study and I go ahead.

Despite this unorthodox approach, David has been very successful. What makes his success even more significant is the fact that his operating environment has not been particularly enabling for an entrepreneur. Years of an interventionist socialist government, coupled with the nationalisation of nearly all the country's major businesses, has meant that few people in Mozambique have any real business experience. David diplomatically explains:

> It is tough because Mozambique is coming out of a war, and democracy is a learning curve and learning for politicians is slow. We have only been out of the war for 10 years but we are working hard. In Mozambique you work hard or you don't get a lot of money.

And that is what keeps him driven and motivated. Unsurprisingly, the biggest influence in his life is the poverty and hardship of his past:

> It was my history that influenced me to fight for a better life. My father was a fighter; he was always fighting for us to get more. I want more for my wife and my children, more than I had.

At 40, David has already given his wife and children much more than he had growing up. Although the poverty of his past still haunts him, his future certainly looks very, very bright.